THE CHICANO EXPERIENCE

The Chicano Experience

An Alternative Perspective

Alfredo Mirandé

University of Notre Dame Press
Notre Dame, Indiana 46556

Library of Congress Cataloging in Publication Data

Mirandé, Alfredo.
  The Chicano experience.

  Bibliography: p.
  Includes index.
  1. Mexican Americans—Social conditions.
2. Mexican Americans—Economic conditions. I. Title.
E184.M5M553 1985   305.8'6872073   84-40292
ISBN 0-268-00748-9
ISBN 0-268-00749-7 (pbk.)

Manufactured in the United States of America

Para Alejandro Xavier Mirandé Enríquez
"mano man"

y en memoria de,
Xavier Mirandé Salazar
Alejandro Mirandé González
Alejandro Mirandé Garmendia
Gabriela Mirandé Garmendia

Contents

Acknowledgments

A number of persons have contributed directly or indirectly to the successful completion of this volume, and they deserve acknowledgment. Unfortunately, space limitations allow me to name but a few of these individuals. First, I would like to acknowledge the pioneers of Chicano sociology, especially Dr. Octavio Romano, who blazed the trail for subsequent generations of Chicano scholars. Over the past ten years a number of students at the University of California, Riverside have aided my intellectual growth and development by challenging my ideas. Father Gustavo Luis Benson provided valuable input on the chapter on religion. Gilbert Cadena gave me feedback on the manuscript and prepared the index. The Research Committee of the Academic Senate at the University of California, Riverside provided financial support for the project. I would also like to thank Josie Tamayo and Gil Nava, staff members at the University of California, Riverside library for their help and support. I owe immense gratitude to Clara Dean, who not only typed the entire manuscript but carefully proofed and corrected my many errors. I am also indebted to Evangelina Enríquez for her excellent work as in-house editor and critic. Although our exchanges have not always been harmonious, they have spurred me on in the quest for excellence. Eva deserves special recognition for her contribution. Yet, perhaps my greatest debt is to my *raza* for giving me a rich heritage which has endured centuries of economic, political, and cultural oppression and instilled an undying sense of pride and dignity in our people.

1

Introduction: Toward a Chicano
Social Science

One of the consequences of the civil rights movement of the 1960s was a reevaluation of the role played by social science in the continued subordination and exploitation of racial/ethnic groups. Social science typically was written from the perspective, and reflected the values of, the dominant society and culture. Oppressed groups sought recognition of their own perspectives (Moore 1973, p. 65), arguing that both history and social science should be reexamined and evaluated from female, black, and Chicano[1] perspectives, for example. Over the past decade major changes in social science paradigms have been proposed, changes so radical that they hold the potential for a scientific revolution which would incorporate the world view of the oppressed. But acceptance of these changes would mean a complete revamping of social science and a rejection of prevailing paradigms. In sociology Joyce Ladner (1973), Robert Staples (1973, 1976a and b), and others (Wilson 1974; Watson 1976) have sought to develop a black perspective. A distinctive female view of sociology has also emerged (Freeman 1975a and b; Firestone 1972; Ladner 1971; Smith 1977).[2]

While research on Mexican-Americans is extensive, to date a coherent framework or perspective on Chicano sociology has yet to be developed. A number of scholars including Octavio Romano (1968a and b), Nick Vaca (1970a and b), Miguel Montiel (1970), and Deluvina Hernández (1970) have written incisive critiques of historical and social-science depictions of Mexican-Americans, but their works have been published primarily in Chicano journals and have not been incorporated into mainstream academic circles, and their impact on social science as a whole has been minimal. These early works were typically revisionist and did not fully develop alternative frameworks or conceptualizations. While more sophisticated and sympathetic works on Chicanos have recently appeared (see for example, Murguía 1975; Barrera 1979; Moore 1978; Baca Zinn 1979b, 1981) such works tend to neither build on or extend Chicano perspectives nor attempt to revamp social science but, rather, simply apply existing paradigms to Chicanos. Although their orientation is clearly less pejorative than mainstream views, their ultimate frame of reference remains social science, not Chicanos; hence they are largely reformist.

1

This chapter proposes a Chicano perspective on sociology and social science, arguing that it is both badly needed and long overdue. A basic thesis advanced is that prevailing views, even if well intended, reflect the biases and misconceptions of the dominant society and perpetuate a mythical conception of Chicano culture.[3] Specifically, the chapter attempts to (1) point out flaws and limitations in traditional frameworks, (2) demonstrate the need for a Chicano sociology that would call into question the more traditional sociology of Mexican-Americans, (3) show how the ethic of scientism may help keep Chicanos and other minorities in a subordinate and exploited condition, and (4) propose a new perspective which will not only serve as the underlying framework for this work but might also assist in guiding or directing future research and writing on Chicanos. Although tentative, this paradigm should provide a corrective for former views of Chicanos which now prevail and in contrast present a new depiction of Chicano culture, values, and characteristics which is not only more accurate but also more consistent with a Chicano world view.

The Need for Chicano Sociology

Much of the research and writing subsumed under the rubric "the sociology of Mexican-Americans" has simply taken existing perspectives and applied them to Mexican-Americans. A basic problem is that the sociology of Mexican-Americans has not developed new paradigms or theoretical frameworks that are consistent with a Chicano world view and responsive to the nuances of Chicano culture.

Traditional social-science depictions of Mexican-Americans have been extensively critiqued (see, Romano 1968a and b; Vaca 1970a and b; and Montiel 1970), so that only a brief overview of such characterizations is necessary.[4] Suffice it to say that they have reinforced a negative conception of Mexican-Americans that sees them as (1) controlled and manipulated by traditional culture, (2) docile, passive, present oriented, fatalistic, and lacking in achievement, (3) victimized by faulty socialization which takes place in an authoritarian family system, dominated by the cult of *machismo*, and (4) violent and prone to antisocial and criminal behavior. The sociology of Mexican-Americans thus leads to the inevitable conclusion that most of the problems encountered by Chicanos are the result of deficiencies in their own culture and family system.

Even those social scientists who are sympathetic to the plight of the Chicano often reveal a lack of sensitivity to contemporary Chicano values and culture. The pervasive use of "Mexican-American," for example, fails to recognize that "Chicano" is a word self-consciously selected by many persons as symbolic of positive identification with a unique cultural heritage. Many have not realized that Mexican-American is analogous to Negro or colored, whereas Chicano is analogous to black. Both terms denote persons of Mexican extraction living in the United States, but they have very different connotations. By using Mexican-American in lieu of Chicano one consciously or unconsciously makes a political choice. A label that connotes middle-class respectability and eschews ethnic consciousness and political awareness has been selected. Hispanic reflects a similar insensitivity in that it downplays our Indian heritage in favor of the European and fails to distinguish us from other Spanish-speaking groups.

A cornerstone of the Chicano movement has been a very positive identification, culturally and biologically, with our *indio/mestizo* roots and overt rejection of our Spanish or European heritage. Duran and Bernard (1982, p. 3) observe:

> It is this emphasis on the physically conquered but spiritually vibrant Indian aspect of raza that is central to the Mexican and Chicano identity. For, like the Mexicans, Chicanos have chosen their Indian heritage as the symbolic force of their identity. The area where most Chicanos live is not called the Southwest or el Sudoeste, but Aztlan, after the mythical origin of the Aztecs perhaps in what is now Colorado or New Mexico. The name Chicano itself is derived from Mexicano, the word used in Mexico today to refer to the 1.5 million people who still speak Nahuatl (Aztec).

In 1969, at the National Youth Conference in Denver, Corky Gonzales resurrected the word Chicano and proclaimed the Southwest, Aztlán. The name Chicano captured the unique position of *mexicanos* living in the United States, who had opted to identify neither as American or Mexican.

> . . . too often, "Mexican" became "meskin" in much the same way "negro" was slurred by Southerners as "nigra"; . . . But "Chicano", like "black" for "negro", cut through all the problems of tags and labels. "Chicano" was to become a badge of brown pride embraced by the activists while it was uncomfortably digested by the moderate and conservative Mexican-Americans. (Castro 1974, p. 130)

Mexican-American or Hispanic-American is often preferred over Chicano not only because they are devoid of radical or militant meaning but because they instantly transform Chicanos into "another" hyphenated ethnic group like Irish-Americans, Italian-Americans, or Polish-Americans. Such terms imply that we, too, are immigrants faced with problems of acculturation and assimilation not unlike those faced by white European immigrants and can therefore be studied with the same paradigms.

Chicanos strongly resist the notion that we are somehow transplanted or imported Americans. The Chicano has been in America for a long time. In fact, as Luis Valdez (1972, p. xxxiii) has pointed out, we did not come to the United States, but rather the United States came to us. However,

> Now the gringo is trying to impose the immigrant complex on the Chicano, pretending that we "Mexican-Americans" are the most recent arrivals. It will not work. His melting pot concept is a sham. . . . the Anglo cannot conceive of the Chicano, the Mexican Mestizo, in all his ancient human fullness. He recognizes him as a Mexican, but only to the extent that he is "American"; and he accepts Mexican culture only to the extent that it has been Americanized, sanitized, sterilized, and made safe for democracy. (Ibid., pp. xxxii-xxxiii)

Chicano sociology can serve as a corrective for the many misconceptions and erroneous characterizations which have been perpetrated by the sociology of Mexican-Americans. Beginning with the premise that Chicanos are not a recent immigrant group but native to the Southwest and the American continent, the relationship between Chicanos and the dominant society becomes one, not of a voluntary, mobile, immigrant group and a host society, but of an indigenous people and an invading nation. The initial introduction of Chicanos into United States society was forced and involuntary, as in the case of blacks and native Americans, and came at the conclusion of the Mexican-American War in 1848. Domestic racial and ethnic minorities thus have much in common with Third World nations that were similarly colonized by European nations.

The birth of the Chicano, then, can be traced directly to the military conquest and forceful incorporation of Mexico's northern territory and its inhabitants into the United States, ratified with the signing of the Treaty of Guadalupe-Hidalgo. Chicanos today are not colonized in the classic sense of the word, but they remain "internally colonized." Internal colonialism differs from the classic variety in that it entails not the subordination of a distant land but the acquisition of contiguous territory. Once territory is acquired, local elites are deposed from power and indigenous institutions are completely destroyed. The "classic" colony is recognized formally and legally, while the "internal" colony has only an informal existence.

The informality of internal colonization makes it more insidious and oppressive, however, because the existence and legitimacy of native institutions and culture are not recognized. The culture, values, and language of Chicanos thus have had no formal or legitimate standing within American society. It has not been atypical, for example, for Chicanitos to be punished in school for speaking their native tongue or for expressing familial or cultural values that run counter to dominant societal values (Steiner 1970, p. 210; U.S. Commission on Civil Rights 1974, pp. 4-5). Although Chicanos may have formal and legal equality, they are informally excluded from full participation in the educational, economic, and political system.

Since Chicanos are a de facto colony, the process of colonization has generally gone undetected. Many would argue that while Chicanos were once conquered militarily, today they are a volunteer immigrant group. Few Chicanos, after all, trace their ancestry to the preconquest inhabitants of the Southwest—they are said to be immigrants or descendants of immigrants who came here of their own free will in the hope of improving their economic position. But to view Chicanos as an immigrant group is to miss the essence of internal colonialism. A person of Mexican ancestry living in the United States, whether a recent arrival or native to the Southwest, is subjected to the same colonial condition. An individual may be a "voluntary" immigrant, but he or she enters a colonial situation nonetheless. Colonization, after all, is a relationship between groups or nations, not among individuals.

Escape is possible for individual members of a subordinate group if one is more Caucasian in appearance or if the culture and values of the larger society are adopted. This, ironically, makes a person not a "noncolonized Chicano" but rather a "noncolonized non-Chicano." "The apparent semi-permeability of the colonial barrier for Chicanos is illusory, since there is no escape from the colonial status for an individual *as a Chicano*" (Barrera, Muñoz, and Ornelas 1972, p. 485). Typically the cost of acceptance into mainstream society and upward mobility for colonized people has been rejection of both their cultural heritage and ethnic identity: a choice, in other words, between subordination and cultural genocide.[5]

The conception of Chicanos as immigrants reflects the world view of the dominant group. Such a conception ignores the fact that the border was established and imposed by the conquering nation and that our ancestors are indigenous to this continent. It is a historical and political rather than a cultural border, and for many who cross it "illegally" the boundary is, and has always been, arbitrary and capricious.

One can subscribe to the internal colonial model, however, without accepting the view of Chicanos as a conquered people. Mario Barrera has attempted a synthesis of internal-colonialism and class-segmentation approaches. He holds that "Colonialism historically has been established to serve the interests of merchants, industrialists, and would-be landowners, or of the state which ultimately safeguards the interests of the dominate classes" (1979, p. 212). Chicanos are found within all classes, but they constitute a subordinate segment within each. These different Chicanos segments share common interests bases on discrimination and a common culture (ibid., p. 216). It is interesting to note that although Barrera does not link internal colonialism to a conquest perspective, neither does he endorse the immigrant-group model.

It is clear, then, that a sociology of Mexican-Americans, which is based on an immigrant-group model of society, cannot adequately describe the Chicano people. Its emphasis on "acculturation" and "assimilation" makes the model inappropriate for Chicanos and other groups who first entered United States society involuntarily, and it should therefore be discarded (these models are discussed more fully in chapter nine.

Although the assimilationist model was severely criticized in the late 1960s and early 1970s (see Moore 1970; Memmi 1965; Almaguer 1971; Acuña 1972; Barrera et al. 1972; and Barrera 1979), many social scientists continued to adhere to an immigrant-group model in interpretating the Chicano experience.[6] From the early work of Bogardus to the present, sociologist, in particular, have demonstrated an inordinate concern with acculturation, assimilation and integration. Much contemporary research on Chicanos still focuses on differential rates of social mobility, intermarriage, achievement, occupational and educational aspirations, and the like, and despite greater methodological sophistication its underlying theseis is still that the ultimate fate of ethnic minorities is assimilation into the melting pot.[7]

Scientism and Chicano Sociology

In its quest to gain recognition and legitimacy as an academic discipline, sociology has attempted to model itself after natural science. The cumulative effect of these efforts has been the emergence of "scientism," or what has been termed "the pernicious exaggeration of both the status and function of science in relation to our values" (Kaplan 1964, p. 405). Scientism places undue emphasis on objectivity, standardized research instruments, universalistic generalizations, and value-free science. Accordingly, the social scientist is expected to be objective, detached, and void of all value positions, and his or her observations are to be unaffected by personal, social, or political considerations. The tenets of scientism not only discourage the emergence and incorporation of minority paradigms but neutralize attempts by Third World scholars to modify prevailing world views.

Objectivity has been extolled as a virtuous trademark of science. Since the scientist is to be objective and detached rather than subjective or partisan, commitment and emotional involvement introduce bias. Proponents of this ethic assume that observations are somehow more valid and accurate if one is affectively neutral toward the phenomenon under study and, conversely, that the expression of value preferences necessarily invalidates or prejudices observations. But this characterization of science is in conflict with the actual conduct of scientific inquiry. The fact "that a scientist has values does not of itself imply that he is therefore biased; it may mean just the contrary" (Kaplan 1964, p. 381). The pursuit of the scientific enterprise, after all, is based on deeply ingrained and cherished values such as the search for truth and the extension of knowledge.

Closely related to the cult of objectivity is a belief in value-free sociology. If sociologists are to attain a true state of objectivity, it is argued, they should refrain from making value judgments or moral pronouncements. Those who make such judgments or pronouncements are viewed as ideologues, not as pure scientists. The value-free position, like the belief in objectivity, is based on a dualistic separation of reason and faith, of knowledge and feeling, and the doctrine of value-free sociology is an attempt to reconcile the tension between these two conflicting conceptions of man (Gouldner 1962, p. 212).

The belief in value-free sociology has been criticized by a number of persons who reject this view of the relationship between sociology and science. Alvin Gouldner likens belief in value-free sociology to belief in minotaurs. The existence of minotaurs, creatures that are half man and half bull, cannot be disproved since "a belief in them is not so much untrue as it is absurd" (Gouldner 1962, p. 199). Given that one cannot avoid making value judgments and value decisions, the belief in value-free sociology is equally absurd. "Those who use ethical neutrality or similar arguments as an excuse for inaction, for not 'choosing sides,' are . . . adopting a philosophical stance that was undermined decades ago" (Hoult 1968, p. 6). Since not to decide is one kind of decision, those who adopt the stance of ethical neutrality opt to support the status quo. The value-free ethic is also in conflict with a basic premise of sociology and cultural anthropology, cultural determinism. "If behavior is strongly shaped by societal or cultural forces as we maintain, how can we escape the realization that our activities as anthropologists also are so controlled?" (Sorenson 1964, p. 8). Social scientists have thus resisted applying a sociocultural perspective to their own behavior.

A final characteristic of scientism is adherence to the norm of universalism or omniscience. Before sociology can hope to attain scientific status, it must be capable of making valid generalizations that apply to numerous individuals and groups across time and setting. Science is by definition universalistic rather than particularistic. The norm of universalism has led to an emphasis on the quantification of behavior and the development of a rigorous methodology. Sociologists have sought not only to quantify behavior but to standardize instruments and techniques—to develop scales and measures that are validated or standardized across different populations or groups. Universalism holds, moreover, that "the acceptance or rejection of claims entering the lists of science is not to depend on the personal or social attributes of their protagonist; his race, nationality, religion, class and personal qualities are as such irrelevant" (Merton 1963, p. 553).

The cult of objectivity, the value-free ethic, and the norm of universalism contribute to the subordination of oppressed groups. "Objective" social scientists have used research to reinforce numerous societal myths, stereotypes, and misconceptions about Chicanos. The cult of objectivity has become a shield that hides cultural myopia. Ethnocentric anthropological descriptions of alien cultures as primitive, simple, and underdeveloped have their counterparts in more recent depictions of Chicano culture as traditional, passive, and present oriented.

The biases of the dominant culture are also reinforced by the norm of universalism. Most research instruments in the social sciences are "validated" and standardized on members of the majority society and are then applied to Chicanos and others. The norm of universalism, however, contains an inherent bias that remains unchallenged: a bias against culturally different groups whose values deviate from those of the mainstream society. The attempt to make Chicanos "fit" into inappropriate paradigms designed for volunteer immigrant groups is itself an outcome of the quest for omniscience.

A latent consequence of scientism has been to institutionalize and legitimize the biases and prejudices of the dominant society. Joan Moore (1973, p. 66) has remarked that "it is beginning to be generally acknowledged that the field in *some* way reflects the biases and limitations of the 98 percent Anglo white composition of the profession." Chicano sociologists have found it difficult to escape this web. Trained at institutions controlled by culture-bound researchers, they are often pressured to accept racist and pejorative formulations in the guise of scientific objectivity. The values of science themselves, it should be noted, are a product of Western traditions and reflect the dominant ethos of Protestantism.[8] Sampson argues that the ethos of Puritan Protestantism had a profound impact on the development of modern science. "The democratization and pursuit of equality that marked the religious ethos likewise influenced the scientific paradigm and its search for general and universal laws that, in the social realm, applied to all persons, that is, a value for truth that would apply to everyone equally" (Sampson 1978, p. 1336). Protestantism also affected the emergent scientific paradigm through its emphasis on individualism. "Individualism . . . facilitated the development of an analytic and atomistic scientific model" (ibid.). The basic and fundamental element in society was the individual, not the totality.

These values are alien to many Chicano researchers whose cultural heritage is based on subjectivity, particularism, and the mergence of truth and feeling, a heritage which also gives priority to the collective. For these Chicanos, socialization into an individualistic, atomistic, distant, objective, and impersonal ideology is not only more difficult but perhaps self-alienating. Rejection of one's culture often becomes a subtle prerequisite for entrance into academic life and for success within the academic establishment (defined as being a promising scholar or becoming a successful contributor to "scholarly" journals). The norm of omniscience also provides an impetus to internalize and espouse the ideology that one is a "scientist" or a "sociologist" first and a Chicano second. Mentors and colleagues will openly acknowledge that what is most critical in training or recruiting minority scholars is that they be competent or qualified. Ethnic minorities and women are often asked to hold their ethnic or sexual identification in abeyance, that is, to accept without question the dominant or prevailing world views. Women tend to be accepted to the extent that their femaleness is neutralized; Chicanos, to the extent that they become noncolonized non-Chicanos.

In proposing a sociology for women Dorothy E. Smith contends that women's consciousness is not accepted as a legitimate source of knowledge, experience, and relevance.

> . . . Women do not appear to men as men do to one another, as persons who might share in the common construction of a social reality where that is essentially an ideological construction. There is, we discover, a circle effect—men attend to and treat as significant what men say and have said. The circle of men whose writing and talk has been significant to one another extends back in time as far as our records reach. What men were doing has been relevant to men, was written by men about men for men. Men listened and listen to what one another said. A tradition is formed, traditions form, in a discourse with the past within the present . . . women have been almost entirely excluded. When admitted, it has been only by special licence, and as individuals, never as representatives of their sex. (Smith 1977, p. 3)

The value-free ethic is especially effective in neutralizing or cooling out racial/ethnic minorities and women. Attempts to correct existing biases or to view situations from a different perspective are likely to be discounted as provincial, biased, partisan, or simply unscientific. The sacred commandment of value-free science—"thou shalt not commit a value judgment" (Gouldner 1962, p. 199)—has been broken.

Whose Side Are We On?

If to have values is to be human and if it is not possible to do research that is free of personal or political values, "the question is not whether we should take sides, since we inevitably will, but rather whose side we are on" (Becker 1967, p. 239). Howard Becker has observed that the issue of bias is usually raised when one takes the side of the oppressed or disadvantaged. Research from the perspective of the superordinate group—that is, those in positions of power, authority, or responsibility—tends to be accepted as objective, balanced, and value-free. A hierarchy of credibility exists so that "in any system of ranked groups, participants take it as given that members of the highest group have the right to define the way things really are" (Becker 1967, p. 241). We all know, for instance, that the police are more responsible than criminals and that their statements should be taken more seriously. The question of bias generally comes into play when the subordinate point of view is assumed, because then both the hierarchy of credibility and conventional wisdom are being challenged. By debunking prevailing myths the dominant order is questioned.

Researchers on Chicanos and other minorities should question whose side they are on. By adopting the perspective commonly found in the sociology of Mexican-Americans, they knowingly or unwittingly take the side of the dominant society, as do those who profess to be value-free. Chicano sociology, on the other hand, admittedly takes a stance both with respect to Chicanos and sociology as a whole. Chicano sociologists approach all social science, not just the study of Chicanos, from a Third World perspective, that is, as members of an oppressed group.

Critics of this perspective might counter by saying that Chicano sociology or Chicano social science represents a form of reverse racism. Merton has criticized black claims to monopolistic and privileged access to particular forms of knowledge as an elitist and racist doctrine, not unlike the Insider doctrine espoused by the Nazi regime (1972, pp. 11-13). He would reduce the claims of Chicano social science to a debate between Insiders (Chicanos) and Outsiders (Anglos). Chicano sociology would become the Insider claim to exclusive access to knowledge not available to those outside the group. But if only Chicanos can understand Chicano culture, it follows that only Anglos can understand Anglo culture. "Once the basic principle is adopted, the list of Insider claims to a monopoly of knowledge becomes indefinitely expansible to all manner of social formations" (Merton 1972, p. 13). The Insider-Outsider doctrine traps us, as it were, in a never-ending circle. Since we are all Insiders and Outsiders relative to certain groups, our observations are always limited and biased. As rational people, Merton would argue, we are forced to conclude that outside perspectives are as valid as inside perspectives.

Are we to be inundated by a multitude of perspectives, each equally valid? The Insider-Outsider doctrine has some validity, but carried to its logical extreme, it is not only seductively simple but misguided. Based on an order-pluralistic consensus model of society, Merton's critique of "Insiderism" ignores the issue of inequality. The perspective is valid only in situations where relations between the groups under consideration are relatively equal. When a power differential is present, as it often is, the critique of Insiderism is of dubious value. Since all things are not equal in society, truth is not obtained by simply averaging or combining the views of the oppressed and their oppressors. Oppression is not simply "in the eye of the beholder," as some labeling theorists would have us believe; it has an objective basis in reality. A relationship such as that which exists between Chicanos and the dominant society is based on oppression. It can therefore be argued, contrary to conventional wisdom, that the two sides of every story are not always equally valid. Oppression will be perpetuated unless one takes the side of the oppressed.

The intent of advocating a Chicano perspective is not to reverse roles and oppress Anglos or to champion reverse racism. Such a stance would simply reinforce the Insider-Outsider doctrine. The intent rather is to propose a broader and more humanizing perspective that is sensitive to the needs and concerns of all groups. The aid of sympathetic persons who are sensitized to the dehumanizing character of society and the limitations of established science is therefore welcomed. A number of Anglo social scientists have made valuable contributions to the development of minority-oriented paradigms, and, conversely, many social minorities subscribe to the dominant world view. The issue is not one between Insiders and Outsiders but between existing culture-bound paradigms and emergent views.

Some would use this outlook to argue against the establishment of separate minority paradigms. While nonminority scholars are capable of making important contributions to the development of minority paradigms, they do so largely to the extent that they successfully adopt a minority world view. Robert Blauner, for example, has done much to enhance our understanding of racially oppressed groups, and his work reflects considerable sensitivity. While sympathetic and perceptive Anglos are able to articulate the needs and demands of minorities, they neither create these needs and demands nor experience them directly; they simply respond to them. The point is that Chicanos experienced the devastating effects of colonial oppression long before sociologists theorized about it, and in this sense internal colonialism is much more than a theoretical model; it is also a way of life.

Toward a Chicano Theoretical Perspective

The harmonious incorporation of anomalous findings has been the exception rather than the rule in the development of science. New paradigms have not been readily accepted because their acceptance would mean rejection of older, more established, perspectives. Scientific revolutions entail the supplanting of older paradigms with newer incompatible ones (Kuhn 1962, p. 90). Not only are scientific revolutions discontinuous but paradigm choice itself is inherently polemical and beyond the purview of science.

> . . . Like the choice between competing political institutions, that between competing paradigms proves to be a choice between in-

compatible modes of community life . . . the choice is not and cannot be determined merely by the evaluative procedures characteristic of normal science, for these depend in part upon a particular paradigm, and that paradigm is at issue. (Kuhn 1962, p. 93)

The debate between models is necessarily circular, since proponents of a particular paradigm use that paradigm to defend its virtue (Kuhn 1962, p. 93). Paradigm choice may therefore be beyond the scope of both logic and science.

This chapter calls for the development and acceptance of a new perspective on Chicano sociology. Such a perspective is part of a broader movement to develop nontraditional paradigms in the social sciences by racial and ethnic groups and by women. Since these paradigms hold the potential for a scientific revolution, they will meet with resistance from established social science, for their acceptance would entail discarding prevailing world views.

This chapter concludes now by isolating some of the major components of an emergent perspective or theoretical framework. Although admittedly tentative and suggestive, this framework should serve as a model or starting point for future research and theorizing on Chicanos. Ultimately, perhaps, a full-fledged Chicano paradigm will emerge.

(1) Theories and paradigms developed for volunteer European immigrant groups are inappropriate for Chicanos and other racial/ethnic groups whose initial entrance into American society resulted from force or conquest.

(2) Chicanos are not a volunteer immigrant group but an internally colonized one excluded from full participation in the legal, political, and economic system. They have formal or legal equality but are informally exploited, and their culture and values are not granted legitimacy by the dominant society.

(3) Chicano workers have much in common with Anglo workers who are also exploited economically by the capitalistic system, but they differ in that they are a subclass excluded from the primary labor market and are subjected to cultural and linguistic control.

(4) By virtue of their membership in an internally colonized racial/cultural group, Chicanos tend to be relegated to subordinate status regardless of their birth or economic status. Chicanos may move out of such subordination but only largely to the extent that they reject their language and cultural heritage.

(5) Unlike European immigrants who blend into the melting pot, Chicanos have retained a viable and relatively independent culture outside of mainstream American culture.

(6) Chicano culture is not disorganized and pathological, as depicted in much social-science literature, but is an integrative force that organizes and guides the activities of its members, enabling them to cope with oppression.

(7) Because social science has traditionally reflected the values and ethos of the dominant culture, established paradigms are typically based, overtly or covertly, on negative and pejorative views of Chicanos and their culture. They have tended to look for defects inherent in Chicano culture and values to explain their subordination rather than to external factors.

(8) The prevailing ethos of scientism also works to maintain the subordination of Chicanos and other disadvantaged groups through its predominant emphasis on objectivity, value neutrality, and universalism.

(9) Although less openly pejorative perspectives have recently emerged, they continue to subscribe to the tenets of scientism, and rather than rejecting or revamping traditional perspectives, they tend to make Chicanos "fit" into existing paradigms.

(10) There is a need to develop a Chicano perspective on social science that not only is sensitive to the nuances of Chicano culture and sympathetic to Chicanos but one that transcends the limitations of prevailing theoretical perspectives and establishes links with other oppressed groups.

(11) Acceptance of a Chicano sociology or Chicano social science as well as the perspectives of other minority groups requires challenging existing paradigms and world views.

(12) Chicano sociology and similar approaches will generally be resisted by establishment science on the grounds that they are polemical, partisan, and otherwise incongruous with the norms of science.

(13) The choice between minority paradigms and prevailing world views tends to be political and beyond the scope of science and logic. The choice appears ultimately to be political and/or moral.

(14) Those who subscribe to existing paradigms and eschew new Third World perspectives perpetuate directly or indirectly the oppression of such groups.

PART I

Displacement of the Chicano

2

Chicano Labor and the Economy

Perhaps it is appropriate that an analysis of the displacement of Chicanos begin with the economy, for no single institution impinges more directly and affects Chicanos more profoundly. The economy is important not only in its own right but in relation to other institutions. An evaluation of the position of Chicanos within American society would not be complete without looking at Chicano labor and the economic status of Chicanos both historically and in contemporary society. This chapter begins with an overview of Chicano labor from after the Mexican-American War to the end of the century. It then turns to an examination of Chicano labor and the economy from 1900 to the present.

Chicano Labor during the Nineteenth Century: From Rancheros to Colonial Labor Force

The American take-over of the Southwest was much more than a military and political victory; it also initiated Anglo penetration of the economy and eventual control of the entire society. Rather than being immediate and complete, the take-over was gradual and hotly contested by the native Mexican population. California during the period immediately preceding and following the take-over will be used to illustrate the process of Anglo penetration and control of the Mexican economy.

Prior to 1846, when war broke out between the United States and Mexico, the secularization of the missions and of the California economy had been effected. The Secularization Proclamation of 1834 called for dismantling of the missions and bringing them under secular control. According to Albert Camarillo

The secularization of the missions had profound effects on Mexican California society. On the one hand, the economic and political influence of the mission padres was eliminated, even though the religious influence of the Catholic church persisted. On the other hand, mission secularization radically changed the system of land tenure and land disposal in California. In fact, the breakup of the

17

California mission lands was the signal event for the introduction of what has been called the Golden Age of the *ranchos*, the period from 1834 to 1846. (1979, p. 9)

Between 1834 and 1846 land ownership became increasingly concentrated in the hands of a few wealthy *rancheros* who had been awarded large land grants by the Mexican government (ibid). The mission/*presidio* economy gave way to a pastoral economy characterized by four major social strata. The top of the socioeconomic system consisted of the *rancheros*, mission fathers, and government administrators. This small group laid claim to direct Spanish ancestry and separated itself socially from the next strata made up of *mestizo* small ranchers and farmers. "The third identifiable sector, which formed the bulk of the majority mestizo population in the pueblo, was composed of artisans, other skilled workers, laborers, and seasonal *matanza* workers all employed in occupations related to the pastoral economy" (ibid., p. 11). At the bottom of the class structure was a small group of ex-neophyte Indians who served as a chief source of manual labor.

The American take-over of the Southwest entailed not only the imposition of an alien culture, language, and religion but the introduction of a different economic system. In the aftermath of the Mexican-American War the pastoral Mexican economy was supplanted by Anglo capitalism. Within much of California, especially the northern sectors, this change came quickly as the massive influx of Anglos caused the Mexican population to be suddenly outnumbered and lose economic control. In other areas, however, where the Mexican population maintained a numerical majority and the *ranchero* class was firmly entrenched, Anglo control of the economy proved more difficult.

From 1850 to the late 1860s the Mexican influence prevailed in Santa Barbara. The *ranchero* class owned much of the land and dominated the pastoral economy. Despite a persistent Anglo threat *mexicanos* managed to retain control of the political scene, the judicial system, and education. Until 1870 common council minutes were recorded in Spanish; Mexican juries seldom convicted Mexican defendants. English language instruction was not available until 1858 (ibid., pp. 14–25). However, as the Anglo population grew, Americans gradually gained in political power. At the same time that Californios were losing political control, they also experienced economic and occupational displacement. By 1873 the *ranchero* class had lost its hold on the economy and was replaced by a rapidly growing professional and merchant class that was non-Mexican. Thus the infusion of capitalism and Anglo ascendancy went hand in hand.

By the 1880s not only had Anglos gained economic ascendancy but Santa Barbara had been transformed from a Mexican pueblo into an American city. One consequence of Americanization was the initiation of a process that has been termed *barrioization* of the Mexican community, which entailed "the formation of residentially and socially segregated Chicano barrios or neighborhoods" (ibid., p. 53). The process was more than simple segregation and intertwined economic, social, and demographic forces. *Barrioization* meant the virtual elimination of the Mexican from the social and political life of the community at large; through isolation Chicanos became invisible, if not nonexistent. Conversely, barrios offered Chicanos security and insulation from American influence and the forces of assimilation.

Santa Barbara is an important case study because it represents a Mexican stronghold where Anglo encroachment was actively and forcefully resisted. In the end, however, economic displacement prevailed not only in Santa Barbara but throughout the Southwest, so that by the 1870s Chicanos found themselves at the bottom of the socioeconomic order. They thus went from being an elite *ranchero* class to being a source of cheap and dependent labor within the working class.

While the economic position of Chicanos declined during the American period, patterns of economic displacement varied from community to community. Even within Southern California there were significant differences in the experiences of *raza*. It appears, for example, that the *ranchero* class was less firmly established in Los Angeles, and their deposition from power came more quickly than in Santa Barbara. In the study *The Los Angeles Barrio, 1850–1890* Richard Griswold del Castillo points to the "need to refine our understanding of the economic and social history of Spanish-speaking nineteenth-century California and to move beyond class-determined generalizations" (1979, p. 32). The Californios who lost their lands subsequent to 1848 were, after all, a landed minority which constituted about 3 percent of the total population (ibid., p. 31). It is therefore important to look at the fate not only of this landed minority but of members of the Mexican population as a whole. After carefully examining census data for the pueblo of Los Angeles from 1850 to 1880, Griswold del Castillo concluded that the thesis of decline applied most clearly and directly to California landowners. It is also clear "that the process of property disenfranchisement was well under way before the 1860's" (ibid., p. 47).

In 1850 61 percent of *raza* heads of household owned land valued in excess of 100 dollars, but by 1860 the percentage had been cut in half and stood at 29 percent (ibid., p. 46). By 1880 those Chicano families that owned land consisted of new arrivals to the city rather than of families who had been landowners prior to 1850 (ibid., p. 49). Commercial growth during the three decades (1850–1880) resulted in changes in the occupational structure. "For the developing professional and skilled classes, American domination brought a slight increase in opportunities. For the mass of Mexican-American laborers, there was little change in socioeconomic mobility from the Mexican era" (ibid., p. 61). The majority remained at the bottom of the economic hierarchy of Los Angeles.

The economic decline of Californios followed a similar pattern in San Diego. Mario T. García notes that in 1850 "Compared to the Anglo population the economic resources of the colonized Mexicans, specifically the 'gente de razón' or upper class, were much greater" (1976, p. 56). The rise of commerce meant that the colonial Mexican feudal society would give way to an expansionist capitalistic system. By 1860 these powerful Mexican families had lost much of their wealth and land.

A somewhat different pattern is found southeast of Los Angeles in San Salvador, which refers to the joint communities of La Placita and Agua Mansa. Established by Mexican colonists who migrated from New Mexico to California in the early 1840s, San Salvador became the first permanent settlement in the valley of San Bernardino (Vickery 1977, p. 19). The decline of San Salvador was abetted by a flood which virtually wiped out the community in 1862 and by the economic expansion of the Inland Empire (ibid., pp. 68–69). The community was rebuilt, but its decline continued as the surrounding Anglo communities of San Bernardino and Riverside developed.

> The settlement of the valley by midwestern and New England Protestants, such as the early Riversiders, changed not only the economic basis of the area, but also the social and cultural atmosphere. Within thirteen years, the Riverside community reached the point where it could be incorporated as a city with a stable economic base. Obviously, it was to prove a powerful force to be reckoned with by its neighbors in the La Placita area now known as "Spanishtown." (ibid., pp. 78, 80)

As Riverside developed and prospered, Spanishtown declined. With diminished economic opportunities within the community, many *Salvadoreños* were forced to seek employment elsewhere. Some worked for the Arlington Heights Citrus Company in Riverside, in the mines of The Gavilan Hills, or as common laborers (ibid., p. 82).

In what has now become a classic study of the social history of the Spanish-speaking Californians, Leonard Pitt (1966) documents the decline of the Californios. The processes involved in displacing northern and southern Californios differed, but the end result was the same. While the cow counties of Southern California remained a Mexican stronghold during the 1850s, the northern *ranchos* were quickly decimated. Squatters, speculators, and crooked lawyers who sought to acquire land through legal and extralegal means were aided in their efforts by the legislature through the passage of such bills as the California Land Law of 1851. The bill, proposed by Senator William

Gwinn, encouraged Americans to "homestead" on Mexican-owned land and placed the burden on the latter to prove that they held valid titles. It established a three-person Board of Land Commissioners, empowered "to weed out the valid titles as defined by Spanish and Mexican Law, the provisions of the Treaty of Guadalupe-Hidalgo, the principles of equity, and the precedents of the United States Supreme Court" (Pitt 1966, p. 86).

Although the board's decisions could be appealed to the district court and ultimately to the United States Supreme Court, Californios were clearly at a disadvantage. The law actually encouraged squatters to challenge the validity of Spanish and Mexican land grants and abrogated provisions of the Treaty of Guadalupe-Hidalgo which guaranteed Chicanos "the enjoyment of all the rights of the United States according to the principles of the Constitution; and . . . shall be maintained and protected in the free enjoyment of their liberty and property." Many attorneys took advantage of the precarious position of the Californios. Pitt notes that "since most Californios scarcely understood English, much less the technical language of the courts, they had to depend greatly on their attorneys, whom they usually paid in land itself and only rarely in cash. Sad to say, of the fifty or so attorneys who specialized in claim law in the 1850's, most were shysters who lacked not only honesty but also knowledge and experience" (1966, p. 91).

By 1856 a massive change in landownership had been effected. As a result of force, armed conflict, legislative manipulation, and outright purchase much of the land was now in Yankee hands. Juan Bandini, a prominent citizen of San Diego, expressed the feeling of betrayal common among Californios whose landholdings were devastated by decisions rendered by the Land Commission:

> Of the lands mentioned some have been in the quiet possession of the proprietors and their families for forty or fifty years. On them they have reared themselves homes—they have enclosed and cultivated fields—there they and their children were born—and there they lived in peace and comparative plenty. But now—our inheritance is turned to strangers—our houses to aliens. We have drunken our water for money—our wood is sold unto us. Our necks are under persecution—we labor and have no rest. (Garcia 1976, p. 71)

The Chicano felt betrayed not only by the United States and its unjust and discriminatory laws but by the Mexican government which had "sold them" to the Americans.

Although the demise of the Californios came more slowly in the south and was actively resisted throughout the state, their ultimate fate was seldom in doubt. In the 1850s Chicanos sought and often obtained almost every available public office (Pitt 1966, p. 147). In the south of California they maintained a numerical majority until the 1870s. The Californios retained political and economic influence in Los Angeles through the 1850s and in Santa Barbara into the 1860s. The ultimate economic decline of the Californios in the south was brought about by an economic depression in the 1860s. In 1861 the sagging cattle economy was further damaged by natural disasters: a rainstorm and floods followed by a severe drought which persisted for three years and crippled the entire cattle industry:

> For many ranching families, 1864 meant the end of solvency; their names generally went on the delinquent tax list and stayed there until they had sold their property. . . . Before the catastrophe, practically all land parcels worth more than $10,000 had still been in the hands of old families; by 1870, these families held barely one-quarter. A mean and brassy sky thus eventually did in the south of California what lawyers and squatters had accomplished in the north—the forced breakup of baronial holdings, their transfer to new owners, and the rise of a way of life other than ranching. (Ibid., p. 248)

The economic and political losses were accompanied by an assault on the culture of the Californios. Anglo settlers were openly disdainful of the culture and customs of the Mexican. Dr. John S. Griffin, a noted pioneer doctor and civic leader in Los Angeles, reveals such antipathy in a letter to a friend dated March 11, 1849:

> The Pueblo has changed much since you left. It is now thronged with Soldiers, Quartermaster's men, Sonorians, & C., the most vicious and idle set you ever beheld. Gambling, drinking, and whoring are the only occupations, and they seem to be followed with great industry . . . monte banks, cock fights, and liquor shops are to be seen in all directions, and the only question that is asked is whether a man has been successful at monte. (Griffin, 1976, p. 9)

He is no less harsh on California women. His response to members of the "fair sex" being transported to a dance via carriages was one of shock and incredulity: "to think of sending a carriage for a California woman to a dance!" (ibid., p. 17). As the Americans ascended politically, they also sought to impose their culture and supplant that of the Spanish-speaking inhabitants. It is therefore not surprising to see that the 1850s have been characterized as a period when "Hispanophobia" prevailed.

Lynchings and hangings of Mexicans were common occurrences in the mines and fields of the north, and many sought refuge in the Mexican cow counties of the south. Chicanos suffered injustices not only from Anglos but at the hands of the legal and judicial system as well. Crime was rampant in Los Angeles where Anglo-Mexican relations degenerated into a race war.

Dissatisfied with the efficacy of the legal and judicial system, Anglos frequently took the law into their own hands. "Vigilante justice had a distinctiveness in Los Angeles, however, in that every important lynch-law episode and most minor ones involved the Spanish-speaking" (Pitt 1966, p. 154). The Californios themselves were split so that the *ricos* frequently sided with the Yankees in persecuting the "lower and undesirable element." Pitt distinguished two principal types of lynchers:

> . . . At El Monte lived one key group, an enclave of Texans who had served in the Texas Rangers during the Mexican War, and who, in any event, considered themselves experts at "dealing with" Mexicans. Going by the name of rangers and not vigilantes, they generally tendered their services to the vigilante committees or to the sheriffs, but sometimes took separate action. Another group, the vigilante committeemen, generally included "respectables"—old-time ranchers, merchants, lawyers, and government officials. Since they owned land titles or had a smattering of legal knowledge, the town looked to them for leadership. (Ibid., p. 155)

Even the *ricos* were not immune from persecution as illustrated in the infamous Lugo case. The Lugos, sons of the owner of Rancho San Bernardino, were charged with the murder of two men. "Although the defendants were ultimately acquitted and the case was dismissed in late 1852, the incident set off explosive ethnic tensions, led to the attempted lynching of the Lugos by an Anglo-American gang, and resulted in the wiping out of the lynch gang by Cahuilla Indians who worked for the Lugos" (Cortés 1976, p. 1).[1]

The pattern of political and economic repression that existed in California was repeated throughout the Southwest, but nowhere was it more intense than in the Texas territory. The conflict between *mexicanos* and Anglo Texans was fierce and culminated in the Texas Revolt for Independence in the 1830s, an event which preceded the Mexican-American War and the incorporation of Mexico's northern territories into the United States.

Fearing possible annexation of this sparsely settled area by France, England, or the United States, the Mexican and Spanish governments encouraged colonization by awarding generous land grants to prospective settlers (Meier and Rivera 1972, p. 57). In 1821 Spain granted Moses Austin an *empresario* land grant which permitted him to bring in 300 Spanish families from Flordia. Austin died before he could effect this goal, but his son received a comparable grant from the Mexican government in 1823 (ibid., p. 58). This signaled the beginning of an Anglo influx, and eventually twenty such *empresario* grants were awarded. The conditions of the grant were simple: all settlers were required to be of good moral character, to be Catholic or to convert to Catholicism, and to swear allegiance to Mexico. Austin took great care to abide by these terms but most *empresarios* ignored them (ibid.). Anglo settlers were disdainful toward Mexicans and did not recognize the authority of the Mexican government, tending to ignore or disregard Mexican customs and laws. When Mexico tried to enforce the provisions of the grant in 1826, it led to a short-lived crisis known as the Fredonia Revolt (ibid.).

By 1830 Anglo Texans outnumbered the Mexicans by more than five to one. Many of these were not legal settlers but illegal aliens from the South who sought to develop cotton cultivation and to import slaves (ibid.). Mexico, fearing that the United States would move to annex Texas, began to take measures to stem the tide of illegal aliens. In 1829 Mexico abolished slavery by executive decree. After intense protest by Texans the decree was quickly suspended, but in 1830 Mexico passed a law which prohibited the importation of slaves and attempted to severely restrict Anglo settlement. Another law set up customhouses and presidios along the border (ibid., p. 59). Mexican soldiers were also sent to Texas to enforce Mexican laws, including laws pertaining to immigration.

Conflict heightened, and by 1835 the Texas Revolt was in full swing. Santa Anna's victories at the Alamo and Goliad were short-lived, and on April 21, 1837, he was soundly defeated at San Jacinto. Although Santa Anna had agreed to Texas independence by signing the Treaty of Velasco in exchange for his freedom, the treaty was not recognized by Mexico. Texas eventually obtained de facto independence, although annexation to the United States did not come until 1845. The annexation of Texas set the stage for an all-out war between the two nations, as Mexico, fearing total annexation, broke off diplomatic relations with the United States.

Anglo contempt of the Mexican during the Mexican period grew into open hatred and hostility following Texas independence. Racial tension was exacerbated not only by economic and cultural conflicts but by deeply ingrained racist attitudes. "Since more than 80 percent of early Anglo migrants to Texas came from the deep South, racial attitudes toward black people were readily transferred to Mexicans. . . . Mexican Americans were considered innately inferior and an obstacle to a progressive economy and society" (ibid., p. 88). Hostility toward the Mexican was further aggravated by the chauvinism of Mexican *tejanos* (Texans) who saw themselves as separate and superior to the *mexicano*.

Unlike California where the Mexican landed elite were firmly entrenched, *tejanos* constituted a small and relatively insignificant group. In 1840 *tejanos* represented only 10 percent of the population; by 1860 their numbers were reduced to 6 percent. The one notable exception was south Texas, especially the area between the Nueces River (the international boundary prior to the Treaty of Guadalupe-Hidalgo) and the Rio Grande, which remained heavily Mexican (ibid., p. 89).

This is not to suggest that *tejanos* were not displaced from their lands, but rather that the process of displacement began long before the war between Mexico and the United States. During the Texas Revolt many *tejanos* were forcibly driven form their lands (Nance 1963, vol. 1, p. 547), and the Treaty of Velasco simply fueled the expansionist fervor. According to Meinig (1969, p. 46) "much of the Hispano population was driven out of Bexar, and took refuge along the Rio Grande or beyond." Although the Treaty of Guadalupe-Hidalgo recognized Mexican land titles as legitimate in principle, they were not protected in practice. As in California legal and extralegal means were used to deprive Mexicans of their land. A favorite target was the *Espíritu Santo* grant, a 260,000-acre parcel awarded to Don José Salvador de la Garza in 1782 along the northern bank of the Rio Grande. In 1848

> . . . A horde of American businessmen, squatters, and ex-soldiers arrived on the Espíritu Santo lands, many bore headrights, bounty warrants, and Texas veteran's land certificates. There was a general claiming that the land around Brownsville was "vacant," or national land, and thus public land under Texas law by right of conquest. (Fehrenbach 1968, p. 511)

Charles Stillman, an unscrupulous merchant, established the city of Brownsville on 1,500 acres that were part of the de la Garza grant.

Many Mexicans, especially those with small landholdings, also had their land taken away by force and intimidation. Even the *hacendados* were stripped of their property (ibid., p. 510). Walter Prescott Webb observed that a dual standard of justice emerged, so that " 'One law applied to them [Mexicans], and another, far less rigorous, to the political leaders and to the prominent Americans' " (ibid., pp. 509–10). A Mexican who killed an American would surely be hanged, but a white man could injure or kill Mexicans with impunity (ibid., p. 510).

Given this double standard of justice, it is not surprising to see that many Mexicans found it necessary to take the law into their own hands. Although the lower classes were more likely to be victims of Anglo abuse and violence, the Mexican upper classes were by no means immune:

> The imposition of American law infuriated most Mexican landowners. They had to defend their ancient titles in court, and they lost either way, either to their own lawyers or to the claimants. In these years the humbler classes of Mexicans were finding that they were treated with contempt, and that the American law would not protect

their persons; now the upper class felt that American courts were not upholding their ancient rights. (Ibid., p. 511)

One disgruntled Mexican elite was Juan Nepomuceno Cortina, also known as the "Red Robber of the Rio Grande." Cortina, born into the upper class, had seen his mother give up a square league of her property in order to keep the rest. Cortina made it a practice to go into Brownsville and drink coffee with friends. On July 13, 1859, he began his career as a revolutionary somewhat unwittingly as he confronted a marshal who used excessive force in arresting a drunken Mexican who had previously worked as a servant for Cortina. Words were exchanged, and Cortina shot the marshal and rode out of town with the servant on the back of his horse (see Fehrenbach 1968, pp. 511–21; Goldfinch 1949). Two months later the Red Robber of the Rio Grande led a group of one hundred men who raided Brownsville, released all the prisoners from the jail, shot three Americans, and shouted "Death to the gringos" as they raised the Mexican flag. He returned to his mother's ranch, Rancho del Carmen, and issued a proclamation:

> Mexicans! When the State of Texas began to receive the new organization which its sovereignty required as an integrant part of the Union, flocks of vampires, in the guise of men, came and scattered themselves in the settlements, without any capital except the corrupt heart and the most perverse intentions. Some, brimful of laws, pledged to us their protection against the attacks of the rest . . . ; while others, to the abusing of our unlimited confidence, when we intrusted them with our titles, which secured the future of our families, refused to return them under false and frivolous pretexts. . . . Many of you have been robbed of your property, incarcerated, chased, murdered, and hunted like wild beasts, because your labor was fruitful, and because your industry excited the vile avarice which led them. . . .
>
> Mexicans! My part is taken; the voice of revelation whispers to me that to me is entrusted the chains of your slavery. . . . (Valdez and Steiner 1972, pp. 113–16)

Cortina organized an army and led an open rebellion against Anglo control which aimed at "reconquering" Texas for the *mexicano*. Although unsuccessful, Cortina emerged as a hero and symbol of Chicano resistance against oppression.

As in California, displacement of the Mexican from the land was hastened by economic expansion. The cattle boom in the 1860s and also railroad expansion put pressure on Mexicans to relinquish their land (Barrera 1979, p. 31). Pressure was also exerted by ongoing political instability and the precarious position of the Mexican. Fearing that their land would ultimately be taken away, many sold it at ridiculously low prices, sometimes as little as 1.6 cents per acre (Taylor 1934, p. 181):

> . . . While Mexican titles were confirmed by Texas statute in 1852, there was a debate on the floor of the state convention of 1845 in which some favored confiscation of the Texas property of Mexicans who gave aid to Mexico against Texas. Even had Mexican owners known with certainty that their titles would be protected, that alone could not remove all apprehension from foreign domination. . . . It was under the pressure of these conditions that the grants passed to Americans (Ibid., pp. 180–83)

Paul Taylor notes that at the beginning of the Texas Revolt in 1835 every foot of land in Nueces County was held under Mexican land grants, two years prior to the Civil War all but one had passed out of Mexican hands, and by 1883 none was held by Mexicans. In 1928 twenty-nine Mexican farmers owned land in the county, but, interestingly, rather than being descendants of grantees, all were recent purchasers who had risen from laborer to farmer status (ibid., p. 179). Table 1 illustrates the process by which land passed from Mexican to American hands in Nueces County.[2]

The pattern of displacement of Chicanos occurred throughout the American Southwest. With the exception of New Mexico where Chicanos retained landed interests and political power, by 1880 they had been deposed from power and reduced to second-class-citizens status. Relative to the ever-expanding capitalistic economy the Chicano became an important source of cheap and dependent labor.

Chicano Labor during the Twentieth Century: The Emergence of a Chicano Proletariat

Not only were Chicanos displaced from the land and their economic position altered radically but they were also reduced to the status of a numerical minority throughout the Southwest, with a few notable exceptions such as south Texas and parts of New Mexico. Although Chicanos constituted a numerical majority in Southern California until the 1870s, by 1890 they comprised only 10 percent of the population (Meier and Rivera 1972, p. 86). In Santa Barbara Chicanos represented 46.8 percent of the total population in 1870, 26.8 percent in 1880, and only 20 percent by 1890 (Camarillo 1979, pp. 58–59). Similarly, they made up 75.4 percent of the population of the Los Angeles pueblo in 1850, 37.7 percent in 1870, and declined to less than 20 percent (19.3) by 1890 (Griswold del Castillo 1979, p. 35). Thus, by 1890 the social, political, economic, and numerical displacement of the Mexican had been effected. The decline of the pastoral economy and capitalistic expansion had transformed the Chicano into a source of unskilled labor. The numerical and economic ascendancy of the Anglo brought with it the loss of political power. At the same time distinctively Mexican communities were transformed into American cities, the Chicano population was concentrated within ethnic enclaves, barrios. Schrieke observed,

TABLE 1

Spanish and Mexican Grants to Land Lying Partly or Wholly within Nueces County, Texas, as Bounded in 1929[1]

| | | ORIGINAL GRANT | | FIRST DEED TO AN AMERICAN | |
| | | | | | |
Name of Grant	Grantee	Date Granted	Date	Name	
Casa Blanca	Juan de la Garza Montemayor and four sons	1805	1848	Wm. Mann	
Barranco Blanco	Vicente Lopez de Herrera and sons and Gregorio Farias	1806	1852	James Carter[2]	
Rincon de los Laureles[3]	Juan Perez Reyes, Juan Perez Reyes Rey, and Manuel Garcia	1807	1853	Charles Stillman[2]	
Puentecitas	Andres Fernandez de la Fuente	1809	1858	Conrad Meuly	
San Antonio de Agua Dulce[4]	Benito Lopez de Xaen	1809	1848	Wm. Mann	
Padre Island[3]	Juan Jose de Balli	1829	1846	1846[5]	
Villareal	Enrique Villareal	1831	1840	Henry L. Kinney[6]	
El Rincon de Corpus Christi	Ramon de Ynojosa	1831	1845	John Schatzell	
San Antonio del Alamo	Policarpio Farias	1834	1845	Wm. H. Lee	
Santa Petronilla	Jose A. Cabasos	1834	1845	Wm. H. Lee	
Agua Dulce[4]	Rafael Garcia	1834	1859	Richard King	
Palo Alto	Matias Garcia	1834	1853	Charles Stillman	
El Chiltipin[3]	Blas Maria Falcon	1835	1880[7]	Mifflin Kennedy	
Paso Ancho de Arriba	Manuel Farias	1836	1857	James Grogan and	
Paso Ancho de Abajo	Luciano Rivas	1836	1857	John L. Haynes	

Source: Taylor 1934, p. 180.
1. The above data were obtained principally through the courtesy of Mr. H.S. Guy.
2. Transfers from the grantee to other Mexicans preceded transfer to the American.
3. Grant lies only partly within present Nueces County.
4. These grants overlap.
5. Title still in litigation, but supposed to have passed to Americans by a series of deeds of interests or acreages, the first dated 1846.
6. First deed dated 1840; the remainder of the grant was deeded to Kinney within a very few years.
7. An earlier deed of two leagues in 1857 was made to an attorney who in court action recovered the grant for Falcon. The remainder of the grant was finally deeded away by Falcon in successive portions in 1880, 1882, and 1883.

. . . In the towns separation of domicile is general: the typical Mexican area is "The other side of the tracks." . . . the "Mexican" community is sometimes the original settlement. . . . In this case the "Anglos" sometimes strive to remove the Mexicans, as the Mexican area is judged to be an "eyesore." (1936, p. 51)

Chicanos became foreigners in their own communities and the barrio the last link to their Mexican past. With reference to Santa Barbara Albert Camarillo remarked that

. . . During the last quarter of the nineteenth century the processes of barrioization and Americanization created a new reality for Mexican people in Santa Barbara. As the Anglo capitalist economic order became dominant during the 1870s, Chicano workers tied to the dying pastoral economy experienced increasing privation. This impoverishment was reflected in the general appearance of the residentially segregated and isolated barrio of Pueblo Viejo. Made politically powerless through various methods of disenfranchisement and gerrymandering and without political leaders, the Chicanos were defenseless within a dominant society that regarded them as foreigners. (Camarillo 1979, pp. 77–78)

As the process of barrioization was effected in communities throughout the Southwest, Chicanos were transformed into an internal colony within the United States. The Chicano went from being the colonizer of a region to being the colonized, albeit a de facto one that was not formally or officially recognized. A people that had previously controlled the economy, political system, and culture had been rendered subordinate and dependent.

Perhaps no force was more critical to the subordination of the Chicano than the development and expansion of the economy of the Southwest. The three main areas of economic expansion were in agriculture and ranching, the railroads, and mining (Barrera 1979, p. 35). Between 1850 and 1880 ranching decreased and agriculture increased in importance. As agriculture became increasingly specialized and mechanized, subsistence farming declined, and there was an increased need for cheap agricultural labor. The extraction of natural resources followed a similar pattern. The development of a sophisticated technology and mechanization meant that the individual miner was replaced by the wage worker (ibid., p. 37). Although Chicanos had been pioneers in mining, they now constituted a common labor force. Economic expansion of the Southwest was greatly facilitated by the railroads.

. . . The development of mining and agriculture depended heavily on the transportation provided by the railroads, and as these sectors boomed the need for labor increased accordingly. Railroads had other significant ramifications. By triggering land booms, they hastened the displacement of Chicanos from the land. . . . The displaced Chicanos often entered the labor market as a consequence and out of sheer necessity, generally in very disadvantaged positions. (Ibid.)

What emerged during the latter part of the nineteenth century was a segmented labor force that functioned within a colonial labor system. A system, in other words, "where the labor force is segmented along ethnic and/or racial lines, and one or more of the segments is systematically maintained in a subordinate position" (ibid., p. 39). Chicanos were not the only group to serve as a subordinate labor force, however. Prior to passage of the Chinese Exclusion Act in 1882 the Chinese had been used in this capacity as colonial labor in agriculture, the mines, and the railroads. Japanese labor was used extensively after that until Japanese immigration was limited by the so-called "Gentlemen's Agreement" of 1907 (ibid., p. 40). It was not until the early part of the twentieth century that the importation of Chicano labor began on a massive scale. During the twentieth century their position as a colonial labor force was solidified.

Mario Barrera isolates five characteristics of a colonial labor system (ibid., pp. 40–48).

1. *Labor Repression.* Chicanos were "unfree labor," being relatively immobile and almost under total control of employers.

2. *The Dual Wage System.* Chicanos typically received a lower wage than Anglos who performed the same task. The practice was so common in the Arizona mines that there was an "Anglo wage" and a "Mexican wage."

3. *Occupational Stratification.* A key dimension of occupational stratification is that those jobs that are considered least desirable and which receive the lowest wages are occupied by the colonial labor. Agricultural field labor in the Southwest, for example, was performed almost exclusively by Chicanos during the twentieth century.

4. *Reserve Labor Force.* Capitalistic expansion in the Southwest was facilitated by the establishment of a large labor force in the twentieth century. This large reserve force keeps wages down by being able to expand the work force without raising wages. "Secondly, a group of unemployed workers can be used by employers as leverage in bargaining with or controlling their workers. If workers can be easily replaced, as in a strike situation, their power is greatly reduced" (ibid., p. 47).

5. *Chicanos as Buffers.* A related principle to a reserve labor force is the use of Chicanos as buffers to "absorb" the shock of economic fluctuations. During times of high unemployment colonial labor can be

laid off, whereas during times of economic expansion or during strikes they are hired once again.

Robert Blauner (1972, pp. 53–70) has isolated three characteristics of internally colonized groups that overlap somewhat with Barrera's classification. The first is group entry and lack of freedom of movement. Unlike immigrant groups who enter the host society more or less freely and as individuals or families, internally colonized people are incorporated into the society by force and en bloc as a result of conquest, enslavement, or the implementation of a labor policy based on race. According to Blauner

> The essentially voluntary entry of the immigrants was a function of their status in the labor market. The European groups were responding to the industrial needs of a free capitalist market. . . .
> Because the Europeans moved on their own, they had a degree of autonomy that was denied those whose entry followed upon conquest, capture, or involuntary labor contracts. (1972, pp. 55–56)

Because immigrants enter the society by choice and their freedom of movement is less restricted, they are more likely to identify with and assimilate into the host society. Blauner concludes that "this element of choice . . . must have been crucial in influencing the different careers and perspectives of immigrants and colonized in America, because choice is a necessary condition for commitment to any group." (ibid., p. 56)

A second characteristic identified by Blauner, the colonial labor principle in the United States, is very similar to Barrera's description of a colonial labor system. The development of the Western Hemisphere has followed a colonial labor principle based on race and color, according to which free labor was associated with white Europeans and unfree labor with non-European people of color. Colonization and control of non-Western nations has been critical to the development of Western capitalism, yet capitalism and free labor were largely reserved for white Europeans, while the colonized native participated in forced labor systems. A similar process occurred within the United States:

> . . . In an historical sense, people of color provided much of the hard labor (and the technical skills) that built up the agricultural base and the mineral-transport-communication infrastructure necessary for industrialization and modernization, whereas the Europeans worked primarily within the industrialized, modern sectors. The initial position of European ethnics, while low, was therefore strategic for movement up the economic and social pyramid. The placement of nonwhite groups, however, imposed barrier upon barrier on such mobility, freez-

ing them for long periods of time in the least favorable segments of the economy. (Blauner, 1972, p. 62)

The third characteristic isolated by Blauner is the systematic destruction of the culture and social organization of internally colonized groups. Unlike white European immigrant groups who were encouraged to assimilate into the dominant society, people of color were not readily incorporated. The cultures of people of color were not considered whole or viable. In fact, in order to implement the colonial labor system, it was necessary to attack and demean the culture of the colonized.

> . . . The colonial situation differs from the class situation of capitalism precisely in the importance of culture as an instrument of domination. Colonialism depends on conquest, control, and the imposition of new institutions and ways of thought. Culture and social organization are important as vessels of a people's autonomy and integrity; when cultures are whole and vigorous, conquest, penetration, and certain modes of control are more readily resisted. (Ibid., p. 67)

Thus, in addition to exploiting their labor and restricting freedom of movement, the dominant society seeks also to exploit their culture and to render it subordinate and dependent. Although other ethnic groups have, at various times, experienced prejudice and persecution, it should not be equated with the racism directed against colonized groups who experienced an all-out assault on their culture. In the decades following the war with Mexico legal attempts were made to restrict Mexican customs. According to Leonard Pitt (1966, p. 197)

> Under the lash of an ill-defined puritanism and nativism, the 1855 legislature passed six laws—sumptuary, labor and immigration— which bluntly or obliquely injured the Spanish-speaking. The first was a Sunday law prohibiting the operation of any "bull, bear, cock or prize fights, horse race, circus, theatre, bowling alley, gambling house, room or saloon, or any place of barbarous or noisy amusements on the Sabbath," on pain of a $10 to $500 fine; the second was a separate gambling-control act.

> . . . Other acts which had important implications for Chicanos included a $50 head tax aimed at discouraging immigration of persons not eligible for citizenship, a new foreign miners' tax, an antivagrancy law (openly referred to as the "Greaser Law"), a temperance referendum, and the failure of the legislature to translate laws into Spanish as required by the California constitution. (Ibid., p. 198)

Another aspect of colonial control identified by Blauner is external control and manipulation of colonized groups. The essence of internal colonization is the absence of power and control over vital social institutions. The colonized lack control over the economy, the political system, education, the law, and other institutions that impinge on them. Barrioization was but a simple extension of colonization.

It was through these various processes that Chicanos were rendered a conquered people. Although Mexico had been defeated in 1848, it was not until around 1880 that the Mexican inhabitants of the Southwest became economically, politically, and culturally dependent. Leonard Pitt (1966, p. 296) summarizes the downfall of the Californios:

> . . . In the final analysis the Californios were victims of an imperial conquest. . . . The United States, which had long coveted California for its trade potential and strategic location, finally provoked a war. . . . At the conclusion of fighting, it arranged to "purchase" the territory outright, and set about to colonize, by throwing the gates open to all comers. Yankee settlers then swept in by the tens of thousands, and in a matter of months and years overturned the old institutional framework, expropriated the land, imposed a new body of law, a new language, a new economy, and a new culture, and in the process exploited the labor of the local population. . . . To certain members of the old ruling class these settlers awarded a token and symbolic prestige, at least temporarily; yet with that status went very little genuine authority. In the long run Americans simply pushed aside the early ruling elite as being irrelevant. (Ibid.)

By the latter part of the twentieth century Chicanos were concentrated in the least desirable, most menial, and lowest paying occupations. In Southern California, for example, Chicanos went from working largely within a pastoral economy to being part of an urban proletariat. In 1860 30.5 percent of the Chicano population in San Diego worked as ranchers or farmers, 39.1 percent as skilled workers, and only 15.9 percent as unskilled workers (Camarillo 1979, p. 128). By 1880, however, less than 2 percent were in pastoral/ranching, 4.8 percent in skilled, and 80.9 percent in unskilled laborer occupations (ibid., p. 133). In Santa Barbara 24.3 percent were in ranching or farming in 1860, 9.9 percent in skilled trades, and 47.9 percent were unskilled laborers. By 1880 only 4.7 percent were rancher/farmers, 3.1 percent skilled workers, and 79.7 percent unskilled workers (ibid., p. 133).

The same general pattern was not supported by Griswold del Castillo's study of the Los Angeles barrio. He found very little change in the occupational structure of Los Angeles between 1844 and 1880. The vast majority of Chicanos remained at the bottom of the occupational structure throughout the Mexican and American period. Yet, information on the occupational structure may be misleading in that the categories are broad and obscure internal changes within categories. Griswold del Castillo presents data which suggest that the economic position of the Chicano did decline subsequent to the American takeover. The percentage of Mexican families who owned property was 61.4 in 1850 and the average value of property was $2,105, in 1860 the percentage declined to 28.8 with an average value of $1,228, and by 1870 it was only 21.2 percent and an average value of $1,072. Thus, fewer and fewer families owned land, and the value of the property was on the average worth about half as much (Griswold del Castillo 1979, pp. 46–47).

By 1860 the "ricos" in San Diego had already lost most of their wealth. While Mexicans had held almost all the property in 1850, within a decade out of a total real estate value of $206,400 only $82,700 (or less than 30 percent) was held by Mexicans (García 1976, p. 70). The population of San Diego fell from 650 in 1850 to 539 in 1860. Despite efforts to quickly transform San Diego from a pastoral to an urban/commercial economy, the 1850 Census for the Township of San Diego showed

> . . . that only eleven merchants remained; that only five farmers (as defined by the Census) could be found in San Diego, and only nine Anglo rancheros as compared to 25 Mexican rancheros. Twenty-four people were listed as "professionals," and 66 as skilled laborers (miners, teamsters, seamen, vaqueros) of which 43 were Anglos and 23 Mexicans. Finally, 30 persons fell in the category of unskilled labor (19 Mexicans and 11 Anglos). (Ibid., p. 77)

Although urbanization and economic expansion during the first part of the twentieth century resulted in a large influx of persons from Mexico, their economic positions remained relatively constant. Chicanos continued to be concentrated in the lowest- and least-skilled occupations.[3] In Santa Barbara in 1900 3.7 percent of the Chicano population occupied professional, 2.3 proprietorial, 10.2 skilled, 15.7 semiskilled, and 57.4 unskilled occupations. Thus, more than 70 percent were semiskilled or unskilled low blue-collar workers. By 1930 only .4 percent were in professional occupations, 3.4 percent proprietorial, 8.9 percent skilled, 12.7 percent semiskilled and 55.6 percent unskilled. The slight decrease in semiskilled and unskilled workers was offset by decreases in the proportion of Chicanos in professional occupations (Camarillo 1979, p. 173). Further analysis also revealed "that the large majority of Spanish-surnamed workers who remained in Santa Barbara from one decade to the next were occupationally immobile" (ibid., p. 175). Thus, although Chicanos entered the United States in record numbers during the 1920s, they did not partake in the American Dream according to which subsequent generations of immigrants are readily assimilated into the economic order. They remained a source of cheap and dependent labor.

The pattern was repeated in other cities throughout Southern California. Between 1910 and 1930 "the total percentage of Mexican male heads of household who were low blue-collar workers (primarily unskilled laborers) ranged from 68 to 73 percent in San Diego, from 74 to 81 percent in San Bernardino, from 65 to 69 percent in Santa Barbara, and a constant 79 percent (for 1910 and 1920) in Los Angeles," while the percentage in professional occupations ranged from 0 to 2 percent in the four communities (ibid., pp. 217-18).

The assumption that the downfall of Chicanos was attributable to the fact that they became a numerical minority in Southern California is quickly dispelled as one examines Chicano progress in communities where they retained numerical superiority. The city of El Paso was established in 1827, initially a suburb of Paso del Norte, of Ciudad Juárez, México (Martínez, 1980, p. 5). Between 1850 and 1880 the community more than doubled in population (from 300 to 736 inhabitants) but remained predominantly Mexican. With the coming of the railroads "The economy of El Paso and other centers in the Southwest received a strong stimulus as the demand for raw materials increased in the eastern United States. By 1900, El Paso had become a leading supply, processing, smelting, and refining site for the rich mining districts in the surrounding territory" (ibid., p. 7). In 1910 El Paso had been transformed into a major urban center with a population of almost 40,000. These economic changes had a significant impact on Chicanos of El Paso as the Anglo minority gained economic and political control and relegated them to a position of powerlessness.

Ethnic tensions were exacerbated by its proximity to the border and territorial disputes. Shortly after the signing of the Treaty of Guadalupe-Hidalgo, the communities of Ysleta, San Elizario, and Socorro, located near El Paso on an island formed by shifts in the Rio Grande, sought to remain in Mexico (ibid., p. 7). Their attempts were thwarted, however, as the United States claimed jurisdiction over the area. "To make matters worse, the newcomers often disregarded local rules and traditions in their drive to acquire property, inflicting native Mexicans with heavy losses in communally-held farm land, timber, and salt" (ibid.). Perhaps the most infamous of these examples was the El Paso Salt War in 1877-78, which literally became a race war. The salt beds had been discovered in 1862, but they were held as community rather than as individual property. A group of Anglo politicians, the Salt Ring, sought to gain control of the salt beds in the 1870s (Acuña 1981, p. 38). In 1877 Charles Howard, an Anglo entrepreneur, laid claim to the salt beds and attempted to charge Mexicans for salt that was removed (Sonnichsen 1961). Led by an Italian priest, Antonio Borajo, residents of San

Elizario violently resisted the Anglo take-over. The Mexicans eventually shot Howard, and this set off the so-called Salt War.

Although El Paso grew at an impressive rate during the twentieth century and Mexicans contributed to this growth, they remained grossly underrepresented economically, politically, and educationally. Martínez found that between 1910 and 1970 Chicanos were largely concentrated in low-skill, poorly paying jobs, while Anglos were concentrated in skilled and professional occupations (Martínez 1980, p. 9). "Entry of Spanish surnamed individuals into white-collar positions has been extremely restricted, with only 3.4 percent falling under ths designation as late as 1960, and a slightly improved 6.3 percent by 1970. By contrast, the Anglo labor force has experienced considerably greater expansion at the top since 1910" (ibid., p. 9). In 1910 57.4 percent of the Spanish-surname population worked as unskilled laborers and 17.0 percent as semiskilled and service workers, while only 1.6 percent worked in high white-collar occupations. By 1970 23.5 percent worked in unskilled occupations, 33.7 percent in semiskilled and service work, and 6.3 percent in high white-collar positions (ibid., p. 10). Thus, while there are more Chicanos in lower-level management and professional positions, "proportionately these individuals still lag far behind their Anglo counterparts, and Chicanos are largely absent from influential and policy-making positions in El Paso" (ibid., p. 11). Chicanos in high white-collar occupations increased from 1.6 percent in 1910 to 6.3 percent in 1970, but the proportion of Anglos in such positions went from 17.0 to 27.4 percent (ibid., p. 10).

A similar pattern was uncovered in a study of El Paso conducted by Mario T. García. In a more refined occupational analysis than Martínez's, García found that the proportion of Chicanos in professional and managerial positions actually declined between 1900 and 1940 (1981, p. 86). In 1900 3.03 percent of the Spanish-surnamed population were employed as professionals and 3.64 as managers, whereas in 1940 2.42 percent were professionals and 2.42 percent were managers. (ibid.). Significantly, throughout this forty-year period the vast majority of Chicanos were employed as laborers, service workers, or operatives (ibid.).

The dual wage system was also observed in El Paso. According to García (ibid., p. 88) an economist reported that Mexican carpenters received an average wage of from $3.50 to $4.50 at the same time that Anglo carpenters were earning about $8.00 per day. What is most significant is not only that Mexicans generally occupied the lowest, most menial occupations but that within the same occupation they were consistently paid less than Anglo workers. The Dillingham Commission (U.S. Senate Immigration Commission 1911, p. 19) found that in 1909 86.1 percent of the Mexicans who worked on the western railroads earned less than $1.25 per day, whereas only 10.3 percent of American workers earned this little. The commission also found that while most Mexican smelter workers were paid between $2 and $2.50 per day, the majority of other workers earned more than $2.50 per day.

García reports that hearings in El Paso before the Texas Industrial Welfare Commission of 1919 revealed that Chicanas there were consistently paid a lower wage than Anglo women who worked in laundries, department stores, and garment factories (1981, pp. 91-96). Chicanos were generally excluded from unions, and even when they were included, it was not uncommon for union locals to be segregated. "In an occupation, for example, including a significant percentage of Mexican Americans as well as American employees, the AFL endorsed segregated locals" (ibid., p. 97). The Mexican workers were frequently used as strikebreakers, and they were perceived as depressing wage scales. The response of the local AFL in El Paso was strongly anti-Mexican. The *Advocate* encouraged business and industry not to hire the Mexican.

> Cheap labor—at the cost of every ideal cherished in the heart of every member of the white race, utterly destroyed and buried beneath the greedy ambitions of a few grasping money gluttons, who would not hesitate to sink the balance of society to the lowest levels of animalism, if by so doing they can increase their own bank account.
>
> True Americans do not want or advocate the importation of any people who cannot be absorbed into full citizenship, who cannot eventually be raised to our highest social standard, but help to raise that standard to even higher planes; where the avariciously inclined will be relegated to the nether darkness from which they drew their blackened souls. (Ibid., p. 103)

While organized labor generally perceived Mexicans as a menace, they were welcomed by employers (see Hufford 1929, p. 37). The following statements from farmers in Nueces County, Texas, demonstrates why they were favorably disposed toward them:

> "You can't beat them as labor." "I prefer Mexican labor to other classes of labor. It is more humble and you get more for your money." "The Mexicans have a sense of duty and loyalty, and the qualities that go to make a good servant." "They are the best labor we have." "No other class we could bring to Texas would take his place. He's a natural farm laborer." "If a Mexican likes you he will fight for you. One of my Mexicans beat up another Mexican for saying that I beat up Mexicans." "The Mexicans are ignorant, but good laborers." (Taylor 1934, p. 126)

In 1870 almost one-third of the population in Nueces County was Mexican. These and subsequent generations of Mexicans provided the bulk of the cheap labor in the stock industry and the development of agriculture (ibid., p. 100). In the 1860s *vaqueros* worked for about $10 per month and food. By the 1880s Mexican *vaqueros* were earning about $12 per month and Americans $15. Almost all *pastores* (sheepherders) in the county were Mexican, and they worked for as little as $3 or $4 per month in the 1860s, and by the mid-1870s wages were still only between $5 and $10 per month (ibid., p. 117). Mexicans also made up the bulk of the cheap labor in the cotton industry. During the 1880s Mexicans were employed at a rate of 75 cents per day without board; by 1909 they were still earning only $1 per day for 11 hours of labor, and some received less (ibid.).

Inducements were given to the Mexicans in the form of land on halves so that they could maintain gardens or domestic animals, while others provided them with lodging, wood, and water. "The primary purpose of maintaining Mexican share-croppers on halves is to immobilize them so that ample labor will be on hand through the year and a large nucleus to start the picking season" (ibid., p. 121). By maintaining an ample labor supply wages were kept low. Also, by providing all the essentials of life and extending credit Mexicans were maintained in a form of debt servitude. The annual cash income of Mexican families was estimated at between $300 and $350 per year (ibid., p. 122). One family was reported to have earned $1,335, but the family contained two sons who worked all year round, four other children who picked cotton, and the mother who also worked (ibid., p. 123). Most of the Mexican sharecroppers were in debt to the landlord by the time the season for picking cotton arrived. And many remained in perpetual debt. "One large farmer estimated, for example, that 'about 20 out of 24 Mexicans owe me money until the crop comes in. Only one man carried his account over [the end of the year] twice, and he is ahead now'" (ibid., p. 124).

Mexicans were viewed as docile and were generally preferred over Negro or white labor.

> . . . "People here don't want white pickers. They prefer Mexicans; they are content with whatever you give them . . . you handle the Mexican better; they're more subservient. . . . "
>
> "The Mexican is ignorant and you can train him. The white man is socially better than the Mexican; he feels more on an equality and doesn't want to take your orders."
>
> A real estate dealer complained "Whites here will beg before they will work for $2 a day. They think it's a disgrace to work at low wages and with the Mexicans." (ibid., p. 130)

It was also not uncommon to use force to discipline them. Yet when Mexicans complained or struck for higher wages, they were readily denounced.

"Some Mexicans you can rely on the same as a white man, but they are very much in the minority. The majority are worthless; some are most agreeable. . . . They are treacherous." (ibid., p. 127)

While the bulk of the Mexican population in Nueces County was employed in agriculture, a few were found in urban occupations. Almost all track laborers were Mexican, as were most of the laborers in the Corpus Christi fishing industry (ibid., pp. 158-159). They were also employed as mechanics and as carpenters but were largely excluded from the unions and received a lower wage for the same work (ibid., p. 160). The women worked as clerks, dressmakers, cooks, and domestic servants, and in laundries. Mexican laundry workers in Robstown earned between $7 and $9 per week, and in "Corpus" earnings ranged from $9 to $12. Like their male counterparts, Mexican women were preferred because of their willingness to work long hours at low wages.

The exploitation of Mexican labor has been documented by Paul Taylor in a number of other communities throughout the Southwest. The pattern in the Imperial Valley of California is similar to that of Nueces County. Mexican labor is employed "in almost every agricultural crop and operation in the valley" (1930, volume 1, p. 33). It is used in picking grapes, melons, tomatoes, and cotton and in harvesting lettuce. Mexicans provided the bulk of the cheap labor demanded by these various industries. They also were a source of cheap labor in the sugar-beet industry in the valley of the South Platte Colorado and the Winter Garden District of south Texas (Dimmit County). In fact, almost all labor in the fields throughout the Southwest was Mexican (ibid., p. 325).

Contemporary Chicano Labor: An Assessment of Progress since the Great Depression

Changes in the American economy in the more recent period were to have a profound impact on the position of Chicanos. Throughout the second half of the nineteenth century and the first third of the twentieth, Chicanos worked as common laborers within agriculture. With increased urbanization and industrialization, and the mechanization and expansion of agriculture, more and more Chicanos entered urban and industrial occupations. In 1900 farmworkers made up 17.7 percent of all workers, but by 1920 they constituted only 11.7 percent, and by 1970 they were less than 1.8 percent (Szymanski 1972, p. 107). Chicanos, thus, were transformed into an urban colonial labor force, At the same time that Mexican laborers were concentrated largely in unskilled manual occupations, there were signs of an emerging lower middle class, and a few Chicanos were even entering professional and managerial positions.

Mario Barrera (1979, pp. 53-57) has isolated four general economic sectors that were present in the Southwest during the nineteenth century—peripheral, colonized, marginal, and integrated. According to Barrera most but not all Chicanos were found within the colonial sectors. The *peripheral sector* was made up of Chicanos employed outside the mainstream of the newly emerging capitalistic economic order. These Chicanos lived in rural areas and participated in the precapitalistic economic order. An example would be San Salvador, a Mexican community established near present-day Riverside, California. The *colonized sector* included Mexicans who were absorbed by the new capitalistic order but at the bottom in the lowest positions. The *marginal sector* consisted of workers who were displaced by the new economic order, but their labor was not yet utilized or incorporated. Many Chicanos were unemployed or not incorporated into the capitalistic economy, especially in the period prior to 1880. They were in a sense a part neither of the declining feudal nor of the emerging capitalistic order. "The *integrated sector* was at least theoretically possible, although few data can be cited to support its existence" (ibid., p. 57). To be integrated required that Chicanos occupy an equal and nonsubordinate position within the capitalistic order. It required, in other words, the absence of discrimination and subordination. During the nineteenth century, at least, Chicanos remained clearly outside of the integrated sector.

The first part of the twentieth century, according to Barrera, brought significant changes within the four economic sectors. The peripheral sector was eliminated, and the marginal sector did not play a significant role, as most Chicanos were incorporated into the colonial sector (ibid., p. 76).

> . . . As Mexican immigrants flowed into the Southwest and were incorporated into the segmented labor market, the colonial labor force underwent a major quantitative expansion. At the same time, there was still no clear evidence of a distinct integrated sector of Chicano workers at this time. (Ibid.)

Although a few Chicanos began to assume lower- and middle-status white-collar occupations, "Chicanos were not integrated into the Anglo middle class, but were confined to a kind of Chicano subeconomy" (ibid., p. 72). Clerks, for example, "were hired by Anglo stores not to serve the general public, but to bring in Chicano trade. They were paid considerably less than Anglo clerks" (ibid.).

This pattern led Barrera to introduce the notion of class segmentation. In the contemporary period Chicanos can be found across all social classes, although they are concentrated in the working class, but within each class they constitute a colonized class segment. "A class segment is a portion of a class which is set off from the rest of the class by some readily identifiable and relatively stable criterion, such as race, ethnicity, or sex, and whose status in relation to the means and process of production is affected by that demarcation" (ibid., p. 101). Barrera posits that the movement of Chicanos out of the working class has not led to decolonization, for "The different class segments can be considered *together* to constitute an *internal colony*, a dimension of reality that cuts across class lines" (ibid., p. 103). Thus, Chicanos appear to have made some economic progress since the Great Depression, but most have yet to be incorporated into the integrated sector of the economy.

Since 1930 Chicanos have gradually but consistently improved their economic standing (ibid., p. 138; Fogel 1967, p. 195). In 1930 35.1 percent of the male and 19.7 percent of the female Chicano population worked as farm laborers, whereas by 1970 these figures had dropped to 8.1 and 3.0 respectively. The proportion working as unskilled laborers was 28.2 percent of the men and 2.8 percent of the women in 1930, and 12.1 percent of the men and 1.5 percent of the women in 1970 (Barrera 1979, p. 131). Yet, 40 percent of the Chicano population are still unskilled or semiskilled laborers, compared to 20 percent of the general population (ibid., p. 130). Also, although the proportion of Chicanos in professions has increased from less than 1 percent to about 4 percent, 8 percent of the general population are professionals.

Despite these apparent improvements the economic position of Chicanos relative to Anglos has remained fairly stable. Increases in income have generally lagged behind occupational upgrading (Fogel, 1967, pp. 194-95). Briggs, Fogel, and Schmidt (1977, p. 59) found that in 1959 the median income of Spanish-surnamed families in the Southwest was 65 percent of Anglo income, and in 1969 it was only 66 percent. In California, in fact, income declined. Although Barrera notes that "Why the incomes should have declined in California at the same time that there was some occupational upgrading is not clear," a possible interpretation is that Chicanos continue to function as a colonized class segment. If this is the case, the so-called "progress" made by Chicanos since 1930 may be illusory. Chicanos, in other words, may be moving out of the working class without improving their economic position. Skilled and unskilled Anglo workers, for example, earn more than Chicano white-collar workers and, at times, even more than Chicano professionals.

More recent figures show that Chicano income still lags behind Anglo income. Data from the 1980 Census revealed that the ratio of Hispanic to white median family income was .71 in California, .63 in Texas, .74 in New Mexico, .78 in Arizona, and .64 in Colorado (National Chicano Research Network 1982, p. 1). Similarly, in 1976 the median income for persons 14 years and over with income was $6,450 for Chicano males and $2,750 for

Chicano females, while for persons not of Spanish-origin it was $8,981 for males and $3,394 for females (U.S. Bureau of the Census 1977, p. 28). Thus, Chicano male income was 72 percent of Anglo male income, and Chicana income was 81 percent of Anglo female income. Significantly, the median income of Chicanas was only 31 percent of the median income of non-Hispanic males. It should be noted that these averages are based on persons with incomes, and Chicanos have a higher rate of unemployment, so that many who work sporadically (and receive low wages) are not reported in the census.

The income of Chicano families has improved but still lags behind Anglo income. In 1975, for example, the median income of families of Mexican origin was $9,551 compared to an Anglo median of $13,719. Thus median Chicano income was 70 percent of non-Hispanic income (U.S. Bureau of the Census 1977, p. 9). In 1977 the median income of Mexican-origin families was $11,742, whereas the median for families not of Spanish origin was $16,284, or 72 percent of Anglo income (U.S. Bureau of the Census 1978a, p. 10). In 1978 Chicano median income ($12,835) remained about 72 percent of the median income ($17,912) of families not of Spanish origin (U.S. Bureau of the Census 1979, p. 6). By 1979 there was a modest improvement, as the median income of Spanish-origin families ($15,171) climbed to 76 percent of the median income ($19,965) of other families (U.S. Bureau of the Census 1981, p. 6). Approximately 19 percent of Mexican-origin families live below the poverty line, compared to 9 percent of those not of Spanish origin (U.S. Bureau of the Census 1978a, p. 10). Significantly, among individuals of Mexican origin 14 years and over only 1.2 percent had incomes of $25,000 or more (U.S. Bureau of the Census 1977, p. 9). Yet, the proportion of Mexican-origin families with incomes this high was almost 9 percent, as compared to 23 percent of families not of Spanish origin (ibid).

In evaluating the relative economic progress of Chicanos it is important to consider relevant demographic characteristics. Chicanos as a people are much younger than the population as a whole. The median age for persons of Mexican origin is about 21 years, while the median of non-Hispanics is 31 years (U.S. Bureau of the Census 1981, p. 5). Indeed, 42.4 percent of the Chicano population is under 18 years of age, and only 7.2 percent is 55 years or older, as opposed to 21.2 percent of the general population (ibid.). A significant proportion of the Chicano people are dependent children rather than adults. Because Chicanos have a higher rate of fertility and larger families, family income figures tend to obscure their economic subordination. Stated simply, family income is typically divided among more persons, so that even if Chicano families were to attain parity with Anglo families, Chicano *per capita* income would still lag behind. Chicano families have an average of 4.07 persons per household compared to an average of 3.28 for those not of Spanish origin (U.S. Bureau of the Census 1980, p. 12). If one takes the median family income for families of Mexican origin in 1978 ($12,835) and divides it by the total number of persons in the average household (4.07), the *per capita* income is equal to $3,154 (ibid., p. 14). The *per capita* income for non-Spanish-surnamed families, on the other hand, is $5,461. In terms of *per capita* income Chicano median income is therefore only 58 percent of Anglo median income.

The educational attainment of Chicanos is also lower than that of Anglos. Only about 3.9 percent of the Mexican-origin population 25 years and over have completed 4 years of college or more, compared to 16.9 percent of those not of Spanish origin (U.S. Bureau of the Census 1980, p. 5). Similarly, whereas 68.9 percent of the non-Hispanic population have graduated from high school, only 34.9 percent of Chicanos have completed this much schooling (ibid.). Finally, 23.9 percent of Chicanos and only 2.8 percent of the general population have completed less than 5 years of school (ibid.). Although the education of young adults has shown consistent improvements, the Census Bureau concluded that "the gap in education between Spanish and non-Spanish persons 25 to 29 years old was not significantly different from that of persons 25 years old and over" (ibid., p. 4). Data from the 1980 Census indicate that the ratio of the percentage of Hispanics over 25 completing high school to the percentage of whites over 25 having completed high school was .56 in California, .53 in Texas, .66 in New Mexico, .61 in Arizona, and .56 in Colorado (National Chicano Research Network 1982, p. 1).

While there has been some improvement in the occupational distribution of Chicanos, they are far from achieving parity with the Anglo population. The majority of Chicano males (61.3 percent) who are employed are blue-collar workers, 12.9 percent are service workers, 6.4 percent are farmworkers, and 19.4 percent are white-collar workers (U.S. Bureau of the Census 1980, p. 9). For Chicanas who work 28.1 percent are blue-collar, 23.4 percent service, 2.4 percent farm, and 46.1 percent white-collar workers (ibid.). It should be noted, however, that the vast majority of Chicanas in white-collar jobs occupy sales and clerical rather than professional or managerial positions. In fact, while only 6.4 percent of Chicana workers are employed as professionals and 3.5 percent as managers or administrators, 31.1 percent are in clerical positions, 25.0 percent are operatives, and 23.4 percent are service workers (ibid., p. 29). The fact that only 1.3 percent of Chicanas work as laborers suggests not that they have been incorporated into the integrated sector but that they are largely within the marginal sector. When both sexes are considered, 5.8 percent of the Mexican-origin population occupy professional occupations and 5.1 percent are managers or administrators, compared to 16.5 and 11.2 percent respectively of the non-Spanish-surnamed population (ibid.). Approximately 25.8 percent of the Mexican-origin population are operatives, 9.2 percent are laborers (excluding farm), 4.8 percent are farm laborers, and 16.7 percent are service workers (ibid.). Among those not of Spanish origin 14.5 percent are operatives, 4.2 percent are nonfarm laborers, 1.0 percent are farmworkers, and 13.4 percent are service workers (ibid.).

Even more significant than the level of movement of Chicanos out of unskilled and semiskilled occupations is the question of whether they receive comparable pay as Anglos when they do move into nonmanual positions. Table 2 shows that within almost each occupational category persons of Spanish origin earned less than their counterparts who were not of Spanish origin. The category "not of Spanish origin" of course is a gross one that in-cludes blacks and other groups that are not white. It also includes persons who do not know or did not report on origin. The figures are therefore conser-vative estimates of Anglo income. The median income of Spanish-origin male professionals was $13,478, or 71 percent of the median earnings of non-Hispanic professionals ($17,483). The median income of non-Hispanic pro-fessionals who are self-employed was $22,888, and for Hispanic males and females the figure was too low to compute a median. Spanish-origin males who are managers or administrators report a median of $13,257, whereas those not of Spanish origin have a median income of $18,373.

The commonly accepted adage that education is the key to social mobility for social minorities is also called into question by the Mexican-American study project, which reported that even when educational attain-ment is controlled, Chicano incomes are much lower than Anglo incomes (Fogel, 1967, p. 11). Recent census data also show that for each educational level Chicanos tend to earn substantially less. The median income for Chi-canos who graduated from college ($14,691) is, in fact, lower than the median income for non-Hispanic families as a whole (U.S. Bureau of the Census 1980, p. 37). The median income for persons of Mexican origin with 1 to 3 years of college was $11,393, for those who graduated from high school it was $9,565, and for grade-school graduates it was $6,504 (ibid.). The depression of wages is especially apparent among Chicanas. The number of Chicanas with 4 years of college was too low to compute, but for those with 1 to 3 years of college the median income was a paltry $6,393 (ibid.).

Conclusion

This overview of social and economic history of the Southwest illus-trates how Chicanos were transformed from a colonizing to a colonized peo-ple. The first permanent settlements in the Southwest were Spanish, sub-sequently Mexican. The war with Mexico and the military victory of the United States signaled not only the beginning of the destruction of the Mex-

TABLE 2

Median Earnings in 1978 of Civilians 14 Years Old and Over with Earnings,
by Spanish Origin, Occupation of Longest Job in 1978, Class of Worker of
Longest Job in 1978, and Sex: March 1979

OCCUPATION AND CLASS OF WORKER	MALE		FEMALE	
	Spanish Origin	Not of Spanish Origin[1]	Spanish Origin	Not of Spanish Origin[1]
Total with earnings	$ 8,899	$12,327	$ 4,705	$ 5,282
Occupation				
Professional, technical, and kindred workers	13,478	17,483	10,415	9,893
self-employed	(B)	22,888	(B)	2,925
salaried	14,038	17,229	10,652	10,064
Managers and administrators, except farm	13,257	18,373	(B)	8,611
self-employed	(B)	11,629	(B)	3,379
salaried	13,897	19,531	(B)	9,246
Sales workers	7,404	12,174	3,209	2,815
Clerical and kindred workers	10,093	12,025	6,048	6,484
Craft and kindred workers	11,110	13,735	(B)	6,659
Operatives except transport	8,859	10,869	4,972	5,683
manufacturing	9,031	11,356	5,096	6,034
non-manufacturing	8,212	9,823	(B)	3,661
Transport equipment operatives	10,397	11,791	(B)	3,222
Laborers, excluding farm	6,097	4,339	(B)	3,149
Farmers and farm managers	(B)	7,541	(B)	1,436
Farm laborers and supervisors	4,780	2,335	(B)	793
Service workers except private household	6,136	5,496	2,986	2,762
Private household workers	(B)	(B)	1,207	770
Class of Worker				
Private wage or salary workers	$ 8,577	$12,244	$ 4,761	$ 5,066
in agriculture	5,955	3,178	1,388	976
not in agriculture	8,899	12,507	4,954	5,119
Government wage or salary workers	11,502	13,996	5,233	7,694
public administration	14,681	15,766	(B)	8,517
other government workers	9,824	12,335	4,734	7,417
Self-employed workers	10,060	10,249	(B)	1,908
in nonagricultural industries	10,360	11,172	(B)	1,909
Unpaid family workers	(B)	1,179	(B)	944

Source: U.S. Bureau of the Census 1980, p. 30.
1. Includes persons who did not know or did not report on origin.

ican social system and way of life but the imposition of a new economic order. Mexican society was traditional, Catholic, and feudal, whereas American society was predominantly modern, Protestant, and capitalistic. Historically it is difficult, if not impossible, to separate cultural and linguistic conquest from economic penetration. Economic, political, cultural, and religious domination of the Chicano by the Anglo were thus inextricably linked. Economic changes subsequent to the war with Mexico meant that Chicanos went from being part of a feudal order that was internally differentiated to being a colonial labor force and, eventually, an urban proletariat not fully integrated into the modern economic order. So critical was the economic subordination of the Chicano that Raul Fernandez argues that the Mexican-American War and the American take-over of the Southwest is best seen, not as a clash between cultures or a military victory, but as a clash between competing and conflicting economic systems. More specifically, he sees it as the usurpation of a pastoral feudal economy by a capitalistic one.

In examining the United States-Mexico border in general Fernandez isolates three distinct historical periods that correspond to stages of capitalistic development (1977, pp. 6-12). The first stage begins with 1848 and extends to the turn of the century and is characterized by the defeat of a more "backward" economic system by a more "developed" system. The Treaty of Guadalupe-Hidalgo thus simply legitimated the victory of capitalism over feudalism. "After the War of 1848, the battle moved from the economic sphere to the political and judicial levels" (ibid., p. 7). In the decades that followed, Mexican landowners lost their land as a result of legal and coercive extralegal mechanisms, with both Mexican and Anglo landowners giving way to a rising entrepreneural class. The second stage entailed the development of capitalism and the emergence of a demand for a cheap labor force that was needed for capitalistic expansion in the Southwest. Much of this cheap labor was provided by Mexican immigration which began in the 1880s and increased rapidly during the twentieth century. *"The first stage deals with the process that led to the legal establishment of a border that was already being established economically. The second stage is the epoch of coincidence of the legal with the actual economic border. The present stage is one where the legal border is, in some ways, a fiction, and has been left behind by the advance of the integration process"* (ibid., pp. 10-11).

This last stage coincides with the rise of multinational corporations. Fernandez sees the economy of border towns as being "increasingly shaped by the presence of American industry" (ibid., p. 11). The United States-Mexico border cannot therefore be understood independently of economic forces and the dependent relation that exists between the Mexican economy and American-based multinationals.

Chicanos are unique in being an internal colony that borders on its home nation. Blacks were forcefully transported from their native Africa, Indians displaced from their homeland, but the Chicano remains close to his native roots. The proximity of Mexico and the economic dependency of this nation on the United States meant that the Mexican would constitute a permanent and virtually inexhaustible supply of cheap labor, but it also meant that they would actively resist assimilation and incorporation into the melting pot. The following chapter examines the United States-Mexico border and patterns of migration.

3

The United States–Mexico Border: A Chicano Perspective on Immigration and Undocumented Workers

This chapter presents an in-depth analysis of the United States–Mexico border and of Mexican immigration, legal and otherwise, to the United States. Among the questions raised are: What have been the dominant patterns or trends in migration and what factors have affected its flow? Are undocumented workers a drain on the economy and on social services? What are some of the prevalent attitudes toward undocumented workers by employers and the public at large? What are the solutions that have been offered for stemming the tide of undocumented workers and how viable are they? How does the proximity of the border affect the problem of undocumented workers? To what extent is public policy on Mexican immigration shaped by the interests of the dominant society and American capitalism? After examining these and related questions, the chapter concludes with a series of policy recommendations that reflect a Chicano perspective on the issue of immigration and undocumented workers.

Patterns of Migration: From "Natives" to "Wetbacks"

Patterns of migration from Mexico to the United States are closely tied to expansion and contraction of American capitalism. Between 1850 and 1880 there was virtually no movement across the border (Samora 1975, p. 65), as the United States was viewed as a conquering and inhospitable nation. However, by the last quarter of the nineteenth century economic expansion had created a demand for cheap labor. From the 1880s to about 1908 migration increased slowly but steadily. The railroads played a critical role in facilitating this migration. Porfirio Díaz, Mexican dictator from 1876 to 1910, encouraged foreign capital investment. On the eve of the Mexican Revolution of 1910 almost 15,000 miles of railroad had been completed, and one could easily travel from the interior of Mexico to the border (Galarza 1964, p. 27). At the same time that the railroads served as a conduit for transporting Mexican workers, Mexican crews provided much of the labor for the American rail-

48

roads. In 1909 nine western railroads had a common-labor force that was 17.1 percent Mexican, but 20 years later the figure was 59.5 percent (Hoffman 1974, p. 7).

Yet the great wave of Mexican migration was to come between 1910 and 1930. So extensive was this massive movement of people that it has been estimated that perhaps as much as one-eighth of the Mexican population came to the United States during this period (Acuña 1981, p. 123). A number of factors contributed to the mass movement. First, the rapidly industrializing and urbanizing United States created a great demand for cheap unskilled labor to work in the steel mills, mines, meat-packing houses, brick yards, and canneries. Even more significant was the demand for cheap labor in the expanding agricultural industry. Opportunities for crop picking opened up throughout the Southwest—in the Imperial and San Joaquin valleys of California, the Salt River Valley of Arizona, the Lower Rio Grande Valley of Texas, and the sugar beet fields of Michigan, Minnesota, and Colorado. The demand for cheap labor was intensified further by World War I, which depleted the number of U.S. workers, and the Immigration Act of 1917, which restricted foreign labor. The Immigration Act of 1917 set limits on immigration from Europe and established a literacy test and a head tax for immigrants. However, these restrictions were waived in the case of Mexican workers, so that between 1917 and 1920 over 73,000 Mexican temporary workers entered the United States (Samora 1975, p. 66). In addition there were over 100,000 permanent Mexican immigrants (ibid., p. 681).

Political and economic forces within Mexico also gave impetus to the northern migration. During the thirty-four-year dictatorship of Porfirio Díaz the economic position of the Mexican peasant had witnessed a continuous and precipitous decline. Díaz was successful in consolidating not only his own power but also the power of wealthy landowners. The masses were brutally exploited. The rich grew richer at the expense of the poor. Most peones were landless and forced to work for subsistence wages (Silva Herzog 1960, p. 40). Estimates indicate that by 1910 almost half of Mexico was controlled by 3,000 families, and the real wages of a peasant were about one-quarter of what they had been in 1800 (Parkes 1969, p. 306). The economic and political instability of Mexico, however, was not unrelated to American domination and intervention. At the time of the Mexican Revolution American interests were in control of more than three-fourths of the mines and over half of the oil fields. They also held substantial interests in many other industries.

The need for cheap labor was intensified by the Chinese Exclusion Act in 1882, the Gentlemen's Agreement of 1907 which effectively barred Japanese immigration, and restrictions on immigration from southern Europe (Samora 1975, p. 233). Mexican labor was also preferred by American capitalists because the Mexican was willing to work long hours at low wages and because of Mexico's proximity. Much of the employment, especially in agriculture, was seasonal and subject to change. The labor supply and demand could thus be easily manipulated. It was also commonly assumed that the Mexican, being so close to his homeland, did not wish to establish permanent residence in the United States. The Mexican was therefore viewed as an ideal worker. It was believed that they would come, work for long hours and low wages, make few demands, and eventually return to Mexico.

These beliefs were further buttressed by negative racial stereotypes (see Reisler 1974, pp. 210-45). The Mexican was frequently viewed as a subhuman species, as a domesticated animal that would do work that a white person would not. Dr. George P. Clemens, who managed Los Angeles County's Agricultural Department from 1917 to 1939 and was a lobbyist in Congress in favor of unrestricted Mexican immigration, felt that the lowly tasks of agriculture were those "to which the oriental and Mexican due to their crouching and bending habits are fully adapted, while the white is physically unable to adapt himself to them" (Hoffman 1974, p. 10).

Although the Immigration Act of 1917 included Mexicans in its literacy provisions and the head tax was also initially applied to them, pressure from industrialists and growers led to the waiving of illiteracy and head-tax requirements for Mexican immigrants. Between 1917 and 1921 72,862 persons entered the United States legally, and thousands more entered illegally (Neal, 1941, p. 100).

At the same time that capitalistic interests favored an open border and unlimited Mexican immigration, antipathy toward the Mexican and nativist fervor intensified. Nativism was exacerbated by World War I and the prevailing antiforeign sentiment. Negative attitudes toward Mexicans also had an economic basis. Because Mexicans were frequently used as a reserve army of labor and as strikebreakers, they were held responsible for depressing wages.

As a result of a depression in 1921 Mexican laborers quickly became superfluous, and many were stranded throughout the United States without work or money (ibid., p. 130). By 1923 the economy had recovered, and Mexican labor was once again in demand. Nativist and restrictionist feeling continued to grow and resulted in heated debate in Congress over the issue of Mexican immigration. Restrictionists included small farmers, unions, and those with racist ideologies who feared widespread miscegenation. Testimony before the Committee on Immigration of the United States Senate favoring restriction of Western Hemisphere immigration included statements by Dr. Thomas Nixon Carver, professor of economics at Harvard University, who asserted that

> . . . The bringing of cheap Mexican labor brings the same situation in agriculture in California as slavery did in the South . . .

> Slavery in the South . . . drove a wedge that raised those who
> were able to buy slaves to do their work, but lowered those who had
> to sell their labor to compete with that of the slaves. It made aristocrats
> above the wedge and poor white trash below. The same thing is likely
> to happen in California . . . and the introduction of Mexican peon
> labor will bring a problem far worse than caused by the introduction
> of Chinese and Japanese. (U.S. Congress Senate Committee on Im-
> migration 1928, p. 9)

Unrestricted immigration was favored by industrialists and large growers
(see, Lipshultz 1962, pp. 6-10). The Immigration Act of 1921 restricted immigration from eastern and southern Europe. There was considerable pressure
to include Mexicans in the provisions of the bill, but agribusiness was successful in lobbying Congress to exclude them (Acuña 1981, p. 131). Nativist fervor intensified, however, and led to the passage of the Immigration Act of
1924, which excluded most Asians and further limited immigration from
southern and eastern Europe (Acuña 1981, p. 132). Despite heated debate
over the issue in both houses of Congress and intense opposition by those
who saw the Mexican as racially and culturally inferior, Mexicans were once
again excluded from the quota.

While restrictionists failed in their quest to include a quota on Mexican
immigration, they did succeed with the passage of a bill which created the
Border Patrol, an agency charged with the responsibility of enforcing existing
immigration laws. In 1925 $1 million was appropriated for the creation of the
Border Patrol. Although hampered initially by a lack of uniforms and poorly
trained personnel, within seven years after its inception it had captured over
100,000 illegal aliens and over 2,600 smugglers of aliens (Hoffman, 1974,
p. 31).

Although attempts to pass restrictive legislation failed, by the end of
the 1920s Mexican immigration was being impeded via stronger enforcement
of existing laws. By August 1928 visas were being denied to most Mexicans
entering the United States (ibid., p. 32). The three most basic reasons for
their denial were (1) illiteracy, (2) rigid interpretation of the Liable to Become
a Public Charge (LPC) provision of the Immigration Act of 1917, and (3) enforcement of the provision which forbade "contract labor." If a person seeking a visa indicated an advanced commitment for employment, the visa could
be denied, but if he did not, then it was said that he might become a public
charge. By 1929 the State Department had negotiated an agreeement according to which Mexican officials would voluntarily limit the number of visas
that would be issued. In the same year Congress passed a law which made it
a felony to enter the United States illegally. Thus, during the decade Mexican migrants were transformed from being migratory workers who crossed an

arbitrary demarcation with impunity to becoming criminal or illegal entrants into an area that was previously Mexican land. Interestingly, the establishment of the Border Patrol and enforcement of immigration laws created a need for a new entrepreneur—the *coyote*, or person who specialized in transporting undocumented workers for profit.

Jorge Bustamante has isolated several contradictions of American capitalism which are reflected in the ambiguous status of undocumented workers:

> . . . contradictions such as (1) a condemnation of the Mexican worker by defining him as a criminal and, at the same time maintaining a demand for his labor. This is reflected in a steadily increasing flux of Mexican workers each year. (2) penalizing a worker from Mexico for being in the United States without a visa, but not penalizing a farmer for hiring the former. (3) maintaining an agency for the enforcement of immigration laws, and at the same time exerting budget limitations and/or political pressures to prevent a successful enforcement of the law. (1981, p. 46)

Throughout history Mexican immigrant workers to the United States have been at the mercy of fluctuations within the American economy. Their movement has depended on the operation of a number of "push" and "pull" factors. As American capitalism has expanded, the demand for Mexican labor has intensified, but during times of economic contraction the demand decreases. Juan Gómez-Quiñones has classified Mexican immigration into five broad periods: 1848 to 1910, 1910 to 1929, 1930 to 1940, 1941 to 1965, and 1965 to the present. "These periods are related to labor needs, quantity of immigration, and United States immigration laws" (Gómez-Quiñones, 1981, p. 22). During periods of economic depression harassment of Mexican workers has been intense according to Gómez-Quiñones. Persecution was unusually severe in the years 1920-21, 1932-33, 1953-54, and 1974-80 (ibid.).

Mexican immigration grew steadily between 1900 and 1925, but by the 1930s the number had dramatically declined:

1920	51,042	1926	42,638
1921	29,603	1927	66,766
1922	18,246	1928	57,765
1923	62,709	1929	38,980
1924	87,648	1930	11,915
1925	32,378	1931	2,627

(Samora 1975, p. 68)

At the time of the Great Depression nativist feelings had reached a feverous pitch. As a result the Mexican worker was the first to be fired or laid off, and many were forced to go on public relief. Great pressure mounted not only to limit immigration but to expel Mexicans who had entered illegally and who were perceived as burdening the welfare rolls. Thousands of Mexicans were excluded through a program termed "operation deportation" in 1930.

> . . . Although no statistics were kept for this operation, the general procedure was to require all those suspected of being alien, to prove that they were born in the United States. The person who could not satisfy this requirement was expelled from the country under the administrative procedure of "voluntary departure." (Bustamante 1981, p. 43)

In addition to deportations which were forced and coercive, a so-called "voluntary" program of repatriation was also used to exclude surplus Mexican labor. "Repatriation" was technically a voluntary return to one's homeland, but in reality coercion and intimidation were frequently employed. Many were excluded because they were declared indigent and a public charge by local officials. In Los Angeles alone over 80,000 Mexican workers and their families were herded together with their worldly belongings and sent back across the border in special trains. Significantly, many of those excluded were children born in this country and thus United States citizens. The two-pronged program of deportation and repatriation was so successful that the mass migration of the previous era was reversed. Officially 300,000 Mexicans were excluded, but unofficially the figure was probably closer to 500,000 (Kiser and Kiser 1979, p. 33; Acuña 1981, p. 138). The repatriation of the 1930s, however, was not unprecedented, as a sizable number of Mexicans had previously been returned to their homeland during the depression of 1921-22 (Kiser and Kiser 1979, p. 33).

The repatriation program during the Great Depression led not only to the exclusion of thousands of United States citizens but to the separation of families. According to a Mexican newspaper, El Excélsior,

> Another exceedingly serious aspect of the mass deportation of Mexicans is the lack of consideration shown for marriage contracts. Upon being deported to Mexico, Mexicans are separated from their wives, if the latter are Americans.
>
> Notwithstanding the protests and even entreaties of the unfortunate Mexican husbands, or wives, if the husband is an American, the authorities in question show no consideration and separate husbands and wives under the pretext, it itself, an insult, that Mexicans live in a manner irreconcilable with Yankee customs. Neither labor nor marriage contracts are respected. Mexicans being separated from their wives as if they were animals. (Ibid., p. 37)

Repatriation was not limited to the Southwest but extended to distant cities such as Detroit. Ignacio L. Batiza, consul for Mexico, urged Mexicans in Detroit to accept Mexico's offer to aid repatriates:

> As winter approaches, life in this region becomes more and more difficult for persons without work. All of the circumstances which produce the crisis still prevail without hope of amelioration in the near future; for which reason this Consulate reiterates its call to our Mexican residents that for their own interest they accept this opportunity which is offered by the Government of Mexico for their repatriation and return to their country. The Mexican Government, within its power, is disposed to aid these repatriates that they may later make themselves important factors in our national economic structure. (Ibid., pp. 44-45)

Even at the height of repatriation in the early 1930s powerful interests existed which were very much opposed to the program. Primary among these were growers and ranchers who regarded cheap Mexican labor as a valuable resource (Kiser and Silverman 1979, p. 63). These forces were to prevail in the next decade as World War II created a new demand for Mexican labor.

The forceful and brutal exclusionist policy of President Hoover was replaced by the "Good Neighbor Policy of Uncle Sam." The United States, once again at war, welcomed its *amigos* to the south. It is commonly assumed that Mexican contract labor was first introduced via the bracero program of 1942 (see Galarza 1964; Craig 1971; Copp 1963; Anderson 1961). In reality, however, the first bracero program had been established informally during World War I, with the exemption of temporary Mexican labor from the Immigration Act of 1917. "On May 23, 1917, the Secretary of Labor issued an order exempting Mexicans entering for temporary work from the head tax, contract labor, and literacy clauses of the immigration act" (Kiser and Kiser 1979, p. 10).

On August 4, 1942, an agreement was reached between Mexico and the United States that established the bracero program. Except for a brief lapse, the program was to remain in effect until 1964. Like the de facto policies of 1917, the bracero program grew out of pressure from agriculture for Mexican labor. However, unlike the first program which was established unilaterally by the United States, the bracero program was a binational agreement, and Mexico included provisions designed to protect Mexican workers from exploitation and discrimination. The agreement established general guidelines that were to be observed. So that Mexican workers would not be stranded in the United States as in the past, they were to be provided with round-trip transportation (Craig 1971, p. 43). "Other benefits to be guaranteed in contracts included adequate housing, a minimum number of working days, minimum wages or 'prevailing wages' if the latter were higher, and protection against discrimination" (Kiser and Kiser, 1979, p. 68). In addition, braceros were exempted from military service, and they were not to be used to displace domestics or to lower their wages (Craig 1971, p. 43).

Despite the good intentions of the Mexican government the provisions were frequently not observed. The "prevailing wage," for example, was usually the wage growers established, one below the minimum wage for which domestic workers would work (ibid., p. 68). The standard work contract provided that a bracero would receive no less than $2.00 per day. However, after paying board ($1.75) and insurance ($0.09), a bracero would be left with net earnings of only 16 cents per day (Anderson 1961, p. 133). It was not uncommon for braceros to owe money to their employer, as is evidenced by the following statement from a bracero (ibid., p. 137).

> I had a very poor contract. The first two weeks were all right, because we got paid by the hour. The rest of the time we got paid by the contract. Why, I never got enough to pay for my board. In fact, I still owe them money for my board. I left my contract. Right now, I haven't got a penny. Some fellows got 9 cent checks. Some broke even. Some like myself owed the association money at the end of the work period. Many boys quit their contracts. When we told the boss that we wanted to work by the hour, he got angry and said we were all lazy. We told him that we are not afraid of work, but he wanted to get us to work for nothing. He said if we didn't like it to return to Mexico. There are plenty of other men.

Guarantees designed to protect domestic labor from unfair competition were also not upheld (Kirstein 1973, p. 220). At the same time Mexico did attempt to use the bracero program as a mechanism for reducing discrimination against Mexican workers (ibid., p. 70). Excesses were such in Texas that on July 12, 1943, Roberto Medellín, Mexican secretary of labor, announced that contract labor would not be sent until the state took positive action to end discrimination against Mexicans (Morales 1982, p. 109).

> Aware of the need to take action to improve a situation made more acute by acts of discrimination against Mexican-Americans in uniform and visiting Mexican dignitaries, Governor Coke Stevenson had induced the Texas legislature to pass the so-called "Caucasian Race" resolution, which he had approved on May 6, 1943. The resolution affirmed the right of all Caucasians within the state to equal treatment in public places of business and amusement and denounced those who denied such privileges with "violating the good neighbor policy of our state." (Scruggs 1979, p. 88)

The United States government also initiated efforts that, hopefully, would remove the ban on sending braceros to Texas.

Mexico should be credited for its concern over the treatment of braceros. This concern reflected the different goals for which Mexico and the United States entered into the agreement. While the United States saw it as a way of guaranteeing a pool of cheap agricultural workers, Mexico sought to provide safeguards and protection of its workers and to regulate the flow of the work force (García 1980, p. 25). Mexico, however, underestimated the role that special interest groups, especially agribusiness, would play in the operation of the program (ibid.).

The bracero program provided a steady supply of contract labor during the war, but Mexican workers continued to enter the United States illegally. As the flow of illegals increased in the 1950s, pressure mounted to restrict illegal entry. This period proved to be one of intense and open political and social repression against the Mexican. In the height of McCarthyism and the Red scare, Chicano political leaders were repressed, and literally millions of Mexicans were deported under the auspices of Operation Wetback (for a detailed discussion of this program see García 1980). When President Eisenhower requested that Attorney General Brownell devise a way of ridding the country of the "wetbacks," General Joseph May Swing (who had taken part in the expedition into Mexico in 1916) was named commissioner of the Immigration and Naturalization Service and put in charge of Operation Wetback (Samora 1975, p. 71). According to Swing the program "was pursued with military efficiency and the result was that over a million wetbacks were expelled from the country in 1954" (Bustamante 1981, p. 43).

The end of the bracero program in 1964 signaled the beginning of the modern era of United States-Mexican relations, an era when the demand for cheap labor in the United States and growing dependence of the Mexican economy forced Mexicans to cross the border in unprecedented numbers. The flow of illegals continued until 1968 when restrictive legislation was enacted. Yet the number of persons deported increased consistently from only 43,844 in 1964 to 577,000 in 1973 (Samora 1975, p. 70). By 1976 the figure had climbed to 870,000 (Acuña 1981, p. 170). In addition to permanent entrants thousands of Mexicans commute to the United States daily. In 1974 daily commuters were in excess of 40,000 (Kiser and Kiser 1979, p. 215). More recent estimates are that the number is at least 60,000 and perhaps as many as 100,000 to 400,000 (Samora 1975, p. 73).

From the preceding it is clear that while undocumented workers have been in great demand during periods of economic expansion, during economic recessions they have become convenient scapegoats who are seen as increasing unemployment and depressing wages. It is commonly charged that

1. There are many millions of undocumented Mexican aliens.
2. Undocumented workers take jobs away from citizens, particularly minorities. They are in direct competition with poor whites and members of minority groups for jobs.
3. They are a burden on public, social, educational, and medical services, i.e., on the United States wage earner and taxpayer.
4. They are responsible for increasing rates of crime; they are a threat to peaceful society and public morality.
5. Undocumented workers undermine existing wage rates and unionization efforts.
6. Undocumented workers and their families are a "threat" to the ecological balance of the United States.
7. Undocumented workers threaten the political and military security of the United States.
   (Gómez-Quiñones 1981, p. 30)

Are undocumented workers a drain on the economy and the society? A major study of San Diego found that an estimated 59,705 undocumented workers believed to be employed in the county would earn an average of $2.10 per hour and a total yearly salary of $260,791,400 (Villalpando 1977, p. xi). Research results show, moreover, that contrary to popular belief, most employers collect state and federal taxes from undocumented employees. In San Diego 81 percent reported that taxes were deducted from their wages. The estimated tax contribution of undocumented workers was $48,841,017, or 19 percent of their total wages (ibid., p. xii). It was estimated that although 37 percent of the wages earned ($96,722,100) were sent back to the country of origin, 63 percent was spent in this country. Since 37 percent of wages is returned to the country of origin and 19 percent is paid in taxes, the remaining 44 percent ($115,228,283) must be spent on goods and services in the local area (ibid., p. xiii).

The findings of the San Diego study suggest not only that undocumented workers contribute significantly to the American economy by paying taxes and buying goods and services but that they perform jobs that would not normally be performed by domestic workers. As part of the Employer Cooperation Program the Immigration and Naturalization Service vacated 340 job slots held by illegal aliens. Rather than being filled by local residents, however, 90 percent of the positions were filled by guest commuter workers from Tijuana. A similar program in Los Angeles also failed to provide jobs to domestic workers. It was concluded that these jobs were not attractive to local residents because "(1) most employers paid less than the minimum wage rate; (2) the job categories were not appealing to the local resident; and (3) applicants were discouraged by low wages, the difficulty of some of the jobs and the long hours demanded by the employers" (ibid., p. xii). These findings seriously question the assumption that undocumented workers take jobs away from American citizens. They suggest instead that while undocumented workers impact on local social services by an approximately yearly cost of $2,000,000, they contribute far more in taxes ($48,800,000) than they take out in services.

Results of other major studies also fail to support the assertion that undocumented workers take jobs away from U.S. workers and are a drain on local services. North and Houstoun found that the average hourly wage among 793 respondents was only $2.71, and the average wage of those employed in the Southwest was only $1.98 per hour (1976, pp. 5-10). The data in Table 1 clearly indicate that undocumented workers pay much more into tax-supported programs (input) than they take out (output). The vast majority had social security and federal taxes withheld, but a very small proportion collected unemployment or received food stamps, and only one-half of 1 percent received welfare.

Although undocumented workers were typically young, economically disadvantaged adults who came from less-developed nations in search of employment, there were significant differences among them according to country of origin. Respondents whose country of origin was Mexico, for instance,

TABLE 1

Extent of Participation of Apprehended Illegal Alien Respondents in Tax-Paying and Tax-Supported Programs

PROGRAM ACTIVITY	PERCENTAGE OF RESPONDENT PARTICIPATION
Input	
Social Security taxes withheld	77.3
Federal income taxes withheld	73.2
Hospitalization payments withheld	44.0
Filed U.S. income tax returns	31.5
Output	
Used hospitals or clinics	27.4
Collected one or more weeks of unemployment insurance	3.9
Have children in U.S. schools	3.7
Participated in U.S.-funded job training programs	1.4
Secured food stamps	1.3
Secured welfare payments	0.5

Source: North and Houstoun 1976, pp. S-14

earned an average hourly wage of $2.34 compared to an average of $3.05 for other Western Hemisphere respondents and $4.08 for Eastern Hemisphere respondents (ibid., pp. 5-10). Significantly,

> Though Mexico is a more advanced nation than most nations sending illegals to the United States today, the Mexican respondents were substantially more likely than non-Mexican respondents to have come from rural areas, to have been farmworkers in their country of origin, to have had less than a primary education, and to speak no English. The non-Mexican respondents, but in particular those from the Eastern Hemisphere, were more likely to come from urban areas, to have had at least some secondary education, to have been employed in white-collar jobs in their homeland, and to speak English. In brief, the socioeconomic status at entry of EH respondents was close to the U.S. norm; WH respondents clustered well below the norm; while the Mexican respondents fell below the norm of this nation's most disadvantaged peoples, its blacks and Chicanos. (Ibid., pp. 5-15)

Another difference was that most Mexican illegals crossed the border on foot, while a large majority of non-Mexican respondents were visa abusers.

The North and Houstoun study provides at least indirect support for the dual labor-market theory. Most of the respondents were employed within the secondary labor market in low-status, low-wage, unskilled occupations. Less than 25 percent were employed in white-collar or skilled blue-collar positions, and the majority of these worked in crafts (16 percent). Although undocumented persons worked more hours per week, their average weekly wage was substantially less than other workers (ibid., pp. 5-16).

These findings are consistent with those of a study of 919 Mexican migrants in nine Mexican border towns interviewed by Jorge Bustamante before their expulsion to Mexico. Bustamante (1977, pp. 173-74) found:

1. Only 55 percent had been able to find a job prior to apprehension.
2. Only 7.7 percent were paid in cash (compared to 22.1 percent in the North and Houstoun study).
3. Of those paid by check 74.4 percent had tax deductions, and 66.7 percent had social security deductions.
4. Only 0.9 percent said they had ever had children registered in U.S. schools.
5. Only 3.2 percent had received welfare benefits.
6. 7.8 percent had received free medical care in the United States.

In sum, undocumented persons not only assume the least desirable and lowest paying jobs but they pay much more in taxes and other deductions than they obtain in public services. Yet some would still argue that undocumented workers do have an adverse indirect effect on the economy by depressing wages and displacing domestic workers during economic recessions (Jones 1965, p. 103). Vernon M. Briggs, Jr., maintains, "The massive flow of illegal immigrants has caused, is causing, and will continue to cause a serious disruption in the normal labor force adjustment processes throughout the Southwest and, increasingly, in some northern cities (e.g., Chicago, Lansing, and Detroit)" (1975, p. 25). He sees such aliens as a "shadow labor force" whose impact is felt but usually not seen. "In the industries in which they congregate, they depress wages and working conditions to such a degree that native workers cannot compete with them. The native workers must either choose to work and live as does the illegal alien, move to another region, or seek another occupation" (ibid., p. 26).

The group that suffers the most from the presence of undocumented workers, according to Briggs, is the Chicano (ibid., p. 29). Since the 1940s they have not only been a factor in pressuring Chicanos to move from rural areas but have forced them to leave the border region and join the migrant stream. They have also thwarted unionization efforts by depressing wages and serving as strikebreakers. In short, "the influx of illegal Mexican immigrants and commuters has set in motion a process whereby poor Mexicans make poor Chicanos poorer" (ibid., p. 27). Briggs suggests, moreover, that undocumented workers have impeded the Chicano struggle against discrimination and unequal treatment.

> For decades this minority group has been struggling against discrimination and seeking economic assimilation into American life. Now, in the aftermath of the civil rights revolution of the 1960s, Chicanos have come closer than ever before to attainment of their elusive goal only to see their gains eroded by the unfair competition of Mexican workers. (Ibid., p. 29)

Although Briggs is ostensibly sympathetic to the plight of the Chicano, the danger in his position is that it blames undocumented workers, not the dominant society or capitalism, for the low economic position of Chicanos. In addition he fails to provide empirical support for this argument. Even if the presence of undocumented workers were found to depress wages in an area, one can hardly blame them for "causing" the problem. Briggs also cannot account for why the position of Chicanos has not improved radically when the flow of undocumented workers has been stemmed or in areas that do not have an abundance of illegal entrants.

The "further-higher" hypothesis, similarly, proposes that the prevalence of illegal workers causes wages to rise as one moves away from the border (Fogel 1978, p. 117). In California wages should thus be highest in San Francisco, next highest in Los Angeles, and lowest in San Diego. When applied to Texas, wages should be highest in Dallas, lower in San Antonio, and low-est in El Paso. Although there is some equivocal support for the hypothesis, it is difficult (if not impossible) to impute such differentials to the relative availability of undocumented workers. Fogel (ibid., p. 121) found a south-north differential between San Antonio and Dallas, but the differential held across occupations and not just among unskilled workers as predicted by the hypothesis. Not only is the "further-higher" hypothesis difficult to test but it is one filled with both logical and operational flaws. Fogel notes, for exam-ple, that

> . . . it is not clear that Mexican workers are less willing to go to Los Angeles than to San Diego, even though the latter is much closer to the border. Operationally, it is very difficult to test the further-higher hypothesis unless all of the factors which cause differences among the three cities can be identified. . . . San Francisco has historically paid higher wages than the two southern California cities, a phenomenon which has never been well explained. (Ibid., p. 118)

In short, the "further-higher" or north-south, hypothesis appears sim-plistic and poorly conceived. Rather than seeing undocumented workers as filling a need in the capitalistic system for cheap and dependent labor, it blames them for the problems of the very economic system which produced the need for their labor. The fact that Chicano migrant streams stretch from south Texas to Michigan and North Dakota and from Southern California to Washington suggests that Mexican workers will go where there is work and that the demand for cheap labor extends well beyond the border.

A more plausible explanation is that it is American capitalists who, seeking to maximize profits, locate near the border and create a demand for cheap labor. It is in the best interest of capitalism to create and maintain a reserve army of cheap labor that can act as a shock absorber in response to economic fluctuations. Commuters, or "guest workers," who live in Mexico and cross the border daily to work in the United States are said to contribute to this labor surplus and to further depress wages, increase unemployment, and discourage union organization (Ericson 1979, 238; Fogel 1978, p. 124; North 1970, pp. 52-53).

Fernandez sees the emergence of the "border town" as a phenomenon that is somewhat unique to the United States-Mexico border. Ultimately the border town and its attendant characteristics are a product of the economic dependency of Mexico on the United States.

> The present border area and the border towns included in it are continuing the trends of rapid growth, urban sprawl, high unemploy-ment, and squalor experienced during the 1950s and 1960s. The econ-

omy of these towns is increasingly shaped by the presence of American industry, the transport of vegetables northward, the flow of tourists southward, the flow in both directions of contraband items (including weapons), the flourishing of prostitution, and the dynamics of illegal traffic in hard drugs. (Fernandez 1977, p. 11)

If illegals were to displace domestic workers, it would obviously be those workers who occupy the lowest and poorest-paying positions. "Much direct testimony was given to a subcommittee of the House Judiciary Committee in 1971 that legal U.S. residents, usually persons of Mexican origin, are refused employment or laid off from employment because of the availability of illegals" (Fogel 1978, p. 126). However, data on the extent of such displacement is not readily available. Interestingly, proponents on either side of the argument have tended to make bold assertions without the benefit of empirical data. Also, rather than being displaced, it might be more accurate to say that most native workers refuse to work long hours at a very low salary. Illegal workers, moreover, are preferred by employers.

> The relative docility of illegal workers is a major reason for their attractiveness to employers who offer low wages, substandard working conditions and wage supplements, as well as little opportunity for advancement. . . .
>
> They are productive because they have often had experience at hard physical labor . . . and they frequently put forth extraordinary work efforts because of their insecure employment status and their lack of alternative income support. The alternatives available to domestic workers—unemployment compensation, welfare, family support—are not realistically available to most illegals. (Ibid., p. 133)

A point that is all too often overlooked is that, in addition to their contributions as individual workers and taxpayers, the presence of undocumented workers is costly to the Mexican economy. Gómez-Quiñones (1981, p. 17) has observed:

> Immigrant labor represented a direct subsidy from Mexico to the United States economy. It generated billions of dollars in goods and services. It provided labor power and lower cost. Each worker cost the Mexican economy approximately $40,000 to produce, a savings for the United States economy. Whether or not the laborer received the minimum wage, the importance was the differential between what was paid the undocumented worker and what would be paid a legal resident. The difference has been significant for profit. Approximately two-thirds of the earnings of undocumented workers were spent in the United States, and one-third of the earnings were remitted to Mexico. This may have amounted to as much as one-half to two billion dollars a year; a sum

important to the Mexican economy and to the individual families who received it. The money provided an added cash flow in local communities, it created employment which helped stabilization. This has been beneficial to the United States.

Alternative Solutions

Despite increased enforcement efforts the flow of undocumented workers continues unabated. The problem, moreover, is one of immense proportions that defies simple solutions. Weintraub and Ross are emphatic when they observe:

> THERE IS NO GOOD WAY to solve the problem of illegal migrants from Mexico. We deal in this area with degrees of uncertainty about the underlying facts and, hence, of the economic and labor market impact of the flow of persons into the United States. (1980, p. 52)

Proposed solutions range from those that would seal off the border by stronger enforcement, increased raids by INS, or the building of a "tortilla curtain," to those that call for an open border and complete amnesty for undocumented workers. Most proposals, however, lie somewhere between these two extremes. Vernon Briggs, for example, suggests a number of policy changes which he believes are necessary to control the problem. First, he advocates legislation which would make it a criminal offense to employ illegal aliens. Second, sanctions should be provided against employers, and the manpower and budget of the Immigration and Naturalization Service needs to be substantially increased (Briggs 1975, pp. 35–36). A vigorous apprehension drive should be initiated by the Immigration and Naturalization Service. Although civil liberties would be protected, "the message should be made clear: illegal alien workers from any country are unwanted guests" (ibid., p. 36). Finally, strong sanctions against both employers and illegal aliens would be coupled with a program of foreign aid that would help to develop the economy of northern Mexico. For, according to Briggs, "Without U.S. assistance the more restrictive border policies proposed would condemn most of the would-be illegal Mexican aliens to lives of squalor" (ibid., p. 36).

Others have expressed concern not only with the plight of the undocumented worker but with that of those whose task it is to enforce immigration law. Johnson and Ogle note that while there has been great concern with the rights of alienated Mexican poor, little attention has been given to

> . . . the human rights of Americans whose lives are affected, often adversely, by illegal immigration. And very little attention has been given to the emotional and physical toll which the enforcement

of immigration law has had on INS and Border Patrol officers. . . .

What is truly remarkable is that despite the anomaly of what many Border Patrol and INS officers believe to be a government in Washington that wants only an "acceptable level" of law enforcement, hence an acceptable level of lawlessness, I have found that a high degree of professionalism, dedication and pride still exists throughout the service. (1978, p. iv)

Johnson and Ogle proceed to isolate five possible alternative solutions to the problem (ibid., pp. 130–40). Alternative one, to do nothing, is not tenable according to the authors. The second is to propose legislation that would impose severe penalties on employers who hire illegal aliens. A third alternative would consist of the establishment of a treaty with Mexico that would provide temporary contract labor as was the case in the bracero program. Such contract labor would be guaranteed a decent wage, good living conditions, humane treatment, and transportation back to their country of origin. The fourth alternative is to create "Fortress America" by completely closing off the border. Although this alternative would be adopted only as a last resort, the authors "suspect that many United States citizen residents of the border are prepared to 'Fortress America,' indeed they have told us so. They fear that the border may get 'moved north' " (ibid., pp. 131–32). The last alternative is at the opposite extreme, and that is to create an open border and abolish all immigration laws. The authors, however, are leary of this alternative.

. . . This might work if we could also abolish or absorb the Mexican political system. We had the chance to do that in the war of conquest against Mexico which ended with the peace treaty of 1848. That was our opportunity to absorb Mexico. It is probably utopian to speak of it today, unless of course Mexico just becomes totally bankrupt financially and asks to be absorbed. (Ibid., p. 132)

They conclude by noting that each of these policy options would have its consequences and adding, "Take your choice!" (ibid., p. 140). Yet, on the issue of amnesty the authors are unequivocal. "The entire idea of rewarding lawbreakers is highly demoralizing to U.S. law enforcement officials at all levels who are expected to defend the citizenry, not rob them as is the case throughout much of Mexico" (ibid., p. 135). Dedicated border patrol officers, moreover, "say it is hard to maintain professionalism in law enforcement if criminals are routinely given pardons" (ibid.).

Weintraub and Ross are also opposed to complete amnesty; they favor a program that would increase the number of temporary visas so that workers could work legally, have rights, and return to Mexico. Their position is based on the premise that undocumented workers help more than they hurt the

American economy. "The current system is more cruel than a system of temporary work permits, since an illegal immigrant has no rights after he or she is squeezed, whereas a person legally admitted to the United States would have rights" (1980, p. 56). The flow of such workers is best regulated by a program that would bring temporary workers to the United States for periods of six months to a year. More specifically, they propose the following three-pronged program:

1. Adjustment of status for those who have acquired a stake in our society;
2. A significant contract labor program declining on a preagreed time schedule;
3. A cooperative binational effort to regulate the movement of migrants in order to minimize the number of illegals entering the United States. (1980, p. 56)

Walter Fogel's approach to the problem is to increase the yearly quotas for Mexican immigration, while at the same time instituting penalites against employers and undocumented workers. He also recommends a national identity card that would facilitate enforcement of immigration laws and enable employers to refuse work to anyone without such a card (1978, pp. 171–72). A national identity card could be initiated with relative ease, according to Fogel, since it would simply constitute an extension of the Social Security card system. He acknowledges that there will be resistance to a national identity card by those who believe that it would constitute an invasion of privacy and a threat to civil liberties and others who see it as a costly "bureaucratic nightmare," but with the cooperation of those agencies involved and adequate funding, the program could be easily effected.

Fogel, however, fails to address a fundamental issue—How would such a program impact on the Chicano population? Chicano civil-rights groups and organizations have long held that a system of national identification would constitute an additional infringement on their civil liberties. White persons, they argue, would be presumed to be U.S. citizens, whereas "brown people," regardless of their place of birth, would be presumed to be foreign. Even without a national identity card many Chicanos, born in the United States and American citizens, are subjected to daily harassment and abuse at the hands of the Border Patrol.

Such abuses have led to an increased concern over the rights of undocumented workers. The "human rights" position contains at least four basic demands:

1. oppose repressive legislation
2. cease raids and deportations of the undocumented worker
3. unconditional amnesty for the undocumented worker

4. full human and civil rights for the undocumented worker. (Gómez-Quiñones 1981, p. 33)

Although the treatment of undocumented workers is a vital human-rights issue, it is important to keep in mind that such proposals address the consequences rather than the causes of illegal immigration. As Juan Gómez-Quiñones observed, "Amnesty provisions in and of themselves are not immigration options; they have been a juridical response to the phenomena of resident undocumented workers already in the United States" (ibid., p. 29). Proposals that would punish employers or workers would also constitute a threat to civil liberties by creating a vast system of surveillance. "A more benign approach would be equal and fair wage and work rights for all workers" (ibid).

While proposals for bracero-type programs have considerable appeal (see Cornelius 1977), such proposals tend to address the effects rather than the root causes of the problem. First, they reinforce the colonial labor principle by creating a dual wage structure for foreign and for domestic workers. Second, they work to depress wages for domestic workers by formally establishing a reserve army of surplus labor. Third, they would seriously impede unionization efforts by domestic workers. Finally, such programs do not appear to curb illegal immigration. During the 1950s, for example, at the same time that 293,000 legal immigrants and over 3 million braceros were entering the United States, more than 3.4 illegal aliens were apprehended (Samora 1975, p. 71).

Another commonly proposed solution is to provide foreign aid to Mexico, thereby encouraging economic development and reducing unemployment. While such proposals may be well intentioned, ironically they have the effect of increasing rather than decreasing the economic dependence of Mexico on the United States. At the heart of the problem is that Mexico is already one of the most indebted nations in the world, with a foreign debt approaching 80 billion dollars (Eisner 1982), and much of this indebtedness is to the United States government and American banks (see Sommers 1981, p. 160; Russell 1977, pp. 82–85; Fernandez 1977, p. 109).

Perhaps the most essential first step in resolving the problem, then, is recognition that it is a binational issue that cannot be extricated from the historical context of conflict between the United States and Mexico. A final solution will not emerge unilaterally from within either nation but will come instead from a change in the economic relation between them. Since the source of the problem is Mexico's economic dependence on the United States, the solution is ultimately tied to Mexico's quest for economic development and independence. Another critical factor will be the involvement of Mexicans on both sides of the border in the struggle for self-determination and liberation.

A Chicano Perspective on the Border

Having reviewed and critically evaluated the major issues and proposed solutions relative to Mexican migration, the chapter concludes with a series of policy recommendations that are consistent with a Chicano perspective.[1] A Chicano perspective is needed not only because the issue is one which is critical to and impinges directly on the Chicano community but because specialists on the subject typically reflect the interests and perspective of the dominant society both in their analyses and solutions to the problem.

One of the least sympathetic and most openly condescending of such works is Arthur F. Corwin's (1978) *Immigrants—and Immigrants*. In the epilogue to the book Corwin has this to say about the Chicano:

> As never before, this Spanish language soul culture has a flourishing network of educational and indoctrination programs with media pipelines to Mexico. Thanks in some degree to the workings of the American melting pot, Mexico America is now institutionalized. . . .
>
> For all its vitality and deep historical roots, however, Mexico America is essentially a foster child of the Great Society. . . . As such, its present status would have been inconceivable without the affirmative action bureaucracy and the daily spread of millions of HEW dollars. . . .

With regard to the growth in brown power he notes that Anglo-Americans will have to either adjust to it or learn to manipulate the imported *reconquista* ("reconquest") mentality, as have elites in Mexico.

> Perhaps, after all, there would be little justification for "white flight" from the Mexican renaissance or for taxpayer revolts. Many Raza leaders, exhilarated at the swelling ranks of brown power, have promised to be generous with their former Anglo conquerors and patrons, and, moreover, to provide new sources of cultural enrichment and a better cuisine: just keep the border open, you'll see. Such is the nature of the subject. (1978, pp. 353–54)

A Chicano perspective is also needed in order to expose the political nature of immigration law. Estevan Flores (1981, p. 7) has noted that while there is discrimination against persons of Mexican origin, regardless of place of birth or resident status, there is a great effort to differentiate within the population according to residency or legal status. "It was the *strategy* of pitting one group against another through the Bracero Program and *creating a hierarchy of social and economic differences* between the groups that resulted in agribusiness' successes in the fields during the 1940s and 1950s" (ibid.). Ernesto Galarza commented on how braceros and Chicanos were pitted against each other. Domestic workers, for example, resented that they were not privy to many of the guarantees extended to braceros.

> . . . Discrimination, which was prohibited in the agreement, thus pervaded the program as a whole, operating on the principle that equal guarantees were not to be extended to American citizens because of their national origin. The domestic workers of California had long seen the point. Among them there was a saying that the way to get a contract and hold a job in agriculture was to go to Mexico and come back as a *bracero*. (Galarza 1964, p. 257)

In testimony before the United States Senate Committee on Immigration in 1928, Mr. Edward H. Dowell, president of the California State Federation of Labor and a member of the San Diego City Council, spoke in favor of restricting Mexican immigration. He argued:

> When it comes to Mexican competition, I want to assure you it is not only menial work. At the beginning the Mexican immigrant and the oriental immigrant always does the lowest menial work, but mind you, the sons and daughters of these immigrants are American citizens, they are the first-generation Americans, and they do not perform menial work. If you are going to let the Mexicans flow in here, if you are going to experiment for a number of years while they are drifting in here by the hundreds of thousands, then you are going to fill up the great West of our country with Mexicans. (U.S. Congress Senate Committee on Immigration 1928, pp. 6–7)

All too often Chicano interests have been muted or ignored by those who shape public policy. The recommendations proposed, we hope, represent a more viable approach and a solution that recognizes basic human rights for all persons regardless of nationality or immigrant status. A Chicano perspective is not blind to economic, residency, and legal-status differences among persons of Mexican origin, but it recognizes that the accentuation of such differences by policy experts creates invidious comparisons and divisiveness. It also creates the illusion that undocumented workers somehow are responsible for the problem.

Public policy should be guided by the following principles:

1. The U.S.-Mexico border is a political border that was arbitrarily and forcefully imposed on a natural geographic, cultural, linguistic, and economic region. Many persons have crossed, are crossing, and will continue to cross this artificial demarcation. This mass movement is exacerbated by the economic dependency of Mexico on the United States.

2. The proximity of Mexico and its economic dependence on the

United States have provided a cheap, elastic, and virtually inexhaustible supply of labor.

3. Undocumented workers are not a threat to the economy or a drain on social services but a valuable asset. They contribute much more to the economy than they take out.

4. Rather than displacing domestic workers and increasing unemployment, they typically assume jobs that domestic workers do not want because of their difficulty, long hours, and low pay.

5. When domestic workers are displaced, it is because wages and working conditions fall below prevailing minimum standards.

6. The issue of displacement of domestic workers by undocumented workers would be moot if legislation were passed that insured a decent minimum wage and equal pay for *all* workers regardless of citizenship or immigrant status.

7. Undocumented workers should be granted equal protection of the law and full human and civil rights. Provisions of the Treaty of Guadalupe-Hidalgo shoud be honored, especially those that guarantee Chicanos the enjoyment of all the rights of citizens of the United States according to the principles of the Constitution.

8. Health care, social services, and public education[2] shall be provided to *all* persons regardless of citizenship or immigration status.

9. Temporary "guest-worker" programs should be rejected on the grounds that not only are they ineffectual but they perpetuate the dual wage system and impede unionization efforts.

10. The organization and unionization of workers across national boundaries should be supported.

11. The establishment of a national identification system should be opposed not only because it is costly and difficult to administer but because it constitutes an infringement on civil liberties.

12. There should be a declaration of unconditional amnesty for all undocumented workers residing in the United States and a ceasing of all surveillance efforts by INS and the Border Patrol.

13. Current policy which has sought to control "illegal" immigration through increased militarization of the border should be abandoned.

14. The border should be declared free and open, and the Border Patrol abolished.

15. The United States and Mexico should embark on a joint binational program whose ultimate aim is to end Mexico's economic and political dependence on the United States and the exploitation of Mexican workers on both sides of the border by capitalism.

4

El Bandido: The Evolution of Images of Chicano Criminality

Introduction

The history of relations between Chicanos and the legal and judicial system is fraught with conflict. From the signing of the Treaty of Guadalupe-Hidalgo to the present a dual standard of justice, one for Anglos and the other for Chicanos, has existed to maintain and perpetuate the social, economic, and political oppression of the Mexican-American people. The conflict between Chicanos and the legal and judicial system has been especially evident in the relationship between themselves and the police, a relationship frequently characterized by open hostility, distrust, resentment, and violence. Just as the military has been used to pacify conquered peoples in occupied distant lands, so have the police served as a domestic military force that seeks to keep order in the barrio while maintaining Chicanos in a dependent position within the borders of the United States. The U.S. Commission on Civil Rights, in perhaps the most systematic and far-reaching study of Chicanos and the legal and judicial system, found strong evidence of a pattern of systematic harassment and abuse of Chicanos by the police. The commission concluded that "Mexican American citizens are subject to unduly harsh treatment by law enforcement officers, that they are often arrested on insufficient grounds, receive physical and verbal abuse, and penalties which are disproportionately severe" (1970, p. iii). Widespread patterns of police abuse and mistreatment of Chicanos have also been documented by Armando Morales (1972) in *Ando Sangrando* (I Am Bleeding) and, more recently, by the Mexican American Legal Defense and Education Fund (MALDEF 1978a and b), and the National Hispanic Conference on Law Enforcement and Criminal Justice (1980).

Given that Chicanos have typically been victims of police abuse and injustice, it is ironic that they have also been portrayed as a violent and criminally prone people. If there is a persistent image of the Mexican which has perdured, it is that of a ruthless, bloodthirsty bandido (Trujillo 1974; Martínez 1969). While taking various forms such as the "greasy bandido" of the Old West, the zoot-suit or pachuco gangs of the 1940s, or contemporary low-

70

riders and youth-gang members, the image persists nonetheless. Emphasis continues today both in the media and in the public at large on issues such as gang violence and criminality among Chicanos. Media portrayals are especially significant, for they help in shaping and reinforcing public conceptions of Chicanos which are held not only by members of the dominant society but by Chicanos themselves.

This chapter addresses the question of how it is that images of Chicanos as a criminally and violently prone people persist in the face of widespread patterns of police abuse and lawlessness perpetrated against them. It asks, in other words, why a group subjected to a double standard of justice has been labeled as criminal and lawless. While a definitive answer to such a broad and complex question is beyond the scope of this chapter, an overview of the relationship between Chicanos and the legal and judicial system will be presented. In the process some possible explanations for this apparent paradox will be suggested.

A basic thesis is that although the Treaty of Guadalupe-Hidalgo officially ended the war between Mexico and the United States, it marked the beginning of hostilities between Anglo-Americans and Chicanos, displaced Mexicans who now found themselves within the territorial boundaries of the United States. As legal and extralegal mechanisms were used to take land and power away from the Chicano, the police, military, and Border Patrol were employed to maintain them in a subordinate position. The "bandido image" emerged as Chicanos responded to such injustices and to the lawlessness on the part of the dominant society. If an Anglo took the law into his own hands, he was typically labeled a hero or rebel, but a Chicano who engaged in lawlessness was somehow a bandit (see Paredes 1958). It is precisely because Chicanos did not passively accept exploitation that they became bandidos.

Force was thus integral to the colonization of the Southwest. Although the acquisition of Mexico's northern territories by the United States closely parallel the pattern found in classic colonial situations, Chicanos subsequently entered an internal colonial relation with the dominant society.

In classic colonialism one group militarily subdues another and forcibly imposes a foreign culture and language, yet because the conquerors are typically outnumbered, native elites are co-opted to aid in not only the initial colonization but its subsequent administration. The point is that classic colonialism is not as complete or total as internal colonialism because although native culture, institutions, and language are modified, they are still retained. Also, the classic colony is in a dependent relationship but is not totally absorbed.

Internal colonies have no formal or legal standing, but they persist nonetheless. The Treaty of Guadalupe-Hidalgo protected the land and water rights of Chicanos, ostensibly safeguarded their linguistic, religious, and cultural autonomy, and "guaranteed Mexicans the enjoyment of all the rights of citizens of the United States according to the principles of the Constitution." Such guarantees, however, were either ignored or wantonly violated. Today Chicanos are technically free and equal, but they are informally excluded from full participation in the legal, educational, economic, and political system. They lack power and control over vital institutions.

As Chicanos have moved from a classic to an internal colonial position, force and coercion continue to play a prominent part in maintaining their subordination, but more insidious methods have also evolved. Such methods are consistent with an internally colonized situation in that they create the illusion of equality while maintaining the subordination of the colonized group.

One mechanism of indirect control is co-optation: elevating token representatives of the minority group who do not really represent the interests of that group to positions of power. These are the "Uncle Toms" or "tio tacos." A second technique is gerrymandering, and yet another is to "divide and conquer" (Barrera et al. 1972, p. 489). A very important but relatively unexplored technique is the mobilization of bias against the colonized group. The concept is discussed more fully in chapter eight, but, briefly, it involves the manipulation of symbols in such a way that they perpetuate myths about the inferiority of Chicanos (Barrera et al. 1972, p. 490). Since Chicanos lack power over the schools, the media, and other agents of socialization, most prevalent images of them are externally induced. The mobilization of bias is not a totally new phenomenon but one that is exacerbated by the proliferation and pervasiveness of the mass media as well as other external impersonal agents of socialization. While the mobilization of bias is a broad and inclusive process that shapes many images, the focus of this chapter is on how the mobilization of bias has propagated the image of the Chicano as criminal and lawless. It contends that the mobilization of bias is an effective, if subtle, mechanism of control, for by depicting the Chicano as violent and criminal, emphasis is shifted away from the exploitation and subordination of Chicanos and toward problems and inadequacies within the barrio. Bias mobilization becomes, in short, a way of "blaming the victim" for his own oppression while giving tacit approval and legitimation to police abuse. Police abuse is thus viewed no longer as abuse but rather as badly needed and corrective law enforcement. The effects of the mobilization of bias are maximized when Chicanos internalize and espouse such negative images.

The Evolution of the Bandido Image

In the aftermath of the Mexican-American War treaty provisions designed to protect land and water rights and the cultural and religious autonomy of Mexican citizens were not honored. The legal and judicial system, rather than serving as an objective and impartial institution, became a vehicle for advancing the interests of Anglo-Americans. In a word, justice became a mockery for Chicanos.

Yet, ironically, it was the Mexican who was accused of perpetrating crime against American citizens. In response to the establishment of a commission which was sent by the president of the United States to investigate robberies allegedly committed by Mexicans and Indians, the Mexican government set up its own commission in 1873 to carry out an independent evaluation of these charges. The work of the Mexican Border Commission was impressive. It visited all the towns and many ranchos along a 450-mile stretch of the border, culled archives, and interviewed nearly 300 witnesses. In the end the various reports and appendices covered 17,688 pages (Comisión pesquisidora de la frontera del norte, 1875, p. ix). The commission concluded that

> . . . the complaints of the Texans are groundless, inasmuch as the cattle stealing done among them is not the work of any residents in the adjoining country, but of Indians belonging to the United States, and their own outlaws disguised as Indians. If either of the two nations can complain of Indian and other depredations—as it is now demonstrated— it is Mexico, some of whose entire States have been ruined by Indians and banditti from the United States, who still depredate there to a certain extent, robbing horses and perpetrating other outrages. The origin of those evils on both banks of the river, it is clearly proved, consists, in a great measure, in the encouragement given to the Indians for plunder by the traffic carried on with them ever since 1835, tolerated and consented by the American authorities. (Ibid., pp. iii-iv).

As a response to these inequities many Chicanos were compelled to go outside of the law to defend rights and property that should have been legitimately theirs. Mexican social bandits such as Joaquín Murieta, Tiburcio Vasquez, and Gregorio Cortez, for example, challenged the dominant order (see Castillo and Camarillo 1973; Paredes 1958; Hobsbawm 1959 and 1969). Labeled as "bandidos" and bloodthirsty outlaws by Anglo society, they became heroes to their own people—men who were respected and admired and whose exploits were romanticized and idealized in *corridos* (ballads).

Even in these early days the mobilization of bias was evident. Gregorio Cortez, for example, was one of the most feared "bandits" in the history of Texas even though it is doubtful that he ever committed a crime. He was actually a victim of injustice (Castillo and Camarillo 1973, p. 117). Gregorio acted alone as he fled to escape pursuing posses and became a legendary hero to Chicanos because of his horsemanship and cunning in evading hundreds of pursuers. Yet, "as news of Cortez spread among the Anglos, many believed him to be the ringleader of a statewide Chicano gang 'conspiring' to rob and kill the Anglo Texans" (Castillo and Camarillo 1973, p. 117). Thus, a young tenant farmer who killed a sheriff in self-defense was transformed into a notorious bandit and ringleader of a Chicano gang.

In California Joaquín Murieta was also said to have terrorized the Anglo population (see Nadeau 1974; Ridge 1955; Latta 1980). Like Cortez, Murieta was the victim of injustice when he was forced from his mining claim by a group of Anglos. Joaquín was allegedly beaten and his female companion raped. Later, when his half-brother was hanged by an angry mob, he "declared to a friend that he would live henceforth for revenge and that his path should be marked with blood" (Ridge 1955, pp. 12-13). While there is a great deal of mythology surrounding Joaquín and numerous versions of his life and career, all accounts agree on one point—he was pushed into a life of crime in order to avenge injustices committed against him and other Mexicans. Within a very short span of time in 1851 he is said to have terrorized the entire California countryside. Fear of the "Bloody Bandit of the Mother Lode" became so widespread that crimes hundreds of miles apart were attributed to him. In the midst of a crime wave ascribed to Murieta the *Sacramento Union* reported the capture of a bandit believed to be a member of his gang. He was broken out of jail by a mob and "tried before judge lynch." When he refused to talk, "he was escorted to that fatal Oak Tree, fronting the Astor House, which was now destined for the fifth time to bear a peculiar kind of fruit" (Secrest 1967, p. 16).

A reign of terror ensued in the Mother Lode, with retaliation against Mexicans being rampant:

> . . . Three hundred armed miners assembled on Sunday, January 23rd, and commenced a systematic search for the bandits. . . . The posse fanned out over the countryside and in their fear and exasperation, burned Mexicans' houses, took away their arms and told them to leave. The entire Mexican population was driven from San Andreas and the forks of the Calaveras River. Everywhere there were excited groups of men scouring the hills and valleys. (Secrest 1967, p. 14)

In retrospect the mythology surrounding Chicano banditry appears to have been little more than a smokescreen to mask injustices and atrocities perpetrated against Mexicans.

In addition to this individual and somewhat "primitive" form of social protest numerous organized revolts took place. In 1859 Juan "Cheno" Cortina, as noted earlier, led an army into Brownsville, occupying the city and proclaiming it the Republic of the Rio Grande (Goldfinch 1949). In New Mexico *Las Gorras Blancas* (White Caps) emerged in the early 1890s as a response to the Anglo land grab which threatened the traditional pastoral way of life of the region (Schlesinger 1971). This secret organization terrorized residents of Las Vegas through nocturnal raids, fence cutting, and other disruptive activities. Even more ambitious was the drafting of *El Plan de San Diego*, a revolutionary call to arms for Chicanos in 1915 (Gómez-Quiñones 1970; Rosenbaum 1973). Although it originated in south Texas, *El Plan* outlined a military revolt which would lead to the creation of an independent nation in the territory acquired by the United States during the Mexican War.

More recently Reies López Tijerina and *La Alianza Federal de Mercedes* (The Federal Alliance of Land Grants) called for the return of land grants whose ownership was guaranteed by the Treaty of Guadalupe-Hidalgo. While initially using constitutional means to return the land, he later advocated any means necessary for its reinstatement. In 1966 *La Alianza* took two forest rangers into custody for trespassing in the Kit Carson National Forest. The following year it attempted a citizen's arrest of the local district attorney for violation of constitutional rights and interference with local organizational activities in the famous *Tierra Amarilla* courthouse raid (U.S. Commission on Civil Rights 1970, p. 14). Even more impressive than the number and variety of Chicano rebellions has been the intensity of response elicited by them. Such protests typically have been quelled by the massive force of the military and the police.

Historically no other police agency has evoked more fear, resentment, or distrust among Chicanos than the Texas Rangers (*los rinches*). They represent the epitome of police abuse and brutality. Established as an independent state militia for the manifest purpose of putting down Indian uprisings and protecting the Texas frontier against Mexican "bandits," the Rangers were organized in the aftermath of Texas independence from Mexico in 1836. Though formally established on February 1, 1845, as a state militia of five detachments under the command of Captain John C. Hays, they were preceded by volunteer Ranger companies as early as 1823. The Rangers were thus born out of vigilantism. Despite the negative light they have been held in by Chicanos given the many atrocities committed against them by the Rangers, they have been idealized both by American folklore (see Samora, Bernal, and Peña 1979, pp. 3-7) and by apologist historians.

Dr. Walter Prescott Webb, dean of Texas historians, termed them "quiet, deliberate, gentle" men (Webb 1965, p. xv), while of the Mexican he noted, "Without disparagement it may be said that there is a cruel streak in the Mexican nature. . . . This cruelty may be a heritage from the Spanish of the Inquisition; it may, doubtless should, be attributed partly to the Indian blood" (Webb 1965, p. 14). When the Rangers took part in the siege of Mexico City during the Mexican War and committed numerous atrocities, their actions were either applauded or dismissed as "troublesome" behavior or resorting to "rigorous methods." On the basis of their participation in the Mexican-American War Webb concluded that "it was considered by everyone as the most singular and distinctive fighting organization known to the United States Army" (Webb 1975, p. 2). But for the Chicano the Ranger remained a symbol of oppression and exploitation, and the hatred of *los rinches* was recorded in *corridos* (Paredes 1958, p. 146).

> The rangers are very brave,
> That cannot be denied;
> They have to stalk us like deer
> In order to kill us.

Although heralded as protectors of law and order and portrayed as heroic figures in American folklore, there is little doubt that their basic function was to protect the economic interests of Anglo-Texans at any cost (Samora, Bernal, and Peña 1979). The expectation was that the Rangers would either exterminate or drive out the Indian and the Mexican. Webb himself observed, "Texans demanded that the United States should muster the Rangers into federal service, pay them with federal money, and let them run all the Mexicans into the Rio Grande and all the Indians into the Red River" (1965, p. 127).

Given that the Rangers were guilty of numerous abuses, violated the civil liberties of Chicanos, and killed Chicanos and Indians at will, one cannot escape the conclusion that images of the Anglo Ranger and the Mexican bandido not only evolved around parallel lines but were, in fact, mutually reinforcing mythologies. If bias could be mobilized effectively to depict the "Meskin" as a bloodthirsty subhuman species, then those delegated the task of exterminating these despicable creatures were not murderers but heroes to be glorified.

Throughout the history of the Southwest, then, the Rangers have served as a barometer of Anglo prejudice and hostility toward the Mexican. Anti-Mexican feeling has been especially intense when the United States has been at war and hostile attitudes toward foreigners have flourished. On the eve of World War I George Marvin recorded:

> . . . . the killing of Mexicans . . . through the border in these last four years is almost incredible. . . . Some rangers have degenerated into common man-killers. There is no penalty for killing, for no jury along the border would ever convict a white man for shooting a Mexican. . . . Reading over the Secret Service records makes you feel almost as though there were an open game season on Mexicans along the border. (McWilliams 1968, p. 112)

More than half a century later, 1970, the Department of Justice closed its investigative files in a case where a Chicano was shot and killed by a San Antonio police officer on the grounds that "prosecution of a white police officer for the shooting of a Mexican would have little chance of successful prosecution in the Southern District of Texas" (U.S. Commission on Civil Rights 1970, p. 33). The tacit acceptance of police abuses continues to the present day as is witnessed by a recent case in which three Houston policemen received one-year prison sentences after being convicted of murdering a Chicano Vietnam veteran.

The oppression of Chicanos at the hands of the legal and judicial system has been intensified by the proximity of the border and the availability of a vast pool of cheap Mexican labor which can be exploited by American industry and agriculture. It has been said, in fact, that the Chicano is the only racial-ethnic group in the United States that has to contend with both domestic police agencies and an international police force—the Border Patrol. Interestingly, despite the intensity of anti-Mexican feeling during World War I, imported Mexican labor was mobilized to help fill shortages created both by the war and by earlier restrictions on immigration imposed by the Immigration Act of 1917. Restrictionist feelings ran high into the 1920s, but large grower and industrial interests effectively staved off attempts to limit Mexican immigration. During the next decade, however, the Great Depression increased pressure to exclude the Mexican in order to reduce competition over scarce jobs and ease the loads of overburdened welfare rolls. As noted in the previous chapter, thousands of Mexicans were excluded from the United States through a two-pronged program of deportation and repatriation carried out by the joint efforts of the U.S. Immigration and Naturalization Service and local governments. As a result a reign of terror ensued in many Chicano neighborhoods, which were subject to being cordoned off and raided.

Official attitudes toward Mexican labor did an about-face during World War II, as the war created another labor shortage and precipitated a demand for cheap labor once again. Deportation and repatriation gave way to the bracero program, under Public Law 45. The Mexican laborer was welcomed with open arms, at least by American industry and agriculture. Although the bracero plan was heralded by American agriculture, termed symbolic of "The Good Neighbor Policy of Uncle Sam," though a "ticklish experiment in race relations," it did little to obfuscate prejudice against the Mexican. As in World War I, antiforeign sentiment ran high, and much of the hatred and hostility against Germany and Japan were transferred to the Mexican as a very visible symbol of the foreign element in the United States. Perhaps it is not coincidental that the first wave of braceros would enter the U.S. in the summer of 1942 as a reported "crime wave" in Los Angeles, attributed by the media and law enforcement agencies to rampant gangs of zoot-suiters, was ensuing.[1]

No case more clearly symbolizes blatant prejudice and hostility against Mexicans in this period than the famous Sleepy Lagoon case in Los Angeles. The case received much publicity and led to the conviction of seventeen young Mexican boys for conspiring to commit a murder that was never confirmed (see Sleepy Lagoon Defense Committee 1942; Endore 1944). The young men were accused and convicted of conspiring to murder one José Díaz on the night of August 2, 1942, after he left a drinking party on the Williams Ranch near a rock quarry called the Sleepy Lagoon. The conviction was obtained despite the fact that no evidence was ever presented to prove that they had beaten Díaz or that he was even beaten. Evidence indicated that Díaz had been drinking heavily and was probably killed by a hit-and-run driver.

During the course of the trial the boys were not allowed to get haircuts or clean clothing because the prosecution felt that "their style of hair-cut, the thick heads of hair, the duck-tail comb, and the pachuco pants and things of that kind" (Sleepy Lagoon Defense Committee 1942, p. 21) constituted important "evidence." Meanwhile the papers ran sensationalized stories of "Zoot-Suit Gangsters" and "Pachuco Killers" who were terrorizing innocent people. The conviction of the Sleepy Lagoon defendants became a foregone conclusion even before the onset of the trial, for ultimately it was not the boys, but the Mexican-American community, that was on trial (Adler 1974, p. 148). Mr. Ed. Duran Ayres of the Foreign Relations Bureau of the Los Angeles Sheriff's Office summed up prevalent racist feelings in his report to the grand jury, which returned an indictment against the boys. He stated, "The biological basis is the main basis to work from" (Sleepy Lagoon Defense Committee 1942, p. 14).

The Sleepy Lagoon case was but one of many incidents blamed on Chicano zoot-suiters by the police and press. The first incidents of disruption were reported in 1941, and by 1942 and 1943 concern with pachuco crime and violence had reached phobic proportions. Antipachuco feelings reached a peak during the famous zoot-suit riots in June 1943. The riots began on June 3, 1943, with off-duty policemen staging a vigilante hunt for zoot-suiters who had reportedly attacked several sailors in the Mexican district. The following night, according to newspaper accounts, when the police "Vengeance Squad" failed to find the "culprits," 200 sailors cruised through the barrio in a fleet of taxicabs, beating zoot-suiters and ripping their clothing (Adler 1974, p. 150). The police aided and abetted these criminal acts by providing an escort for the rioting sailors and arresting their victims. The violence continued until June 9, when the military declared downtown Los Angeles "off limits."

The role of the press in mobilizing bias against Chicanos and inciting violence against them cannot be overemphasized. Newspapers ran sensation-alized headlines such as "POLICE NAB 300 IN HOODLUM ROUNDUP," "ZOOT-SUITED GANGSTERS ROUNDED-UP," and "HAIR STYLE USED IN IDENTIFICATION OF HOODLUMS." Even before the death of José Díaz the Los Angeles press started building up a "crime wave" among Mexican youth as they ran stories of "Mexican Goon Squads," "Zoot-Suit Gangs," and "Pachuco Killers." So blatant was the racism that the Los Angeles city council passed an ordinance making the wearing of a zoot-suit a crime (Adler 1974, p. 150). As the Sleepy Lagoon Defense Committee observed (1942, p. 10): "Mexican boys were beaten, jailed. 'Zoot-suits' and 'Pachuco' hair cuts were crimes. It was a crime to be born in the U.S.A.—of a Spanish-speaking father or mother."

The Hearst press was especially instrumental in building up the idea of a Mexican "crime wave." Guy Endore, one of the chief protagonists for the Sleepy Lagoon Defense Committee, maintains that the crime wave was the result of a directive from Hearst himself to all Hearst editors. According to Endore (1944, p. 7) the teletype message from Hearst read:

> . . . Chief suggests L.A. editors make survey of crime reports—all types—with particular emphasis on numbers of police bookings of Mex-ican and Negro citizens—and or aliens. Chief suggests L.A. editors transmit findings to all other Hearst editors.

Even though there was no actual evidence of a crime wave among Chicano youth, the press was able to fabricate one by running sensationalized stories and getting "stooges," prominent personalities anxious for publicity, to make statements about Mexican crime.

> . . . even if there is no Mexican crime, there's nothing to stop you from printing what these prominent citizens are saying about Mex-ican crime, even if it is to the effect that it is nothing to be worried about. All this is printed under some sort of scare headline calculated to give the hurried reader the impression that Mexican crime is a real problem. (Endore 1944, p. 8)

Despite the important role played by the press the mobilization of bias was certainly not limited to it. The process was pervasive and extended to local and state politicians, the police, social workers, and social scientists, all of whom saw the Mexican as criminally prone, and they turned either to cul-tural or to genetic defects to explain his criminality (see Adler 1974, pp. 145-48).

While the 1950s symbolize an era of prosperity and a return to nor-malcy for many Americans, for Chicanos, as mentioned in the previous chapter, this was a period of intense and open repression. At the same time that literally millions of Mexicans were deported under "Operation Wet-back," others were being Red baited, and Chicano efforts at political organi-zation were being undermined. In fiscal year 1953 alone 875,000 Mexicans were deported; in 1954 the figure reached over one million (Grebler, Moore, and Guzman 1970, p. 521). These activities were supported by passage of the McCarran-Walter Act of 1952, which authorized the establishment of a Sub-versive Activities Control Board and the building of concentration camps in which subversives were to be interned in the event of a national emergency (Acuña 1972, p. 214). It also set forth a list of conditions under which aliens could be deported or excluded and, more importantly, when naturalized citi-zens could be denaturalized. The threat of "Communism" and subversion provided a rationale for muting Chicano political protest and intimidating Chicano communities. Once again a reign of terror prevailed:

> . . . The viciousness of the present roundup consists in the fact that once such a campaign has been decreed, there is only one way to carry it into effect; namely to make systematic house-to-house raids in every Mexican settlement in the state. In the course of these raids, it is inevitable that some long-time resident Mexicans will be picked up. . . . The mere announcement that the Immigration Service is con-ducting a roundup of this character operates, of course, to spread fear and panic throughout the Mexican settlements. Many of the long resi-dent entrants have married American citizens and have American-born children. (McWilliams 1949, p. 19)

Confrontations with the legal and judicial system continued into the late 1960s and 1970s to the present. *Ando Sangrando* (1972), Armando Morales' classic presentation of Mexican-American—police conflict, is a case study of the 1970-71 East Los Angeles riots. While they did not draw the na-tional attention of the Kent State incident, 35 persons were shot by police in the January 31, 1971, confrontation alone. Other confrontations had pre-viously occurred on January 1, August 29, and September 16, 1970. The mobilization of bias was rampant as indicated by the labeling of the incidents, as the "East Los Angeles riots." Just as it would have been more accurate to term the zoot-suit riots the U.S. Navy riots, so would it have been more ac-curate to term these incidents police riots. The media presented them largely as unprovoked eruptions by the Mexican-American community, however. Channel 7 (KABC) in Los Angeles, for example, presented the following "Moratorium Aftermath" editorial:

> . . . This weekend, a wave of senseless, pointless violence in East Los Angeles left damages totalling over $200,000 in its wake. . . . About a thousand angry youth, perhaps inflamed by rally speeches, cer-

tainly frustrated by the ghetto conditions in which they live, turned to meaningless destruction and violence. . . . The Moratorium was to protest alleged police brutality in the Mexican-American community. But there can be little question about the validity of Sheriff Peter Pitchess' statement that: "They can't say we provoked them this time." Moratorium leaders are already claiming police over-reaction. . . . There's no question that there was over-reaction—but it was initiated by young Chicanos who ignored pleas by Rosalio Muñoz that they disperse peacefully. . . . The Mexican-American community is a vitally-important part of our Southern California society. But such immature displays by a minority of the citizens there are major obstacles in keeping it from gaining the position of respect it deserves. (Morales 1972, p. 119)

The East Los Angeles riots were not isolated incidents, as numerous encounters with police have taken place throughout the barrios of the Southwest. Many of these go unnoticed and receive little publicity, but they are symptomatic of escalating Chicano-police conflict. Unlike the riots of the 1940s, which involved confrontations between racial-ethnic groups and are best termed "communal" riots (Janowitz 1969, pp. 418-24), most Chicano riots today are "commodity" riots involving the destruction or looting of businesses (many of them Anglo-owned). Rather than a direct confrontation between Chicanos and Anglos, "commodity" riots entail a confrontation between them and the police. Yet, the difference between "communal" and "commodity" riots may be more apparent than real, reflecting a more sophisticated form of racial-ethnic conflict. In the 1940s Chicanos were perceived as having made economic progress at the expense of the dominant group, and Anglo hostility was expressed directly at this group (Morales 1972, p. 94). Such hostility undoubtedly continues but is now expressed by the police, the courts, and the mass media, which are predominantly white and reflect the interests of Anglo-American society.

Direct fighting between racial-ethnic groups over contested territory, then, is a rare phenomenon in urban America today. In the case of Chicanos much intergroup hostility is expressed instead through confrontations with the police. Barrios are isolated physically and socially from Anglo society, and the police bear much of the responsibility for enforcing this isolation—that is, for keeping Chicanos in their place. Given this isolation, the mass media assumes an increasingly important role in shaping and maintaining public images of Chicanos.

In a letter to the United States Attorney General, MALDEF (Mexican American Legal Defense and Education Fund) complained of police violence and abuse against Chicanos, providing detailed documentation of 30 incidents taken from 70 reported recent cases of official violence. The document noted that in the last two years alone law enforcement officers in California, Texas, New Mexico, and Colorado have killed at least 16 Chicanos and wounded and physically abused many more. From the MALDEF letter it is clear that the wanton killing of Mexicans along the border is not a distant phenomenon but one that continues to the present day.

One of the most blatant incidents is the infamous Hannigan case which occurred in the summer of 1976 on the ranch of George Hannigan near Douglas, Arizona (see Acuña 1981, pp. 178-79; Arizona Republic 1977; Law 1977; Negri 1977; Blowis 1977). Hannigan and his two sons (ages 22 and 17) forcefully detained three undocumented Mexican workers who were looking for work. After being stripped, stabbed, and burned, with hot pokers, the Mexicans were dragged across the desert. Hannigan and his sons also pretended to hang one of the Mexicans and shot another. George Hannigan died before the case went to trial, but the Hannigan brothers were acquitted in October 1976. There were protests through massive demonstrations by Mexicans on both sides of the border (Acuña 1981, p. 178).

Rather than being carried out by vigilante groups or *los rinches*, killings and beatings are also being carried out more and more by rank-and-file law enforcement officers. MALDEF (1978a) concluded on the basis of its investigation that "official violence against Chicanos had reached epidemic proportions in the Southwest" and "that this violence was a severe, widespread and, for Mexican Americans, highly emotional phenomenon."

Mobilization of Bias Today: "Mi Vida Loca" and the "Myth of Progress"

From the preceding it is clear that Chicanos have frequently been victims of abuse and violence at the hands of the dominant society and the police. Chicanos continue to be subjected to such physical abuse, but as they have moved from a classic colonial relation to an internal colonial relation, more subtle and sophisticated methods of control have emerged.

The schools, the media, and publishing take on added significance for contemporary Chicanos, for these have become the primary vehicles for indirect, symbolic, cultural oppression. They have become, in other words, the primary vehicles for mobilizing bias against the Chicano. Because Chicanos are typically in a dependent relationship, we not only lack control over the transmission of symbols that shape public images of ourselves but are also constantly placed in a defensive posture. One must, for example, insure that the "rights" of Anglos are not violated—that we are not practicing reverse racism or discrimination. The activities of Chicanos who assume token positions of power, in politics or education for instance, are carefully scrutinized to guard against possible "bias" or reverse discrimination. "Any Chicano in public office who self-consciously serves the needs of the Chicano community leaves himself open to charges of 'reverse racism' and divisive parochialism" (Barrera et al. 1972, p. 490). The process can also be illustrated by issues which have recently surfaced in the courts. Litigation and court rulings aimed at protecting the rights of the majority and safeguarding against reverse discrimination show that the mobilization of bias is an effective, if not brutal, mechanism of dominion. The judicial process becomes a mockery when the courts find it necessary to give de jure legitimation to de facto patterns of colonization in the name of protecting the rights of the colonizer. One could hardly devise a more effective method of mobilizing bias than to get the colonized not only to deny their oppression but to believe that *they* are the oppressors.

Since Chicanos function in institutions controlled by the dominant society and are continually exposed to externally manipulated symbols, there is great pressure on them to internalize these negative images. Working within Anglo institutions necessitates obtaining Anglo approval for one's actions.

The view of Chicanos as violent and criminally prone can now be reinterpreted within the context of the mobilization of bias against an internally colonized and economically exploited people. The image of Chicanos as ruthless and bloodthirsty outlaws, as noted earlier, is one which has persisted historically since the Anglo invasion of Mexico's northern territory. The image has evolved over time, as have the techniques for mobilizing bias. Some media coverage of Chicano criminality and gang violence is still blatantly negative and pejorative as in previous times, but much of it is more subtle and indirect. By perpetually reporting criminal activities in the barrio, for example, the media reinforces the image of Mexican-Americans as criminal. Similarly, the media may express interest in the "problem" of gang violence, but by focusing on Chicano gangs it implies to the public that this is largely a "Chicano problem" and that most Chicanos take part in gang activities. These are but two of many indirect and ongoing mechanisms the media can employ to mobilize bias against Chicanos.

The mobilization of bias through indirect techniques is illustrated by a report on the television program "60 Minutes" which depicted the Chicano community of Riverside, California, as "lawless" (Lazzareschi 1979). A fifteen-minute segment narrated by correspondent Harry Reasoner was ostensibly devoted to a special firearms training course developed by the Riverside Police Department. Although prepared in 1978, the report included news film footage of a 1975 disturbance which occurred in the local barrio, Casa Blanca, insinuating that this and more recent disturbances in Casa Blanca were the reasons for establishing the special police program (Gonzales 1979). The broadcast also included an interview with a patrolman who claims to have been shot at several times while patrolling in the community and said

that police drive with their lights out so as not to attract attention, a tac-
tic used in other neighborhoods as well. According to the National News
Council

> . . . the broadcast did create an impression of lawlessness among
> Hispanics in general, which was underscored when it hopscotched
> across the country to Spanish Harlem to show New York police in a
> tense confrontation with apparently lawless elements. (Gonzales 1979,
> p. B-2)

Ironically, as the *Riverside Press* ran a story reporting the reprimand of CBS
News by the National News Council, the boldface feature headline on the
same page was "THREE HELD AFTER RENEWED SNIPING IN CASA
BLANCA" (Gaines 1979). The mobilization of bias is ongoing.

Perhaps even more effective in mobilizing bias against Chicanos than
negative portrayals are those that seek to present violence and criminality as
inherent cultural traits. Such portrayals are found both in the media and in
social-science accounts. Since the first chapter focused on social-science portrayals, attention now turns to how popular writing has worked to mobilize
bias against Chicanos. There has been a recent proliferation of articles about
Chicanos in national magazines. Some would suggest that this is the "Decade
of the Chicano" because press interest in Chicanos appears unprecedented,
yet these articles consistently present a negative and pathological view of the
Chicano and his culture. Although details may vary, the message conveyed
is unchanging—Chicanos live in poverty and squalor amidst affluence in
culturally and physically isolated barrios where crime, violence, and gang
warfare are endemic.

The culture, moreover, is characterized by rigid sex-role separation,
with the *macho* warrior dictating the rules and the woman providing warmth
and support. In an article entitled *La vida loca* which appeared in *New West*
magazine Tracy J. Johnston (1979, p. 38) observes,"The men in the barrios
make the rules, but their sisters and girlfriends provide support and comfort
in the endless gang warfare of East Los Angeles. There is no reason; there
is only pride, revenge and bloodshed." Overwhelmed by poverty and surrounded by wealth, the *vato loco* chooses defiantly to lead *la vida loca*, "where
they can get a reputation for risking their lives without flinching and taking
drugs without caution; where they can die the most glorious death of all—the
death of a soldier fighting for his country, or, in this case, his barrio" (Johnston 1979, p. 44).

A very similar description of Chicano culture and barrio life is found
in Suzanne Murphy's article, "A Year with Gangs of East Los Angeles,"
which appeared in *Ms.* magazine. Murphy is a photojournalist who is said to
have spent more than a year photographing and interviewing gang members.

While focusing on women in gangs, she provides an overall description of gang life. Like *vatos locos*

> . . . *Cholos* (both male and female gang members) generally range in age from 11 to 25. They are often school dropouts with few job prospects. Without steady incomes or cars, they are isolated from everyone except each other. A few hard-core members are even ready to put their lives on the line for a neighborhood as a soldier would in defense of the homeland. (Murphy 1978, p. 56)

Although some women engage in gang activities which parallel those of the men, they typically play the more traditional and supportive roles of girlfriends, morale boosters, and mothers (1978, p. 56).

Through a series of brief case histories Murphy describes a lifestyle fraught with violence, unwanted pregnancies, illegitimacy, family disorganization, drug addiction, and prostitution. A 36-year-old *veterana* comments on gang life:

> . . . I think I was born gang. From eleven on, I identified with *pachucos* and *pachucas*. . . . We drank, we lowrided, and we got into fights with girls from other gangs. Our motto was "This is the way we're going to live, this is the way we'll die, standing up for our gang's name."
>
> I saw a lot of stabbings and killings as a kid. I was frightened, but you can't show it. . . . I had this image to uphold—and it almost killed me because I carried it for so long. (Ibid., p. 62)

Ruth continued this gang life, so that by age 32 "she had a long prison record for narcotics possession and prostitution. Her five children by three different men were in foster homes. Deep into alcoholism and at rock bottom, she finally entered a program for alcoholics" (ibid., p. 62).

A common theme in these articles is that in the barrio "*todo se paga*" (all is avenged). Johnston (1979, p. 46), for example, ends her article with an anecdote of a young boy who stopped playing baseball as she walked by, stared, and told her that she did not belong there, "This is *Mexican* territory . . . *Todo se paga*." *Todo se paga* is the title of another article on Chicano violence. The article provides an in-depth look at a 20-year-old feud between two families in the Southern California community of Riverside. The feud drew the attention of Calvin Trillin (1979), a writer for the *New Yorker* who traveled to Riverside to research the conflict. That a writer for a staid and nonsensationalistic periodical would travel cross country to research an interfamily squabble is curious indeed, except for the fact that the feuding families were Chicano and the incident took place in a barrio with a long history of conflict with police. The feud, which began with a fight between John

Ahumada and John Hernández (plus Hernández's brothers-in-law Marcos and Roman Lozano) that left Ahumada permanently disabled and led to the imprisonment of the Lozanos, has been continued by subsequent generations. According to Trillin (ibid., p. 102) at least four persons have been killed, two have been crippled, and many more sideswiped or shot at. Although Trillin's treatment is less pejorative than Johnston's or Murphy's, he too links the violent family feud to Chicano cultural traits. Trillin concurs that among Chicanos "*Todo se paga*":

> . . . In the *barrio*, the brutal simplicity ordinarily associated with a blood feud—an eye for an eye—is complicated by the element of pride. "You killed my brother, so I will kill your brother" sometimes seems to become "You killed my brother and that makes you think you are stronger than we are and can look down on us, so, to show that's not true, I will kill your brother." (Ibid. p. 103)

Media concern with gang activity has perhaps been most intensely manifested in its coverage of the Mexican Mafia. Numerous stories have been devoted to the Mexican Mafia, a secretive and powerful organization in the California prison system which evolved out of East Los Angeles gangs which control drug traffic on the West Coast. Based on interviews with Eddie Gonzales, an alleged member of the Mexican Mafia turned informant, John Hammarley (1977) wrote "Inside the Mexican Mafia" for *New West*. Hammarley provides detailed information on its structure and activities, alleging it infiltrated Get Going, a self-help group in East Los Angeles. He describes the position and role of "shooters":

> . . . the Mexican Mafia places a special value on its shooters. "The people who kill in the Mexican Mafia are supposed to be the most sincere." Eddie explains. "The shooters are always the ones in line for the top jobs. And their idea of a big shot was being a killer. I guess I looked for people to idolize me in fear. I figured if people were scared of me, they respected me." (Ibid., p. 70)

An Associated Press article on the Mexican Mafia comes to almost identical conclusions. According to the author, Bill Gardner (1977, p. A-1), law enforcement experts believe that "There's no retirement from the Mexican Mafia." Another expert notes, "It's a blood in, blood out organization. . . . You've got to spill someone's blood to get in" (1977, p. A-1). The Mexican Mafia is growing, and its influence is no longer limited to California prisons according to these accounts.

There have also been attempts to link public officials, especially Chicanos or those sympathetic to Chicanos such as former California Governor Jerry Brown, with the Mafia. California State Health and Welfare Secretary

Mario G. Obledo and two of his aides, for example, were subpoenaed to testify in the Michael Delia case. Delia and three other alleged Mexican Mafia members were tried for the murder of Delia's estranged wife, Ellen. Delia was the founder of Get Going, while Ellen served as its executive secretary and wrote grant proposals for the program. Ellen was presumably silenced so that she would not inform authorities about the misuse of federal funds. Although hard evidence linking the Mexican Mafia and public officials has not been forthcoming, these allegations by law enforcement and the media help to re-inforce negative images of Chicanos.

Press concern with Chicano gangs has reached phobic proportions, as the headline of an Associated Press story attests—"THIRD GRADERS SAID MEMBERS OF GANGS." In statements attributed to Father Thomas Fitz-patrick, director of a Bell Gardens youth group, the article notes that "third and fourth graders are among the newest members of the 300 youth gangs in East Los Angeles, and most of those gang members carry handguns." According-ing to Father Fitzpatrick the main sources of weapons for these youth are "smuggling, robberies, and the Mexican Mafia (Associated Press 1978, p. C-4).

Juxtaposed against these stories of crime, violence, poverty, and squalor in urban barrios is a series of articles that ostensibly paint a very positive pic-ture of the Chicano. *New West* (Kirsch 1978) magazine, for example, ran an article entitled "The Decade of the Chicano," while Time's (1978) cover story was "It's Your Turn in the Sun." The ingredients of these optimistic articles, like their pessimistic counterparts, are unvarying. First, they point to population projections which show that Hispanics will soon be the nation's largest minority and that Chicanos are the largest single Hispanic group. They then turn to isolated accomplishments by Hispanics in politics, the arts, and the professions. There is also awareness of a growing assertiveness and political sophistication on the part of Chicanos. When these factors are coupled with the recognition of their potential political clout, the result is a very romanticized and overly optimistic picture of the future of the Chi-cano, frequently depicted as a sleeping giant about to awaken. Governor Jerry Brown, speaking before a MAPA convention (Mexican-American Political Association), could say to the delegates, for example, "It's your turn in the sun and I want to be part of it" (Cover Story 1978, p. 48). The co-optative value of this stance is demonstrated by the fact that MAPA supported Brown and other Democratic candidates and spurned the candidacy of Andres Tor-res, *Raza Unida* candidate for governor.

While these articles appear to be positive portrayals of the "success of Chicanos," they may be even more dangerous in mobilizing bias against them than blatantly pejorative accounts. By reinforcing the "myth of progress" they not only work to minimize problems faced by Chicanos but also provide fodder for those who believe that minorities are already getting preferential treatment. To create the illusion of progress while the bulk of the Chicano population remains in a subordinate and oppressed position is a cruel hoax indeed. Moreover, when the myth of progress is coupled with the alleged persistent violence and criminality of Chicanos, such criminality is likely to be attributed to inherent pathologies and weaknesses in Chicano culture, since it obviously cannot be attributed to poverty or economic oppression. One is led to ask, "Why do they act like animals when they've got it made?"

Despite their trappings the "successful Chicano" articles are negative, for, grounded as they are in the assimilationist perspective, they ultimately turn to failings in the Chicano to explain his disadvantaged position. The cover story in *Time* (1978) commented on their lack of political power:

> . . . There are a number of reasons for the underrepresentation: the Hispanics' relatively *late arrival as a major immigrant group*; their reservations about politics, often the result of once having lived under corrupt, autocratic regimes; their traditional preoccupation with family and community affairs rather than with broad political issues. . . . But the most immediate—and most easily remedied—reason is their failure to register in sufficient numbers. (Ibid. 1978, p. 51; emphasis mine)

Conclusion

Chicanos are a colonized and economically oppressed people who as a result of their military subjugation have had a foreign culture and language imposed by force. Conflict with law enforcement has been commonplace as the police have worked to maintain order in the barrios, literally *colonias* (colonies) within the United States. As Chicanos have moved from a classic to an internal colonial situation, emphasis has shifted from direct, formal, coercive means of control to indirect, informal, symbolic controls. This is not to suggest that Chicanos are no longer subjected to coercive controls, for police violence and abuse is still rampant in the barrio, and Chicanos continue to receive differential and unequal treatment at the hands of the legal and judicial system; but rather, in addition to these direct controls more sophisticated symbolic ones have also emerged. Such controls are designed to maintain the Chicano in a subordinate position. The media, the schools, and other socializing agents have joined the police in suppressing the Chicano. This is accomplished through the projection and reinforcement of negative images. The two forms of control are, in fact, interrelated and mutually reinforcing in the sense that the manipulation of symbols against Chicanos serves to legitimate the formal abusive controls that are used against them. Media interest in issues such as Chicano criminality, gang violence, and the Mexican Mafia helps to reinforce the image of Chicanos as a violent and criminally prone people, even when couched in what is ostensibly a positive, sympathetic, or romanticized approach.

The mobilization of bias against Chicanos can take different and even polar turns. Portrayals of Chicanos as a "successful" or "emerging" minority are perhaps more dangerous than blatantly negative portrayals precisely because they do purport to be positive. The myth of progress not only demonstrates and legitimates the vitality of the system but creates the impression that Chicanos are getting equal, if not preferential, treatment. It serves, in other words, to obfuscate their oppression while creating the illusion that *they* are the oppressors. The greatest danger in the mobilization of bias is that Chicanos, surrounded as they are by these negative images and living in an Anglo-controlled society, are pressured to accept these as accurate images or even to idealize them as positive ones. The *cholo* who goes on national television or grants an interview to a journalist in order to extol his or her "badness" exemplifies this process, as does the "successful Chicano" who wishes to disassociate himself or herself from his barrio counterparts.

A Chicana community organizer who took Johnston into the "heart" of the barrio, for example, observed,

> . . . Don't let them tell you that their life is exciting. . . . These girls have absolutely nothing to do. They fight for one day and hang around for twenty. The girls are mothers, the guys are fighters, and that's it. The girls have no models of women doing anything interesting or positive. . . . People don't grow up here. It's an adolescent culture— full of petty jealousies, paranoia, macho bravado. It's a defeated culture, really. The men think they are shit, and the women are even lower than the men. (Johnston 1979, pp. 42-43)

With a mentor such as this it is little wonder that Johnston arrived at such a pathological view of the barrio. The internalization of such negative images by Chicanos brings the mobilization of bias full circle and reinforces negative images held by the dominant group.

Although the mobilization of bias against Chicanos is prevalent today, it is not a new or recent phenomenon but one that has changed or evolved over time. During the nineteenth century the Chicano was depicted as a bloodthirsty, greasy, mustachioed bandido; in the 1940s as a pachuco killer. Today these characterizations have given way to those of a *cholo* or *vato loco*, but the image of the Chicano as violent and criminal remains unchanged. With the advent of the mass media, control techniques have grown increasingly sophisticated and complex, making it more difficult to counteract their influence. If Chicanos are to be decolonized, it is essential not only that we gain control over vital institutions and counter direct external controls but that we counteract insidious mechanisms of control such as co-optation and the mobilization of bias. Ultimately decolonization will come only when Chicanos are able to eradicate the cultural control which maintains them in a subordinate position. A full understanding of the mobilization of bias and other mechanisms of cultural control is therefore an essential first step in the process of decolonization.

5

Education: Problems, Issues, and Alternatives

As Chicanos have moved from a classic to an internal-colonial situation, we have seen how the emphasis has shifted from direct physical controls to indirect, symbolic ones. Although force remains an effective and prevalent mechanism of domination, it has given way to a considerable extent to more sophisticated and less direct forms of social control such as the mobilization of bias. At the risk of oversimplification, it could be said that force and coercion have given way to persuasion and socialization. Emphasis has shifted from attempts to suppress the Chicano to those designed to keep him in a subordinate position (Barrera, Muñoz, and Ornelas 1972, p. 491). In such a setting socializing institutions such as education and the church assume dramatically important roles. These institutions control ideas and shape images that Chicanos have about themselves and their position within American society. Mind control is essential to colonization, for, when effective, the colonized person comes not only to accept but to deny his oppression. The role of cultural control in colonization has been noted by Blauner.

> . . . Colonialism depends on conquest, control, and the imposition of new institutions and ways of thought. Culture and social organization are important as vessels of a people's autonomy and integrity; when cultures are whole and vigorous, conquest, penetration, and certain modes of control are more readily resisted. (1972, p. 67)

No institution has done more to effect the cultural control of Chicanos or attempted to obviate the impact of Chicano cultural and familial values than the school. This chapter will examine the role of the school in maintaining Chicanos in a subordinate and dependent position. It hopes in the process to demonstrate the Janus-faced character of education. While the school has traditionally served as an instrument of domination and assimilation, "education," in the true sense of the word, holds the potential for liberating Chicanos. More specifically, the chapter will (1) present an overview of Chicanos and education, documenting the history of educational neglect and showing how the school has worked to perpetuate the economic,

educational, political, and cultural oppression of Chicanos, (2) isolate dis-
crepancies between educational goals or ideals and educational functions as
they pertain to Chicanos and other minorities, (3) examine alternative models of education and their relevance for Chicanos, and (4) argue for the development of a Chicano pedagogy of liberation that addresses both their
economic and cultural oppression.

Chicanos and Education: A History of Neglect and Failure

The history of Chicanos' relations with the educational system is a
history of neglect and failure—neglect on the part of the schools and failure
by Chicano students. Chicanos have one of the highest dropout, or more accurately, push-out, rates of any group in the United States.[1] For every 100
Chicano children who enter first grade only 60 graduate from high school
compared to 67 out of every 100 blacks and 86 out of every 100 Anglo youth.
Among those who stay in school and reach the twelfth grade, 3 out of 5 will
be reading below grade level (U.S. Commission on Civil Rights 1971, p. 42).
Whereas 72.8 percent of white persons 25 years and older have completed
at least 4 years of high school, only 54.9 percent of black and 45.9 percent
of Spanish-origin persons have completed this much schooling (U.S. Bureau
of the Census 1983a, p. 54). Of even greater concern is the fact that while
the gap between Chicanos, blacks, and the total population decreased slightly
between 1950 and 1970, the relative position of Chicanos did not change
(Carter and Segura 1979, p. 41). There are also substantial regional differences, with Texas having the lowest attainment level and California the
highest for all groups including Chicanos (ibid., p. 41). By the end of the
eighth grade Chicanos in Texas will have lost 14 percent of their peers; before the end of the twelfth grade nearly half, or 47 percent, will have left
school (U.S. Commission on Civil Rights 1971, p. 42). These figures are even
more appalling when one considers that they are based on Chicanos who
enter school, and many, especially those who are undocumented, never enter
school. Of persons of Mexican origin 25 years of age and older, 23.1 percent
have completed less than 5 years of school and only 34.3 percent have completed 4 years of high school or more. The corresponding figures for the total
U.S. population are 3.6 and 65.9, respectively (U.S. Bureau of the Census
1978a, p. 7).

The gap between Chicanos and Anglos increases with educational level
and is greatest in college and graduate school. Nearly half of the Anglo students who begin first grade eventually enter college, whereas only one out
of every four black and Chicano students enter (U.S. Commission on Civil
Rights 1971, p. 42). While the absolute number of Chicanos in college has
increased, the percentage has remained fairly constant (Carter and Segura

1979, p. 50). Spanish-surnamed persons accounted for only 1.6 percent of all enrollment in higher education in 1968, 2.1 percent in 1970, and 2.3 percent in 1972 (López, Madrid-Barela, and Flores Macías et al. 1976, p. 20). Chicano enrollment constitutes an even smaller proportion of all enrollment, given that Chicanos are only about 60 percent of the *Hispano* population and their educational attainment tends to be lower than other *Hispano* groups.[2] Only 4.3 percent of all persons of Mexican origin living in the United States have completed 4 or more years of college, compared to 16.1 percent of persons not of Spanish origin (U.S. Bureau of the Census 1978a, p. 7). The percentage of Cuban-origin persons who have 4 years of college or more (13.9) is only slightly lower than the percentage for those not of Spanish origin (ibid.).

The push-out rate is important because it is the ultimate measure of school holding power, but it is more accurately an effect rather than a cause of the school's failure. In one of the most comprehensive studies of the educational system in the Southwest done by the U.S. Commission on Civil Rights, a bipartisan agency established by Congress to investigate allegations of denial of equal protection of the law because of race, color, religion, sex or national origin, a series of barriers to equal educational opportunity for Mexican-Americans were isolated. The findings and recommendations contained in six reports indicated that (1974, p. 68):

* Chicanos are instructed in a language other than the one with which they are most familiar.

* The curriculum consists of textbooks and courses which ignore the Mexican American background and heritage.

* Chicanos are usually taught by teachers whose own culture and background are different and whose training leaves them ignorant and insensitive to the educational needs of Chicano students.

* And when Chicano pupils seek guidance from counselors they rarely can obtain it and even more rarely from a Mexican American counselor.

The commission went on to note that Chicanos typically attend inferior, segregated schools, isolated by school districts and by schools within districts (ibid., p. 1). Such schools are sorely underfinanced, even though Chicano parents bear a proportionately heavier burden of the costs of financing schools.

In addition, the commission found that the quality of interaction between teacher and student favors Anglo students. Specifically, Anglo children are praised or encouraged by teachers 36 percent more often than Chicano children, they use or develop the contributions of Anglo children 40 percent more, they respond positively to Anglos about 40 percent more often, and teachers' direct questions to Anglo children 21 percent more often (U.S.

Commission on Civil Rights 1973, p. 43). Predictably, Chicano children also participate less often in class. The commission concluded:

> . . . The findings of this report reflect more than inadequacies regarding the specific conditions and practices examined. They reflect a systematic failure of the educational process, which not only ignores the educational needs of Chicano students but also suppresses their culture and stifles their hopes and ambitions. . . . Having established the conditions that assure failure, the schools then judge the performance of Chicano children. (1974, pp. 67-68)

Discrepancy between Educational Ideals and Realities: A Contemporary American Dilemma

In a classic study of race and ethnic relations Gunnar Myrdal (1944) pointed to what he termed "an American dilemma" between the democratic principles espoused in the Declaration of Independence and the Constitution, on the one hand, and the subordination of certain groups such as black Americans, on the other. The resolution of this ethical dilemma posed a major challenge to the United States according to Myrdal. The dilemma persists, nonetheless, and nowhere is it more clearly evident than in the operation of the public school system.

Even a cursory examination of the stated goals and ideals of the educational institution would reveal that not only is the school the primary mechanism for perpetuating American democratic ideals but that it is also alleged to be the primary vehicle for implementing these ideals. The school transmits an ideology that is best described as the "melting pot," or "Statue of Liberty," view of American society (see Glazer and Moynihan 1963). It holds that in a democratic society education is the "birthright" of its citizenry:

> . . . Democracy makes the many of such paramount political and educational importance because it believes in the essential dignity of all persons. It enjoins that every person be treated always as an end. This injunction holds no matter to which sex a persons belongs, no matter what his color or race, no matter whether he is highborn or low, and no matter what the economic condition. . . . Since every individual counts, it would be a cosmic miscarriage for his capacities to go undeveloped. (Brubacher 1969, p. 57)

According to this ideology the United States is truly the land of opportunity. Children may be born into families of varying economic backgrounds, but such differences are largely inconsequential to their performance, for the school is the great equalizer that works to obviate these differences. The

school, moreover, is a microcosm of the larger society, so that the social, economic, and racial-ethnic backgrounds of children are deemed irrelevant.
Each person is unique and to be judged according to his or her personal characteristics or attributes, not according to social or background characteristics.

The system is not only democratic but meritocratic; achievement and
advancement are based on individual ability, intelligence, and motivation.[3]
A person with a modicum of ability, no matter how humble his origins, can
succeed if he or she wants to succeed. An essential distinguishing and unique
characteristic of American society, then, is its permeability and the prevalence of upward social and economic mobility. Education, not surprisingly,
is the key to social advancement, for societal and economic rewards accrued
to the individual are based on achievement and the acquisition of appropriate
credentials rather than on social or familial background.

Two variants of the melting-pot model have been identified—"permissive" and "exclusive." Ramírez and Castañeda point out that although
the "exclusivist" variant has been the most prevalent, a more "permissive"
form of the model has a history dating back to the eighteenth century (1974,
p. 5). This more positive and idealistic view was espoused by the French-born
writer Crèvecoeur as early as 1782, who held that American society was a
completely new blend both culturally and biologically (ibid., p. 6). The view
is permissive, because the blending is said to have resulted from a natural
evolutionary process and does not entail the coercive or forced imposition of
one culture over another (this variant is very similar to the amalgam model
discussed in chapter nine). Blending produces a uniquely American character
according to Crèvecoeur:

> . . . I could point out to you a family whose grandfather was an
> Englishman, whose wife was Dutch, whose son married a French woman,
> and whose present four sons have now four wives of different nations.
> He is an American, who leaving behind him all his ancient prejudices
> and manners, receives new ones from the new mode of life he has em-
> braced. . . . Here individuals of all nations are melted into a new race
> of men. (Crèvecoeur 1904, pp. 54-55)

The melting-pot view of American society prevailed, and by 1908 a
play by that name appeared and enjoyed considerable success (Ramírez and
Castañeda, p. 6). A line from the play sums up the ideology of the permissive
melting pot: "America is God's Crucible, the Great Melting Pot where all
races of Europe are melting and re-forming! . . . God is making the American.
. . . the real American has not yet arrived. . . . he will be the fusion of all the
races, perhaps the coming superman" (ibid.). Two points are worth noting in
this quote. First, a close reading suggests that it is less permissive or benign
than it appears to be. Second, the statement is racist since it is based on the

espoused superiority of the white race. Note that the so-called melting pot is composed of "all races of Europe" and does not include nonwhites and that the amalgam of this intraracial mixture promises to produce a superior race. The melting-pot model is thus applicable only to white European (largely northern) immigrants and not to people of color such as blacks, Native Americans, and Chicanos whose entrance into American society was forced and involuntary.

The exclusive version of the melting pot is based on the Anglo-conformity (see chapter nine) view of race and ethnic relations. Although it parallels the permissive model in defining American society as a melting pot, the Anglo-Saxon Protestant group is seen as dominant and as assimilating and acculturating other groups into its culture and values. It is assumed to be desirable that English institutions, the English language, and English cultural values be maintained. "Thus, this view is exclusive in that acculturation is viewed as desirable only if the Anglo-Saxon cultural pattern is taken as an ideal. By implication, all other cultural forms are of less value, status, and importance" (ibid., p. 8).

Although they have different emphases, both variants assume that racial and ethnic groups will eventually dissolve into the melting pot and that "American" beliefs and values are inherently superior to foreign ones. Groups who do not acculturate or assimilate are viewed not only with suspicion but as deficient. "The 'damaging-culture' assumption as it has been applied to Mexican Americans has consistently led to the conclusion that the culture of Mexican Americans socialized individuals to become lazy, resigned, passive, fatalistic, nongoal-oriented, docile, shy, infantile, criminally prone, irrational, emotional, authoritarian, unreliable, limited in cognitive ability, untrustworthy, lax, priest-ridden, and nonachievement-oriented" (ibid., p. 9). The failure of Chicanos in school is thus blamed, not on the school or the society, but on Chicanos themselves.

Despite the lofty ideals touted by the melting-pot model, in reality the school has not worked to advance democratic ideals, develop individual abilities, or provide equal opportunity for disadvantaged groups but rather has been an instrument of the dominant society whose ultimate function is to perpetuate the existing order. Schools are controlled by the white middle and upper classes and serve as agencies that advance the values and culture of Anglo society. The ideal of equal opportunity is a myth, a cruel hoax perpetrated on the poor and on Chicanos and other minorities. In fact, the egalitarian ethic which holds that all children should be treated equally and judged according to the same "universal standards" (i.e., Anglo values) works to legitimate the failure of Chicano children (Mirandé 1975, p. 419). Their failure can be blamed on a lack of ability or some defect in the culture because children, after all, were treated and judged "equally."

Models of Education

Having established the conditions in the school that insure the failure of Chicano students and the ideology which legitimates this failure, we now turn to an examination of three dominant models of education and the implications these models hold for Chicanos. The three models are (1) traditional, (2) liberal, and (3) Chicano alternative.

Traditional Model

The traditional model of education has been historically most prevalent and, until recently, almost the only one experienced by Chicanos. The traditional model abets the colonization of Chicanos and the view that their culture and language are inferior. The school thus assumes a critical role in the process of colonization. As the primary institution of socialization and Americanization, its predominant function has been to extinguish the culture of Chicanos and to mute their language. Although lip service is paid to assimilation and amalgamation, the stance of the school relative to Chicanos is exclusionary. Chicanos can be incorporated only if they reject their culture and abandon their native tongue, yet this does not guarantee their success or advancement. Phenomena such as the no Spanish rule, Spanish detention, the banning of Pendletons and khakis, and the practice of subjecting Chicano children to searches for lice emerged out of the traditional model. Anglo control and domination of the school is open and unabashed. Not only are teachers, counselors, and administrators almost exclusively Anglo but the curriculum reflects the values and ethos of the dominant society. School boards and other agencies that establish educational policy are also predominantly Anglo. The school, in short, is for Chicanos a hostile and alien institution that asks them to reject their culture and language and establishes conditions for failure.

Segregation was a common feature of this model. Although segregation based directly on race or nationality was outlawed in the five southwestern states, it was generally justified on other grounds such as the unique educational needs of Mexican children. The Texas educational survey report, for example, argued:

> On pedagogical grounds a very good argument can be made for segregation in the early grades. In the opinion of the survey staff, it is wise to segregate, if it is done on educational grounds, and results in distinct efforts to provide the non-English-speaking pupils with specially trained teachers and the necessary special training resources. This suggestion is not always a practical one, especially in the small school.

This advice is offered with reluctance, as there is danger that it will be misunderstood by some. By others it may be seized upon as a means of justifying the practices now obtaining in some communities. In some instances segregation has been used for the purpose of giving the Mexican children a shorter school year, inferior buildings and equipment, and poorly paid teachers. (Cited in Reynolds 1933, p. 9)

Whenever feasible, separate schools were maintained for Mexican children, especially in the lower grades, or separate classes were established for them (ibid., p. 11). There was a general consensus, however, that by the fourth or fifth grade Mexican children should be educated with white children.

Although the practice of segregating Spanish-speaking children continued, it was challenged in the courts. In Delgado vs. Bastrop Independent School District (1948) in Texas and Mendez vs. Westminster School District (1946) in California, rulings were obtained against segregation. In the Delgado case the major ruling of the court was that:

The defendant, L. A. Woods, as State Superintendent of Public Instruction, is hereby permanently restrained and enjoined from in any manner, directly or indirectly, participating in the custom, usage or practice of segregating pupils of Mexican or other Latin-American descent in separate schools or classes. (Sánchez 1974, p. 14)

As a result of this court order State Superintendent Woods issued a set of instructions and regulations which specified that segregated schools in the state of Texas could only be authorized for persons of Negro ancestry. Woods' order stated that

You will take all necessary steps to eliminate any and all segregations that may exist in your school or district contrary to instruction and regulations. I shall take whatever steps are necessary to enforce these instructions and regulations and to prevent segregation of Mexican or other Latin American descent in the public schools as in the State of Texas as directed by the above-mentioned Court decree.

L. A. Woods,
State Superintendent of Public Instruction,
State of Texas.
(Ibid., p 75)

Despite this order and several court rulings segregation continued well into the 1960s.

Since Chicano culture is viewed as a negative and pathological force, before Chicano children can be educated it is first necessary to "de-educate" them. The extinction of the Spanish language is critical to this process:

The native language of the Chicano child was treated with colonial disdain. His voice was muted. . . . In a conquered land the institutions of culture—theaters, books, libraries, academics—may be visibly suppressed. It is more difficult to eradicate the spoken word. Language then becomes the last resource of cultural survival. (Steiner 1970, p. 211)

In addition to shaming and ridiculing children for speaking Spanish the schools denigrate Chicano cultural and familial values. The culture is seen as being responsible for many of the problems experienced by Chicanos inside and outside of school.[4] It is said to instill low motivation and low need to excel, while stifling creativity and individuality. The family is an authoritarian, male-dominated structure where the needs of the individual are subordinated to those of the group. Parents are thus their own children's worst enemies, and one of the primary functions of the school is to neutralize this negative parental influence. Success in school for many Chicanos is, not surprisingly, often achieved at a heavy cost—alienation from one's culture and family. When this attack on Chicano culture is coupled with the denigration of the Spanish language and the ignoring of Chicano history, the net effect is that schools teach children to be ashamed of being Mexican (see Gómez 1973, pp. 5-12; Rodríguez 1974-75).

The traditional model prevailed in the schools of the Southwest until the 1960s, when Chicanos first began to challenge the racist policies and practices of the school on a massive scale. The East Los Angeles "blowouts" of 1968, the 1969 school boycott in Crystal City, and similar protests in Chicano communities throughout the Southwest can be seen as a direct response to the effects of the traditional model of education. Perhaps no case more clearly illustrates the operation of this model than Cristál (Crystal City). Located in the Winter Garden area of Texas, and about 80 percent Chicano, the community was controlled since its inception by the Anglo minority. With the exception of a few Mexican-American compromisers, businesses, the city council, and the school board were under Anglo control. The school was similarly dominated, and racist policies prevailed. A number of teachers were known to Chicanos and Anglos alike to be blatantly racist and anti-Chicano. These "Mexican haters"

> . . . had precipitated many incidents in their classrooms, occasionally lashing out at all Mexicans, telling them they "should feel privileged to sit next to whites," and in general doing their best to make the Mexicans feel insecure and inferior. (Shockley 1974, pp. 117-18)

When the community was first founded, there was no school for Mexicans. Some improvements were made over time, but by 1951 only as few as

9 percent of entering first graders had graduated from high school, and by 1958 the figure had reached only 17 percent. The median number of years of school completed by Spanish-surnamed persons went from 1.8 years in 1950 to 2.3 years in 1960, compared to a median of 11.2 years for the Anglo population (ibid., p. 117). By 1968 87 percent of the student body had been Chicano, and although a few *raza* teachers had been hired, their numbers were abysmal relative to the composition of the student body (ibid., p. 117).

The first challenge to Anglo control came in 1963 when Chicanos carried out a take-over of the city council that was short-lived ending two years later. The second revolt occurred in 1969 and was sparked by a successful school boycott which led to the founding of *El Partido de la Raza Unida. El Partido* mobilized Chicanos and enabled them to regain control of the city council as well as the school board. That the schools served as a catalyst for politicizing Chicanos is perhaps not surprising. Since the schools reflect the values of the dominant group and are key agents of social control, it seems appropriate that the school would become the battleground for the struggle for equal treatment.

Schools had become the no man's land of the cultural conflict. They are the most visible, best known, and most exposed institutions of the Anglo society in the barrios. On the inside they are the bastions where the language, philosophy, and goals of the conqueror are taught; but to those outside they are the bastions that the conquered can most easily besiege, with common cause, so that their children may be taught the language, philosophy, and goals of La Raza. (Steiner 1970, p. 227)

Liberal Model

The liberal model of education emerged as a response to criticisms of the school and the prevailing traditional model, and is today the most common approach to resolving the educational problems of Chicanos. It is a model which enjoys great popularity among Anglos and Mexican-Americans alike and has largely displaced the traditional model. The models are, however, completely separable only in an analytic sense, and in any given situation one may well find elements of both at work. The point is that the traditional model which is overt both in its racism and ethnocentrism is slowly giving way in the schools of the Southwest and among professional educators to a more sophisticated model that appears to recognize the failure of the school and proposes liberal solutions to these problems. It is a liberal model because it ostensibly attempts to go beyond the status quo, but the proposed solutions are moderate ones that would reform rather than radically alter existing conditions.

The liberal model acknowledges the low educational attainment of Chicanos and their history of failure, but the solutions it offers focus change on the Chicano child rather than the school or society. If Chicano children are to succeed in the educational system, they must acquire the skills and values necessary to compete on an equal footing with Anglo children. Whereas the traditional model was based on a colonial mentality, the liberal model is steeped in assimilationism. Two basic assumptions of the liberal model are (1) minorities share a common human nature and are socializable to the conditions of society, and (2) their low position and general inability to compete reflect unequal opportunity and inadequate socialization to whatever is required to succeed within American society (Horton 1973, p. 30).[5] Thus, while the traditional model accepts the natural inequality of Chicanos and their cultural and racial inferiority, the liberal model is based on a *tabula rasa* conception of man which sees human nature as infinitely maleable. The model is compensatory because it sees Chicanos as disadvantaged or deprived, not as innately inferior. Equality for minorities, according to this model, is achieved by conforming to a dominant set of values and behavior (ibid., p. 30). Equality, in other words, means equal opportunity to achieve the same values as other Americans. Equality is sameness and is gained only by losing one's identity as a Chicano and conforming to dominant values.

A compensatory model such as this places great emphasis on the educational institution as the primary vehicle for socializing Chicanos to the conditions necessary for success and upward mobility in American society. School socialization is more insidious, however. Attention is given to "parental involvement," but it becomes a schooling term, with parents comprising only a small component that fits into the total schooling organization. Similarly, token approval is given to the value of bilingual and, to a lesser extent, bicultural education. A professional educator stance prevails, however, so that programs are to be run by and, to a great extent, for the benefit of professional educators. Although perhaps well meaning and well intentioned, such programs typically wind up benefiting tenured white faculty or provide cultural enrichment for white students. Bilingual programs are too often a means through which school districts qualify for federal monies. Rather than hiring Chicano teachers, Anglo teachers are given "crash courses" in Spanish in order to qualify as bilingual instructors.

Chicana aids are hired to do the difficult core instruction in Spanish without receiving adequate compensation or recognition for their efforts. Under the guise of biculturalism Mexican culture is also usurped. Biculturalism is defined as celebrating Mexican holidays such as Cinco de Mayo, making Mexican flags and sombreros, and perpetuating a mythical view of Chicanos as adherents to a simple, rural folk culture (Carter and Segura 1979, p. 380). Such "bicultural" programs are a disservice to Chicanos, for rather than destroying myths, they perpetuate them. They fail to recognize that Chicanos are overwhelmingly an urban people who are frequently far removed from this mythical pristine past. By focusing on Mexican history the schools also manage to bypass or minimize the importance of Chicano history and Chicano contributions to the development of both the Southwest and the United States. The usurpation of Chicanos is completed when Cinco de Mayo and other such celebrations are transformed into American holidays like Christmas or George Washington's birthday, to be exploited by commercial and political interests. Two things are accomplished in the process: (1) Chicano culture is effectively usurped and commercialized, and (2) the impression is given that something is being done to help Chicanos and improve their condition. *Mariachis*, *tacos*, and *fiestas* are used not to eliminate, but to obscure, the poverty and oppression of the barrios. The liberal model is dangerous and insidious, then, precisely because it creates the impression that recognition is being given and thus something *is* being done.

There is some internal diversity within the liberal model, with variations ranging from openly assimilationist positions that pay only token attention to bilingualism and biculturalism, to sincere but misguided efforts that seek to help Chicanos attain parity. While these more sympathetic efforts openly decry assimilationist perspectives, they espouse a form of multiculturalism that is a more veiled version of assimilationism. Such efforts question the cultural determinist position of blaming Chicano children for their own failure, but they also fall short of blaming the school. In the introduction to *Mexican Americans in School: A Decade of Change* Robert D. Segura credits his coauthor, Thomas P. Carter, for helping him to become "increasingly convinced that school and society are primarily responsible for the continuing underachievement and underattainment in school. We have too long blamed Chicano cultural and personal deficiencies for educational failure" (Carter and Segura 1979, p. 9).

While rejecting the cultural determinist argument and criticizing traditional compensatory and remedial programs, the authors caution against the

> . . . strong tendency to overreact and to deny or downplay the culturally different environment in which many Chicanos grow up and live. . . . The interplay and interrelationship among school, home, society must always be considered also.
>
> One conclusion can be drawn from analysis of the kind of children who succeed in school. They are culturally and personally similar to what the school expects—"normal children from normal homes." The "different" child—whether Chicano, poor, black, deaf, delinquent—rarely measures up at school exit to the so-called standard child. (Ibid., p. 379)

While this may appear to be a reasonable or realistic assessment of the schools, a closer examination suggests that the assimilationist perspective dies hard in educational circles. Who are the so-called "normal children from normal homes" if not middle-class Anglo children or other children who have adopted their value system. Chicano children appear "abnormal" only because a dominant world view has been assumed.[6]

Chicano Alternative Model

As the traditional colonial model fell increasingly into disfavor, the response of the school typically came in the form of the liberal or assimilationist model. Since Chicanos had not been afforded equal educational opportunity, there was a need to reform the school and to make it more responsive to the needs of Mexican-American children. The changes that typically occurred, however, were cosmetic and were concerned more with creating the illusion of change than with actual change. The solution to problems faced by Mexican-American children was to socialize them to the conditions necessary to succeed in American society and, in the process, assimilate them.

Chicano parents have grown dissatisfied with both the traditional model and its liberal counterpart, since neither provides truly bilingual-bicultural education or gives them meaningful input into the operation of the school.[7] One of the most significant outcomes of the blowouts and walkouts of the 1960s was the emergence of Chicano alternative schools throughout the Southwest. Such alternatives ranged from nursery schools and day-care centers to colleges such as Colegio César Chávez (see Macías et al. 1975; Galicia 1973). Chicanos had grown tired of trying to work within the system. The public schools were viewed as racist, reflecting dominant societal values, and as enforcing the status quo.

Chicano alternatives are distinctive in a number of ways. First, they call for genuine bilingual and bicultural programs that not only stress Chicano culture and history but acknowledge the oppression of the Chicano people. Second, Chicano alternatives seek to transform the school from an agent of stability, as it has been traditionally, to an instrument of change and liberation. Third, family involvement and community control are critical components of Chicano alternatives. The school is to be transformed from an Anglo dominated, externally manipulated system to a system designed to serve the needs of the Chicano community and Chicano families. Community control and family input are therefore essential. Family input is more than a token gesture, as the Chicano alternative stresses the importance of the Chicano family, which, in turn, emerges as the cornerstone of the culture. Ideally, parental involvement permeates all aspects of the school—planning, curriculum development, decision-making, and fund raising.

Chicano alternatives also do more than pay lip service to bilingualism and biculturalism. The importance of bilingualism and biculturalism is recognized, but it is also recognized that you ultimately need a bilingual-bicultural society before such programs can be complete and effective. There is recognition, moreover, of the potential danger in traditional "bicultural" approaches where Anglo culture becomes the one common denominator among *all* cultures:

> . . . The danger lies in developing bicultural (Anglo and Chicano) programs for Chicanos, bicultural (Anglo and Native American) programs for Native Americans, bicultural (Anglo and Black) programs for Blacks and mono-cultural (White Anglo) programs for Anglos. The common denominator for the oppressed groups become the oppressor rather than each other. This set of relationships does not change the present situation but becomes another way of "legitimizing and extending" it. (Macías et al. 1975, p. 18)

One solution is to offer culturally relevant programs that serve the needs and values of students in the classroom (ibid., p. 19). But such an approach must go beyond current programs which pretend to be "multicultural" but are, in effect, assimilationist. The typical approach which focuses on the "contributions of minority groups to the development of our great country" (ibid., p. 19) is not only misleading but dangerous since it creates the impression that Chicanos have been integrated into the society and obscures our dependent and antagonistic relationship with the dominant society. Traditional bicultural/multicultural curriculums must give way to a Chicano perspective not only on culture and history but on the relationship between Chicanos and the dominant society. In addition, the Chicano alternative approach holds that the language taught in the schools should be consistent with the language and speech patterns common among Chicanos themselves. All too often the Castilian spoken in bilingual classes is as foreign to Chicano students as English.

Such programs must also recognize the linguistic and cultural diversity of Chicanos rather than impose a monolithic conception of Chicano culture and speech patterns.

> We can find among Chicanos a range of speech that goes from mono-lingual Spanish to mono-lingual English; from a Chicano dialect of English to the rule-governed mixing of Spanish and English languages, from caló . . . to the regional dialects of, for example, Northern New México and Southern Colorado. (Ibid., p. 28)

Such linguistic variation is but one manifestation of the cultural diversity of Chicanos. A curriculum developed for Chicanos in northern New Mexico may well lack relevance for urban Chicanos in East Los Angeles. Alternatives must be developed that are capable of capturing both similarities and differences among Chicanos in various geographical regions, urban or rural locales, and economic-educational levels. Such alternatives need also to capture the uniqueness of the Chicano people without stereotyping or mythicizing them.

Although Chicano alternative schools served an important corrective for both the traditional and liberal models of education, they have not been without their own foibles or pitfalls. One basic weakness is that while they have ostensibly assumed a radical stance relative to the public school, a closer examination reveals that more often than not the approach taken has been a reformist rather than a revolutionary one. The preface to a volume examining the parameters of educational change and the Chicano published by the Southwest Network (1974, p. i) observed that by the early 1970s "the flurry of activity had passed from confrontation to institutionalization." After analyzing several Chicano alternatives, Galicia (1973, p. 14) similarly concluded that they

> . . . are alternative institutions reforming existing concepts of school. They have not challenged the basic notion of school. They rather feel that schools are necessary but that Chicanos must control them. This implies a superficial analysis of the function of school, if the desire by Chicano educational reformers is to break American class structures down. This notion (a) assumes that schools can reform society and (b) accepts the classroom as a viable learning situation.

The belief that the schools can serve to reform society is not new; it is deeply rooted in the American value system. However, since schools are created to serve society rather than the other way around, the society must change before schools can change (ibid.). Prevailing patterns of class and racial domination will not be altered by simply implementing bilingual-bicultural programs or a curriculum that is sensitive to the needs of Chicanos. Economic and political domination will persist if it goes unchallenged. A major pitfall of Chicano alternatives, then, is that they have focused on curriculum and socialization of Chicano children without addressing the basic issue of the relationship between the school and the larger society. *Folkloricos, corridos*, and culturally relevant curricula may enhance the self concept of Chicanitos, but they engender a false sense of security and optimism if they are not coupled with attempts to alter the social structure.

Conclusion: Toward a Chicano Pedagogy of Liberation

The primary function of the school throughout its history has been to perpetuate the status quo. Despite its liberal and democratic rhetoric, the school serves as an agent of the dominant society, therefore helping to maintain the racial and economic subjugation of certain groups.

> . . . Education in this country is simply a perpetuation of the status quo inherent in capitalist society. It merely sustains and reinforces the upward mobility pattern of the dominant majority at the expense of the numerous minorities, maintaining a condescending class system. (Cited in Galicia 1973, p. 3)

For Chicanos the school has directly and indirectly worked to propagate their subordinate position. Historically it has been an Anglo-controlled institution that reflects the values, culture, and language of the dominant society (see Rist 1978). The schools have thus created a system of competition and a set of standards where Chicano children are destined to fail. Having established a system that insures their failure, they then proceed to look for defects in Chicano children and Chicano culture to explain this failure.

If the schools are to serve as vehicles of change on behalf of Chicanos, there is a need to develop and implement a Chicano pedagogy that not only reflects the ethos of the Chicano people but seeks to liberate them from economic, political, and cultural control. Such a pedagogy of liberation must eschew both traditional Anglo alternatives which are devoid of a cultural component, and Chicano alternatives which focus only on cultural and linguistic maintenance without addressing issues of economic and political control. Although initial steps have been taken by a few Chicano scholars (see Macías et al. 1975; Galicia 1973; Southwest Network 1974), a fully developed Chicano pedagogy of liberation has yet to be formulated.

Paulo Freire, a Brazilian educator who questions the foundations of traditional education and focuses on the relationship between student and teacher, provides a possible starting point in his works *Pedagogy of the Oppressed* (1970) and *Education for Critical Consciousness* (1973). Freire points out that schools are based on a "banking concept" of education which assumes that all valuable knowledge is held by the teacher, an outlook which creates a dependency relationship for all information (Freire 1970, ch. 2). Galicia (1973, pp. 7-8) further notes that the classroom centers around the division of students into "knowers" and "not-knowers" and that while the knowers are rewarded for "knowing," those who do not know are considered dumb and lazy. Learning thus becomes a commodity, and students are expected to be passive receptors of information. The banking concept is similar to the liberal model of education in the sense that students are perceived as passive and maleable. Freire notes that the banking concept regards "men as adaptable, manageable beings" (1970, p. 60). That the banking concept is supported by the dominant society is not surprising, for "The more students work at storing the deposits entrusted to them, the less they develop the critical consciousness which would result from their intervention in the world as transformers of that world. . . . The capability of banking education to minimize or annul the students' creative power and to stimulate their credulity serves the interest of the oppressors, who care neither to have the world revealed nor to see it transformed" (ibid.). Freire rejects the banking concept and suggests an alternative form of dialogic education and *conscientización* whereby both student and teacher are learning and simultaneously liberating one another.

Consistent with the concept of dialogic education is the dialectic process of liberation outlined by Freire according to which the oppressed have the power to free themselves and their oppressors. Since oppression is a process that dehumanizes both the oppressed and the oppressor, the key to liberating and humanizing both lies with the oppressed. The oppressors oppress and exploit, but despite their power they are incapable of liberating themselves or those they oppress. "Only power that springs from the weakness of the oppressed will be sufficiently strong to free both" (ibid., p. 28).

If one adopts a Freirian perspective, Chicanos must also be leary of generous liberal programs, as in the liberal model, designed to "help" the oppressed to liberate themselves. We must recognize and reject "false generosity" because "In order to have the continued opportunity to express their 'generosity,' the oppressors must perpetuate injustice as well. An unjust social order is the permanent fount of this 'generosity,' which is nourished by death, despair, and poverty" (ibid., p. 29).

Chicano alternatives have sought to establish bilingual-bicultural programs and community control of the school, an initial first step in establishing a pedagogy of liberation. Yet, because they were established outside of the public-school system, they have been beset not only with severe financial difficulties and problems of accreditation and legitimation (Macías et al. 1975; Galicia 1973) but, more significantly, with ideological shortcomings as well. All too often a shift in focus to language and culture has ignored or neglected the sociopolitical context of Chicano oppression. Although alternative schools have been chosen as the battlefield for waging the Chicano's struggle for equality, it has proved to be a safe battlefield.

    . . . . The conflict in the classrooms may be fought, and won or lost, without threatening the sources of social power. The economic and political control of the barrios will not change, even if the Chicanos were to achieve new textbooks, a curriculum based on the heri-

tage and needs of La Raza, and a wholly bilingual and bicultural teaching system. (Steiner 1970, p. 228)

The schools were safe places to carry on the battle because they could
be "revolutionized" without altering existing patterns of political and economic domination. If Chicano alternatives are to succeed in improving the
position of the Chicano, they must go beyond simply promoting language and
culture. They must, in other words, equip children to deal with, and counteract, the various forms of oppression faced by the Chicano people. In addition
to the "three r's" and cultural maintenance Chicano alternatives should deal
with economic, political, and cultural oppression and provide strategies that
would enable Chicano communities to gain control over vital institutions.
Most importantly, they must engender critical consciousness, or *conscientización*, in Chicanitos.

It would be entirely appropriate, for example, for the curriculum to
scrutinize issues such as the relationship of Chicanos to the legal and judicial
system, and the relationship of this system to the political and economic
order. Specific topics for reinterpretation such as the emergence and perpetu-
ation of the bandido image could be discussed. Why did the bandido image
emerge? What function is served by perpetuating the image of Chicanos as
bandits? Who were the Chicano social bandits and why were they termed
"bandits," while Anglos who engaged in similar behavior were heroes or
vigilantes? Related phenomenon such as police abuse, the role of the Texas
Rangers, the zoot-suit riots, and the Sleepy Lagoon case could also be examined. The idea would be to critically evaluate all facets of the relationship
of Chicanos to the legal and judicial system and to demonstrate how this
system functions to maintain Chicanos in a subordinate position. Other areas
such as the economic position of Chicanos and the oppression of workers on
both sides of the border could also be addressed.

If Chicano alternative education is to prove effective in helping to
liberate Chicanos, it must not only instill a sense of *conscientizacíon* that
equips Chicano children to deal with their own individual oppression but
must also spur collective solutions to problems faced by Chicanos as a group.
Such alternatives could include bilingual-bicultural programs, meaningful
parental involvement, and community control of the schools, but they would
go beyond these by providing a linkage between the schools and other social
institutions such as the economy and the political order. Alterations in the
school will not lead to meaningful social change unless they are accompanied
by efforts to alleviate the overall oppression of Chicanos.

Equally important to the liberation of Chicanos is recognition of the
extent to which we are subjected to cultural control. Reference was made
earlier to how images of Chicanos as a male dominant, pathological culture

and as a violent and criminally prone people are externally induced and manipulated. Educational alternatives must develop mechanisms for coping with, and countering, the insidious effects of symbolic control and manipulation. The school itself has served as an important agency that perpetuates such negative images. One of the more basic ways bias is mobilized against Chicanos is via the democratic and meritocratic ideology of the schools. An ideology is espoused that suggests that American society is open and permeable to those with even modest ability if they are motivated to succeed, while at the same time conditions are created that insure failure. This ideology functions not only to obscure racial, class, and gender oppression but to legitimate the failure of Chicano children. Its effects are thus double-edged, rewarding and extolling those who succeed, while contemning and deriding those who fail. The ideology thus blames Chicanos for their own failure.

While Freire's concepts of education have much relevance for Chicanos, the pedagogy of the oppressed cannot be applied uncritically.[8] It must be modified to account for the unique position of the Chicano and reflect Chicano culture and values. The unit of liberation must be the collective rather than the individual. There must, in other words, be a liberation of entire families and communities, not merely individuals. And the proposed pedagogy of liberation needs to transcend the classroom and incorporate a Chicano world view, for efforts that would look to the school for liberation are bound to perpetuate our oppression.

Even if we establish Chicano schools, if we look to the schools for direction, our educational efforts will remain stultified and limited. "We must look to our own culture to help us define education, and not allow another's cultural institution define it" (Galicia 1973, p. 15). A solid basis for a Chicano curriculum could be derived from those cultural and familial values which have enabled our *raza* to perdure over the centuries and have given us strength and direction in combating economic oppression and colonization: those forces, in other words, which have kept us from being conquered spiritually although we have been colonized. These values include our respect for the land as well as a cultural emphasis on respect, dignity, and honor (Armas 1976, p. 4). According to José Armas the cultural concept of *La Familia* itself contains the basic elements for maintaining a genuinely human way of life (ibid., p. 15). The concepts of *La Familia de la Raza* and *carnalismo* establish a common bond and sense of unity not only among individual families and communities but between Chicanos and all other persons of Mexican ancestry.

> . . . the Chicano cultural concept of "La Familia" provides for us
> a ready-made base from which to build both our emerging identity and
> a humanistic system. Idolizing philosophies of Che, Pancho Villa,

Zapata are for the moment, but for the lasting and sane foundation for a humanistic way of life, we must look to our "Familia." The goals are for a foundation of brotherhood, a respect for people, a defense of the family that keeps us spiritually alive and a compatible attitude toward the land that keeps us physically alive. (Ibid., p. 54)

PART II
Chicano Culture

6

The Church and the Chicano

A perennial quest of social science has been the search for cultural universals, yet cross-cultural comparisons suggest that diversity rather than uniformity has been the norm (Mirandé 1975, p. 453). Among the few universal institutions found in nearly every human society throughout recorded time is religion. In fact, "Three things appear to distinguish man from all other living creatures: the systematic making of tools, the use of abstract language, and religion" (Kluckhohn 1965, p. xi). This is not to suggest that religion has always existed in its present institutional form of churches, clergy, and a bureaucratic structure. Religion has always been universal, while the church is not. Religion might be defined simply "as a set of symbolic forms and acts which relate man to the ultimate conditions of his existence" (Bellah 1964, p. 359). Religious forms have varied historically from "primitive" (simple) ones such as The Dreaming or "the dream time" (Stanner 1965) found among Australian aborigines ("the blacks") to modern, complex structures such as the Roman Catholic Church. Significantly, "at the primitive level *religious organization* as a separate social structure does not exist. Church and society are one" (Bellah 1964, p. 363). The distinction between church and society thus brings forth a separate church structure and hierarchy and is more characteristic of modern, complex religious systems.

Although religion as broadly defined here has been universal, its form and expression vary greatly across settings. In less complex societies religion has been virtually coterminous with society and the value system of the group, whereas in others it has worked to legitimate the exploitation and control of one group over another. Peter Berger (1967) notes that "religion has been the historically most widespread and effective instrumentality of legitimation. . . . Religion legitimates so effectively because it relates the precarious reality constructions of empirical societies with ultimate reality" (ibid., p. 32). Individual acts and social institutions are placed within a cosmic perspective, so that they are no longer merely human responses or instruments of power but sacred creations that "transcend the death of individuals and the decay of entire collectivities, because they are now grounded in a sacred time within which merely human history is but an episode . . . they become immortal" (ibid. p. 37).

Religions have also evolved complex theodicies to explain chaotic or

113

potentially disruptive phenomena in terms of the order created by society (ibid., p. 53). Theodicy helps to explain, or, perhaps more accurately, to justify, not only anomic events but suffering, inequalities, and personal or collective tragedies. It also legitimates the socially created order for both the oppressed and their oppressors, serving as an "opiate" for the former and a justification of the superior status of the latter. In the *Karma-samsara* complex of India, for example, "every conceivable anomy is integrated within a thoroughly rational, all-embracing interpretation of the universe" (ibid., p. 65). A person is thus blamed for misfortune and credited for good fortune.

Religion has played a vital role in the historical development of the Chicano people from their pre-Columbian Indian ancestors to the present and has also been closely intertwined with the colonization of *mexicanos* on both sides of the border. Yet its role has been not simple and direct but complex. Although religion has typically worked to facilitate oppression and exploitation, it has occasionally worked for freedom and liberation of people of Mexican descent. The aforementioned distinction between religion and the church is essential here in order to gain a full understanding of the double-edged quality of religion. While the church has typically served as an instrument of colonization and domination in both Mexico and the United States, individual priests have not infrequently resisted colonization and subordination. Religious theodicies have also been evolved to help the people cope with, or to resist, the insidious effects of colonization and exploitation.

This chapter will examine the complex relationship among Chicanos, the church, and religion and will seek to demonstrate that while the church has generally worked to suppress the Chicano people, religion nonetheless holds the potential for liberating them from cultural, economic, and political control. Specifically, the chapter discusses the (1) relationship between religion and the legacy of conquest of Chicanos, (2) *Virgen de Guadalupe* and her role both as a national and spiritual symbol and as a religious theodicy, (3) relationship between the Chicano and the church in the Southwest during the Spanish/Mexican colonial period, (4) effects of the American takeover on Chicanos and the church, and (5) theology of liberation and its relevance for Chicanos.

Religion and the Legacy of Conquest

Even a cursory examination of history would show that *la raza* has a colonial legacy dating from the conquest of Mexico by Spain in 1519 and that religion has been a primary force in the process of colonization. Economic and political forces undoubtedly played an important role in initiating the conquest, given that both the Spanish crown and the *conquistadores* sought wealth and power in the New World, but while religious conversion may not have been the compelling motive for undertaking these expeditions, once the conquest was under way, religion was used to justify subjugation. Inherent in the religious beliefs of the conquerors was a ready-made theodicy which was used to legitimate the subordination and exploitation of the indigenous population. Since the Indians were commonly considered to be a "heathen people," an inferior race, atrocities were often committed with impunity.

Two separate but mutually reinforcing forces paved the way for the conquest. On the one hand was the Spanish missionary zeal which predisposed them to see native culture and institutions as inferior. This religious fervor was of such dimensions that destruction of the native way of life came to be perceived not only as acceptable but as actually ordained by God. On the other hand were numerous elements in native religion and mythology itself which had prophesied their doom. When these forces conjoined with the military superiority of the Spaniard, the conquest became an almost foregone conclusion. Aftereffects of the conquest were so devastating that it has been termed both a physical and a moral or spiritual conquest (Paz 1961; Ramos 1962; Ricard 1966; and Fuentes 1970).

Since the conquest was divinely willed, the conversion of the natives to Christianity and to a European moral code became essential for pacification. As a result, native codices, temples, and religious relics and idols were destroyed and replaced with Christian churches and symbols (Ricard 1966, p. 287; Moreno 1971, p. 14; and Valdez 1972, p. xx). In his dispatches to King Carlos V, Cortés himself reported:

> I overturned the idols in which these people believe the most and rolled them down the stairs. Then I had those chapels cleansed, for they were full of blood from the sacrifices; and I set up images of Our Lady and other Saints in them. . . . I made them understand by the interpreters how deceived they were in putting their hope in idols made of unclean things by their own hands. I told them that they should know there was but one God, the Universal Lord of all, Who had created the heavens and earth and all things, and them, and us. (Blacker and Rosen 1962, p. 57)

The intense missionary zeal and divine imperative by which the Spaniards were driven was rearticulated by none other than Fray Bernardino de Sahagún, a cleric considered to be sympathetic to the Indian and who is credited with writing one of the most comprehensive and accurate accounts of the conquest. Sahagún asserted:

> . . . Our Lord God (by design) has kept this half of the world in darkness until our times, and by his divine ordinance he has willed that it be illuminated by the Roman Catholic Church, with the intent not

that its natives be destroyed or tyrannized but that the darkness of idolatry they have lived in be enlightened, that they be introduced into the Catholic Church and instructed in the Christian religion, and that they may attain the kingdom of heaven, dying in the faith as true Christians.[1] (1946, 3:10)

He saw Cortés, in turn, to be a brave soldier, acting as an emissary of both the king and God: "through the figure and deeds of the valiant captain D. Hernando Cortés, our Lord performed many miracles in the conquest"[2] (ibid.).

The *requerimiento*, a document generally written in Latin and read aloud before entering battle, reaffirmed Cortés' authority as divinely willed and sanctioned. Ostensibly it was read so that the Indians would understand that "there was one God, that His vicar on earth was the Pope, and that the Pope had granted power to the Spanish ruler, who was now obliged to use this power for the salvation of the Indians" (Blacker and Rosen 1962, p. xvi). If they accepted this authority, they would be granted many favors, but if they did not, the Spaniard informed them that he would "powerfully invade and make war upon you in all the parts and modes that I can and subdue you to the yoke and obedience of the church and of His Majesty, and I will take your wives and children and make slaves of them, and sell them as such, and dispose of them . . . and I will take your effects and will do you all the harm and injury in my power" (quoted in ibid., p. xvi).

Although the Indians obviously did not understand this *requerimiento*, the ritual absolved the *conquistadores* of any wrongdoing in the death and disasters that ensued. Cortés, however, continued to take care to protect the "rights" of the Indian and to provide a moral rationale for his actions. He faithfully affirmed the legitimate presence of the Spanish in the New World by reiterating: "I would have you know that we have come from distant lands at the bidding of our lord and King, the Emperor Charles, who has many great lords for vassals. He has sent us to command your great prince Montezuma to give up sacrifices and kill no more Indians, and not to rob his vassals, or seize any more lands, but obey our lord and King. . . . you must give up your sacrifices and cease to eat the flesh of your neighbours and practise sodomy and the other evil things you do. For such is the will of our lord God." (Díaz Del Castillo 1963, p. 137).

Despite his interest in securing the so-called "rights" of the *indio*, Cortés was painfully aware that he was on shaky moral grounds in overthrowing the Aztec emperor, for "Any attack upon a throne was considered an attack upon the Moral Order of things, and he who was responsible for upsetting the Moral Order would suffer" (Blacker and Rosen 1962, p. xvi). Nonetheless, while Cortés appeared to regret unnecessary bloodshed, he did not hesitate to destroy anyone who stood in his way. In the third dispatch to the emperor he reluctantly acknowledges that he was obligated to grant *repartimientos* in the form of Indians and their services to those who fought alongside him. Since he had failed to find the rich treasures he expected, he was forced to pay off his men in this manner. "In view of all these considerations, I found myself almost forced to place the chiefs and natives of these parts among the Spaniards, to recompense them for the service they have rendered to Your Majesty" (ibid., p. 154).

Much later, as Cortés prepared his will, he continued to wrestle with the moral issues surrounding treatment of the Indians. Extensive court debates had failed to settle arguments over whether Indians were examples of Aristotle's people whose basic nature it is to be slaves, or whether they were human beings who should be treated equally and with dignity, as others maintained. Though the problem was unresolved, Cortés' concern persisted. He noted in his will that "Since there are conflicting opinions as to whether the Natives of New Spain who have been conquered in war or purchased can rightly be held as slaves, and since this matter has not yet been settled, I direct my son and heir, Don Martin, and those who shall succeed him in my estate to diligently verify this matter for the sake of my conscience and their own" (ibid., p. xvii). Statements such as this reveal a very different side of Cortés that contrasts sharply with the image portrayed in the "Black Legend" found in Anglo-Saxon, Protestant countries which attacked both Catholicism and Spain (ibid., p. vi).

The Spanish seige of Tenochtitlán and the subsequent imprisonment of Montezuma could rightfully be justified only because the Aztec emperor was not a Christian and did not therefore rule by the grace of God (ibid., p. xvi). When Montezuma was taken prisoner, Cortés took great pains to explain the reasons for his actions to the Spanish emperor and assured him that his captive was well treated and cared for. Commenting on Montezuma's imprisonment, he noted, "I treated him so well, and he was so content, that frequently, when I offered him his liberty and urged him to return to his own palace, he told me that he preferred to remain where he was" (ibid., p. 48). When Montezuma died, Cortés' report carefully stated that the Aztec emperor was killed by the Aztecs themselves: "as he was preparing to speak to the people who were fighting there, one of his own subjects struck him on the head with a stone with such force that within three days he died" (ibid., p. 72).

As indicated earlier, Spanish religious fervor was reinforced by elements in Aztec religion and mythology which foretold their own demise. Some ten years before the arrival of the *conquistadores* Aztec mythology recorded eight signs or evil omens which predicted their downfall. The omens are contained in the *Codex Florentino*, which was originally written in Nahuatl under the direction of Fray Bernardino de Sahagún, whose Indian students recorded reminiscences of elderly natives who lived through the conquest. The eight omens described by Sahagún's informants were as follows[3] (Leon-Portilla 1962, pp. 4-6):

The first bad omen: Ten years before the Spaniards first came here, a bad omen appeared in the sky. It was like a flaming ear of corn, or a fiery signal, or the blaze of daybreak; it seemed to bleed fire, drop by drop, like a wound in the sky. It was wide at the base and narrow at the peak, and it shone in the very heart of the heavens.

This is how it appeared: it shone in the eastern sky in the middle of the night. It appeared at midnight and burned till the break of day, but it vanished at the rising of the sun. The time during which it appeared to us was a full year, beginning in the year 12-House.

When it first appeared, there was a great outcry and confusion. The people clapped their hands against their mouths; they were amazed and frightened, and asked themselves what it could mean.

The second bad omen: The temple of Huitzilopochtli burst into flames. It is thought that no one set it afire, that it burned down of its own accord. The name of its divine site was Tlacateccan [House of Authority].

And now it is burning, the wooden columns are burning! The flames, the tongues of fire shoot out, the bursts of fire shoot up into the sky!

The flames swiftly destroyed all the woodwork of the temple. When the fire was first seen, the people shouted: "Mexicanos, come running! We can put it out! Bring your water jars . . . !" But when they threw water on the blaze it only flamed higher. They could not put it out, and the temple burned to the ground.

The third bad omen: A temple was damaged by a lightning-bolt. This was the temple of Xiuhtecuhtli, which was built of straw, in the place known as Tzonmolco. It was raining that day, but it was only a light rain or a drizzle, and no thunder was heard. Therefore the lightning-bolt was taken as an omen. The people said: "The temple was struck by a blow from the sun."

The fourth bad omen: Fire streamed through the sky while the sun was still shining. It was divided into three parts. It flashed out from where the sun sets and raced straight to where the sun rises, giving off a shower of sparks like a red-hot coal. When the people saw its long train streaming through the heavens, there was a great outcry and confusion, as if they were shaking a thousand little bells.

The fifth bad omen: The wind lashed the water until it boiled. It was as if it were boiling with rage, as if it were shattering itself in its frenzy. It began from far off, rose high in the air and dashed agaisnt the walls of the houses. The flooded houses collapsed into the water. This was in the lake that is next to us.

The sixth bad omen: The people heard a weeping woman night after night. She passed by in the middle of the night, wailing and crying out in a loud voice: "My children, we must flee far away from this city!" At other times she cried: "My children, where shall I take you?"

The seventh bad omen: A strange creature was captured in the nets. The men who fish the lakes caught a bird the color of ashes, a bird resembling a crane. They brought it to Motecuhzoma in the Black House.

This bird wore a strange mirror in the crown of its head. The mirror was pierced in the center like a spindle whorl, and the night sky could be seen in its face. The hour was noon, but the stars and the *mamalhuaztli* could be seen in the face of that mirror. Motecuhzoma took it as a great and bad omen when he saw the stars and the *mamalhuaztli.*

But when he looked at the mirror a second time, he saw a distant plain. People were moving across it, spread out in ranks and coming forward in great haste. They made war against each other and rode on the backs of animals resembling deer.

Motecuhzoma called for his magicians and wise men and asked them: "Can you explain what I have seen? Creatures like human beings, running and fighting . . . !" But when they looked into the mirror to answer him, all had vanished away, and they saw nothing.

The eighth bad omen: Monstrous beings appeared in the streets of the city: deformed men with two heads but only one body. They were taken to the Black House and shown to Motecuhzoma; but the moment he saw them, they all vanished away.

It is clear, then, that even before the conquest, omens foretelling the arrival of the Spanish and the destruction of the Aztec civilization had been observed. When the Spaniards arrived they amazed and bewildered the *indio* to such an extent that many considered them to be gods or to have godlike qualities. Bernal Díaz Del Castillo, a chronicler of the conquest, comments:

> . . . since these allies of ours from the hill towns and from Cempoala had formerly been very much afraid of the Mexicans, and expected the great Montezuma to send his large armies to destroy them, the sight of his relatives coming to Cortés with presents and declaring themselves his servants and ours greatly surprised them. Their chiefs said among themselves that we must be *Teules* indeed, for Montezuma was afraid of us and had sent us presents of gold. (1963, p. 116)

These surrounding, subjugated tribes lived in constant fear of the Aztecs, and were very impressed with the deference the latter showed Cortés.
The Totonacs and Tlaxcalans were bitter enemies of the Aztecs and were terrorized by them. Not only were taxes collected from them but their women
were raped, and some of their members were taken as human sacrifices (ibid.,
pp. 108-10). While Cortés was in Cempoala, five Aztec tax-gatherers entered
the city. Cortés ordered the natives and the *Caciques* of other Totonac towns
to arrest and hold them prisoner until Montezuma could see that they had
come to rob them, enslave their wives and children, and carry out violence
against them (ibid., p. 111). The *Caciques* were appalled by Cortés' daring
suggestion but finally acceded. They arrested the tax-collectors and beat one
who refused to be tied. "The act they had witnessed was so astonishing and
of such importance to them that they said no human beings dared to do such
a thing, and it must be the work of *Teules*" (ibid., p. 112).

As the Spaniards moved inland, they were able to effect alliances with
several of the tribes held under Aztec domination and to convert many of
their members to Christianity. In Cempoala, for example, after Cortés over-
threw the idols and ordered them burned, he erected a shrine to the Virgin
Mary on the spot where the idols had stood. He explained to his new converts
that since they no longer had false idols to worship in their high temples, he
would leave them an image of "a great lady," who was mother of our Lord
Jesus Christ (ibid., p. 124). Once the altar was erected, a mass was said the
following morning with the most important *Caciques* from the area in atten-
dance. In addition, eight Indian girls, the daughters of *Caciques* and dignitaries
who had been given to Cortés, were brought forth to be converted to Christianity. According to Díaz Del Castillo, "It was explained to them that they
must offer no more sacrifices and no longer worship idols, but believe in our
lord God. They were then instructed in our holy faith and baptized" (ibid.,
p. 125).

The *indios* were so impressed with the godlike qualities of the Spaniards
that some mistook Cortés for a returning deposed god, Quetzalcóatl, who had
been a self-sacrificing penitent god of life, love, and peace. He was the god
of wisdom who represented all that is good in man, and the benevolent father
and creator of man who symbolized the cosmic struggle between good and
evil (Caso 1958, pp. 24-26). According to Indian mythology Quetzalcóatl had
been forced to leave Tula by evil forces and departed to the mythical Tlillan
Tlapallan, or "The land of the black and the red," but he had promised to
return from the east in the year "One Reed" (1519) (ibid., p. 25). Through
a fortuitous coincidence not only did this date coincide with the arrival of
Cortés but his physical characteristics resembled those of the departed god.
Both were fair-haired, fair-skinned, and bearded.

The emperor Montezuma sent emissaries to welcome the supposed returning god and to present him with the treasure of Quetzalcóatl (Leon-Portilla, 1962, pp. 21-26). His five messengers were instructed to welcome the strangers and were admonished to "Do reverence to our lord the god. Say to him: 'your deputy, Motecuhzoma, has sent us to you. Here are the presents with which he welcomes you home to Mexico' " (ibid., p. 25). After receiving the gifts aboard his ship, Cortés responded by asking "And is this all?" and gave orders to chain the messengers by the feet and the neck and had the great cannon fired. This frightened them tremendously, and they fainted (ibid., p. 26). Upon their return to Montezuma the messengers gave the following description of the cannon:

> ... A thing like a ball of stone comes out of its entrails; it comes out shooting sparks and raining fire. The smoke that comes out with it has a pestilent odor. . . . This odor penetrates even to the brain and causes the greatest discomfort. . . . If it is aimed against a tree, it shatters the tree into splinters. This is a most unnatural sight, as if the tree had exploded from within. (Ibid., p. 30)

Montezuma responded with terror not only to reports of their firearms but to those of the animals they rode and their large dogs.

Despite this, Cortés' eventual arrival in Tenochtitlán in November 1519 was heralded by the Aztec emperor as marking the return of the great lord Quetzalcóatl. When he greeted Cortés, he explained that the Aztecs realized they had descended, not from the inhabitants of this land, "but from strangers who came to it from very distant parts; and we also hold that our race was brought to these parts by a lord whose vassals they all were, and who returned to his native country" (Blacker and Rosen 1962, p. 43). He also noted that those who descended from the lord "would come to subjugate this country and us . . . and according to the direction from which you say you come, which is where the sun rises, and from what you tell us of your great lord, or king, who has sent you here, we believe, and hold for certain, that he is our rightful sovereign. . . . Hence you may be sure that we shall always obey you, and hold you as the representative of this great lord . . . you will be obeyed and recognized, and all we possess is at your disposal" (ibid.).

Given these obeisances, it might be hypothesized that the conquest should have been effected with a minimum of bloodshed. In reality, the general greed of the Spaniards prevailed, and the blundering action of Pedro de Alvarado—The Sun—in particular, who in Cortés' absence massacred several thousand defenseless Indians as they celebrated a religious festival in honor of Huitzilopochtli, set the conquest on a different course. The massacre in the main temple signaled the beginning of an all-out war. The Spaniard's attempt to leave the city at nightfall was foiled, and they were routed and met with furious attacks. Cortés sorely lamented the defeat of his troops, and he is said to have wept at the foot of *el arbol de la noche triste* ("the tree of sorrows"). The downfall of Tenochtitlán transpired, however, and was finalized on August 13, 1521, after an intense struggle. It was also accomplished with the aid of the Tlaxcalans, who nursed Cortés back to health and aligned themselves with the Spaniards.

Mexico, or New Spain as it was to be called, remained a colony of Spain, administered by a viceroy of the king, for approximately 300 years. While religion played a critical role in the conquest of Mexico, its part in the movement for independence from Spain was no less significant. Whether as a postive or negative force, religion was to leave an indelible mark both on Mexico and the Chicano people.

La Virgen de Guadalupe: Mexican-Chicano National Symbol or Religious Theodicy

Within ten years after the downfall of Tenochtitlán an event took place that would have a profound impact on the development of the Mexican-Chicano people. This event was the apparition of the Virgin Mary to a young Indian boy who had been converted to Catholicism. While many questions surround the myth of the apparition and some have attempted to minimize its significance by pointing out that *Guadalupe* is but one of literally hundreds of manifestations of the Virgin Mary in Europe and the Americas, none can deny her singular importance to our *raza*.

The basic facts of the event are that during December 1531 *La Virgen* is said to have appeared to a poor *indio*, Juan Diego. Her apparition is significant not only because she appeared to an Indian but because it occurred on a hill at Tepeyac, north of what is today Mexico City, which had been the site of a shrine to the Aztec goddess, Tonantzin, "Our Mother."

The *Virgen* appeared to Juan Diego on four separate occasions. The first apparition reputedly occurred on a Saturday in the early part of December, as the young boy passed the hill. It was daybreak, and Juan Diego heard singing that resembled the sound of precious birds. The music was so beautiful that he was taken by it and wondered if he had uncovered an earthly paradise. As he listened to the celestial song and looked toward the hill, the air filled with silence and someone called from the hill saying: "Juanito, Juan Dieguito." Juan Diego climbed to the hill to see who called him. When he reached the top, he saw a lady standing there who asked him to come closer. As he approached her, she spoke saying:

> Sabe y ten entendido, tú el más pequeño de mis hijos, que yo soy la siempre Virgen Santa María, Madre del verdadero Dios por quien se vive; del Creador cabe quien está todo; Señor del Cielo y de la tierra. Deseo vivamente que se me erija aquí un templo para en él mostrar y

dar todo mi amor, compasión, auxilio y defensa, pues yo soy vuestra piadosa madre; a ti, a todos vosotros juntos los moradores de esta tierra y a los demás amadores míos que me invoquen y en mí confíen; oír allí sus lamentos, y remediar todas sus miserias, penas y dolores. (Valeriano, p. 4)

Know and understand, you the most humble of my children, that I am the Blessed Mary, ever virgin Mother of the true God for whom thou lives; of the Creator of all things; Lord of Heaven and of earth. I deeply desire that a temple be erected here so that within it I can show and give all of my love, compassion, assistance, and shelter, for I am thy merciful mother; for you, for all of the inhabitants of this land, and for the rest of those believers who invoke and confide in me; there I shall listen to their sorrows, and free them from all of their misery, grief, and anguish.

The *Virgen* instructed the boy to go to the bishop in Mexico City, to tell him what he witnessed, and to inform him of her wish to have a temple erected on that site. Following her instructions, Juan Diego went straight to the palace of the bishop, Fray Juan de Zumárraga, with her request. The bishop listened increduously to his story and dismissed it, leaving the young boy saddened and discouraged. Juan Diego returned to the spot of the apparition that same day, whereupon the Virgin reappeared. He bowed to her and related what had happened. He reassured her that he would gladly take her message to the bishop, but he was a humble and unworthy person. She responded that there were many who could have acted as her servant and messenger, but she had chosen him as the person who would manifest her will. She told him not to be discouraged, to return to the bishop once again with her message, and to tell him that she, the Virgin Mary and Mother of God, had sent him.

Juan Diego returned to the bishop's palace the following day. Zumárraga listened attentively, this time asked many questions, but reaffirmed to Juan Diego that he would not believe his story until he had some sign that would demonstrate to him that the young *indio* was indeed a messenger of the Holy Mother.

The third apparition occurred when Juan Diego returned to Tepeyac to convey the bishop's answer. The *Virgen* consented to the bishop's request and asked the young man to return the next day (Monday) for the sign. He was unable to return, however, because on arriving home, he learned that an uncle, Juan Bernardino, had taken ill. On Tuesday the uncle took a turn for the worse, and Juan Diego was sent to Tlatelolco to seek a priest who would minister to him. As he approached Tepeyac, the boy decided on an alternative route so that he would not be waylaid should he run into the *Virgen*.

As he went around the hill, however, she suddenly appeared before him and asked where he was going. Juan Diego was embarrassed, knelt before the great lady, explained his uncle's illness, and told her he was on his way to get a priest who would hear his uncle's last confession. The *Virgen* urged him not to worry and fret, assuring him that he was under her protection and guidance. She told him that Juan Bernardino was now well and asked him to climb to the summit of the hill, where he would find many different flowers that he should cut and bring to her.

Juan Diego was astonished to find a harvest of beautiful roses, for it was winter and the hill was normally barren. The *Virgen* then said to him: "Hijo mío el mas pequeño, esta diversidad de rosas es la prueba y señal que llevarás al obispo. Le dirás en mi nombre que vea en ella mi voluntad y que él tiene que cumplirla" (ibid., p. 12) ("This abundance of roses is the proof and sign which you shall take to the bishop, my most humble son. You shall tell him on my behalf that he accept my will through this sign and that he must carry it out."). She admonished the *indito*, however, not to open his cloak and reveal its cargo until he reached the bishop. Juan Diego went directly to the bishop's palace, but when he asked to see Zumárraga, the palace guards ignored him. They did notice that he carried beautiful roses, but each time they attempted to grab them, they disappeared and appeared, instead, to be painted on the cloak. Juan Diego finally succeeded in gaining his audience with the bishop and told him that he had brought a sign from Our Lady. As he opened his cloak, the bouquet of roses spilled onto the floor, leaving in their wake a miraculous impression of the *Virgen María* on the cloak. The image the bishop then saw is described as showing "a young woman without child, her head lowered demurely in her shawl. She wears an open crown and flowering gown, and stands upon a half moon" (Wolf 1972, p. 150).

Juan Diego reiterated the *Virgen*'s desire to have a church built in her honor at Tepeyac. Zumárraga and others who were present were thoroughly overwhelmed by the image and the roses. The bishop immediately began to cry and prayed to ask the Holy Mother's forgiveness for not having translated her will into action sooner. Zumárraga proceeded to order the erection of a shrine on the site of the *Virgen*'s apparition. Significantly, when Juan Diego returned home, he discovered that his uncle had in fact fully recovered from his illness.

Although some have suggested that the image on the cloak may have been painted by an Indian, or others, that the apparition was nothing less than a hoax perpetrated by the Spanish clergy and Cortés himself, the image has survived for over 450 years. Moreover, extensive scientific testing has failed to reveal its origins or explain its durability. Today Juan Diego's cloak hangs at the Basilica of Our Lady of Guadalupe in Mexico City and remains the object of numerous yearly pilgrimages, particularly by the poor and downtrodden.

La Virgen de Guadalupe is significant for our purposes for a number of reasons. First, as La Virgen Morena (The Brown Virgin) she is believed to be a uniquely Mexican symbol. Second, her appearance to an indio demonstrated that the Indian was not only human but worthy of salvation. Third, she addressed Juan Diego in Nahuatl, an Indian tongue, which confirms her place as the patron saint of a conquered race. Fourth, she described herself to Juan Diego as the protectress of the Mexican people. Fifth, she appeared on the same site as the temple to Tonantzin stood, with the symbolism surrounding her being strikingly similar to that of her Indian precursor. Finally, she was to emerge not only as the patron saint of the mexicano but as a national patriotic symbol. Her image was embroidered on the banner the insurgentes carried as they fought for independence from Spain in 1810. One hundred years later she served as a symbol for Zapata and his followers who sought agrarian reform. More recently she has been a symbol for César Chavéz and the farmworkers in their struggle for equality. Just as she has been a symbol for the indio and the mestizo of Mexico, she is also a symbol of liberation for Chicanos within the territorial boundaries of the United States.

Various explanations have been offered for the emergence of what some have termed the "cult of Guadalupe." Perhaps the most simplistic of these is that she is a transplanted version of the Iberian peninsula's Virgen de Guadalupe. Our Lady of Guadalupe of Estremadura, Protectress of Spanish Christianity, was the precursor of La Virgen. According to tradition a sanctuary was founded in the midst of the Eastern Sierra of Estremadura "after a prodigious apparition of Mary" (Lafaye 1976, p. 218). The origins of the Spanish Virgin, however, are no less clear than those of her Indian counterpart.[4] A Codex of 1440 traces the origin of the Dark Virgin with a child to the Moorish invasion of Spain in the eighth century. As the Christians fled Seville, several priests are said to have taken the statue of Our Lady and placed it in a well-concealed cave (ibid., p. 220). The subsequent apparition of Our Lady to a shepherd bears striking resemblance to the Mexican apparition and is intertwined with the Moorish presence. According to the Codex of 1440, "Our Lady, the Virgin Mary, appeared to a shepherd as he watched his cows and ordered him to go home, call the priests and other people, and return to dig at the place where she was, where they would find a statue of the Virgin" (ibid., p. 219). The Codex adds, moreover, that "after the sword of the Moor had passed through almost all Spain, it pleased God, Our Lord, to comfort the Christians so they might regain the courage they had lost" (ibid.). When the shepherd came home, he found his wife mourning the death of their son. The son, however, was miraculously revived after the shepherd said: "Have no care, for I dedicate him to Holy Mary of Guadalupe, that she may bring him back to life and health" (ibid.). The myth thus shares key elements with the Mexican version in that in both cases the Virgen appeared to a humble person, performed miracles, and declared herself to be the protectress of a vanquished people.

The link between Spanish and Mexican images of *La Virgen* is further reinforced by the fact that Hernán Cortés and his *conquistadores* were ardent followers of *La Virgen de Estremadura*. Cortés was a native of Medellín, a town in Estremadura near the sanctuary (ibid., p. 217), as were many of his men. To assume, however, that the Mexican *Virgen de Guadalupe* is but a transplant of the Spanish Virgin is simplistic indeed, for the differences between the two images are undoubtedly greater than their similarities. To begin with, the actual images or figures of Our Lady of *Guadalupe* and Our Lady of Estremadura are strikingly different. Second, "Since Guadalupe was a toponym, its transfer to New Spain, to a place which already had a name long associated with the site of a religious sanctuary, appears an enigma" (ibid., p. 231). Finally, the cult of Our Lady of *Guadalupe* met with considerable resistance within the ranks of the Spanish clergy. Before 1572 the cult was considered a secular and episcopal affair and was opposed by the Dominican, Franciscan, and Augustinian orders. Homage to *Guadalupe* was seen for a long time as a disguised form of idolatry, since many Indians were said to believe that the painting at Tepeyac *was La Virgen*.

In this context it seems especially significant that the apparition on the hill of Tepeyac took place on the site of an ancient religious sanctuary to the Indian goddess *Tonantzin*. Long before the arrival of the Spaniard, Tonantzin was a principal divinity and had the devotion of the *indio*. Sahagún noted that the Aztecs celebrated solemn sacrifices at several places near hills and that "one of those places is here in Mexico City on a hill called Tepeacac . . . , where they had a temple consecrated to the mother of the gods, called Tonantzin . . . and people came from afar to celebrate these sacrifices" (1946, I, p. 46).

Historically *La Virgen* remains a powerful symbol for persons of Mexican origin living on both sides of the border. Since her apparition in 1531 *La Virgen Morena* has symbolized the suffering and struggle of the Mexican people. As such she is uniquely Mexican. According to Octavio Paz:

> . . . The Virgin is the consolation of the poor, the shield of the weak, the help of the oppressed. In sum, she is the Mother of orphans. All men are born disinherited and their true condition is orphanhood, but this is particularly true among the Indians and the poor in Mexico. The cult of the Virgin reflects not only the general condition of man but also a concrete historical situation, in both the spiritual and material realms. (1961, p. 85)

The cult of the *Virgen* constitutes a true religious theodicy because while on the one hand she represents the Spanish conquest and the involuntary imposition of Catholicism on the *indio*, on the other she is obviously much more than a European Virgin Mary. She is more accurately *Guadalupe-Tonantzin*, and, according to Octavio Paz, her ascendence represents a return to ancient feminine deities (ibid., p. 84). Although associated with the Aztec goddess of fertility (Tonantzin), her basic function is to provide refuge for the poor and oppressed. It is said that "she consoles, quiets, dries tears, calms passions" (ibid., p. 85).

The apparition myth of *Guadalupe* also proved that the *indio* was worthy of salvation. Subsequent to the conquest a basic division existed within the church of Spain between those who felt that the Indian was a subhuman species incapable of conversion, whose labor was to be used and exploited like that of a domesticated animal, and those who upheld his humanity and sought to grant him legal and political rights (Wolf 1972, p. 152). "The myth of Guadalupe thus validates the Indian's right to legal defense, orderly government, to citizenship, to supernatural salvation, but also to salvation from random oppression" (ibid.). The myth thus appealed not only to the conquered *indio* but to the large number of *mestizos* who were illegitimate offspring of Spanish fathers and Indian mothers whose place in the social order was even less clear.

The apparition and emergence of *Guadalupe* as the patron saint of Mexico should then be viewed, not as the simple imposition of a European Virgin on an Indian culture, but rather as the erection and elaboration of a complex Mexican national symbol. Eric Wolf reinforces this argument by observing that the apparition myth constitutes a "master symbol" that "links together family, politics and religion; colonial past and independent present; Indian and Mexican" (1972, p. 153). It is linked to familism because *Guadalupe* is ultimately a maternal symbol, a source of warmth, love, and succorance. According to Wolf even *pulque* (an alcoholic beverage made from the *maguey* plant) is identified with her milk. As a religious symbol, she continues to represent the poor, exploited classes who struggle for liberation from poverty and oppression. She is, in other words, the guardian of the oppressed.

Like other theodicies, the cult of *Guadalupe* evolved in order to explain or justify chaotic events, suffering, and personal or collective tragedies. It legitimated the newly created social, political, and economic order. Belief in the *Virgen* further explained not only the conquest and the exploitation of the *indio* but the imposition of Catholicism as well. The theodicy also cuts across all elements of *mexicano* culture, linking Mexico's colonial past with the present lot of *mexicanos* living in Mexico and the United States. "It is, ultimately, a way of talking about Mexico: a 'collective representation' of Mexican society" (ibid., p. 152).

Interestingly, the cult of *Guadalupe* reached such extreme proportions that it is said to have given "rise to a political wish for a Mexican paradise, in which the illegitimate sons who would possess the country, and the responsible Spanish overlords, who never acknowledged the social responsibilities of their paternity, would be driven from the land" (ibid., p. 153). In a book by Miguel Sánchez published in 1648 the conquest is justified on the grounds that Mexico was chosen as a new biblical paradise and that *Guadalupe* was selected as the one who would lead the Mexican people out of bondage and into the promised land of milk and honey (ibid.). Even more radical is the position of Teresa de Mier, who claimed that Mexico had been converted to Christianity prior to the conquest. Accordingly, the apostle Saint Thomas is said to have brought an image of Our Lady *Guadalupe-Tonantzin* to the New World, making the conquest unnecessary (ibid.)! Mexican independence from Spain according to de Mier symbolizes "the promise of an independent Mexico, liberated from the irrational authority of the Spanish father-oppressors and restored to the Chosen Nation whose election has been manifest in the apparition of the Virgin to Tepeyac. The land of the supernatural mother is finally possessed by her rightful heirs" (ibid.). Thus, through the elaboration of an ingenious theodicy a negative symbol of colonization and oppression is transformed into a positive symbol of decolonization and liberation.

The Missions and Spanish/Mexican Colonization of Aztlán

The colonial heritage of the Chicano extends from the conquest of Mexico to the colonization of what is today the American Southwest. Not long after the pacification of central Mexico, Spanish expeditions began to explore Mexico's northern territories. The earliest of these took place in 1528. The first Spanish missionary to bring Christianity to the pueblos was Fray Marcos de Nija, who along with the Negro slave Estevan set forth from Mexico in 1539 in search of the fabled Seven Cities of Cíbola (Forrest 1965, p. 26). Although Estevan was killed by the Zuni Indians and Fray Marcos turned back without discovering the fabled cities, the promise of gold prompted Coronado's expedition in 1540. Coronado failed to find gold, but several Franciscan friars who accompanied him set up crosses in the pueblos and attempted to gain Indian converts. Some of these priests, like Fray Juan de Padilla and Fray Juan de la Cruz Escalona, remained in order to save souls but were eventually murdered (ibid., p. 28). The priests on the Coronado expedition were pioneers who blazed the trail for future missionaries, although they did not build churches or other permanent structures (Kessell 1980, p. 7).

The first Spanish mission in the Southwest was founded in 1581 on a bluff overlooking the Rio Grande in front of the present-day town of Bernalillo. Bartolome mission at Old Puaray was founded by three priests with the aid of eight soldiers and seven Indian servants (Forrest 1965, p. 33). The mission's existence was to be short-lived, however, as the three priests were killed by the Indians (ibid.).

The first permanent settlement in New Mexico was established at San Juan de los Caballeros (twenty-five miles northwest of Santa Fe) by Don Juan de Oñate in 1598. Significantly, the founding of San Juan occurred nine years before the first permanent English settlement at Jamestown and a full twenty-two years before the arrival of the Pilgrims at Plymouth Rock (ibid.). The only older city in the present-day United States is Saint Augustine, which was founded by the Spaniards in 1565. The dedication of Mission San Gabriel on September 8, 1598, signaled not only the establishment of the first permanent settlement but the beginning of a massive attempt to convert nearby pueblos. After a high mass and a feast of the nativity of the Blessed Virgin, Don Juan Pérez de Donís, Oñate's secretary, read a long proclamation which acknowledged that Govenor Oñate would

> . . . concede, grant, designate, and entrust, the Lord as my witness, from now for all time to the aforesaid Sacred Order of St. Francis and its Friars Observant present and future . . . the following provinces, pueblos, and Indian doctrinas with full faculty and license to build in each of them the churches and conventos they deem necessary for their residence and the better administration of Christian doctrine. (Kessell 1980, p. 8)

Although church claims of the number of Indian converts tended to be exaggerated, it is estimated that in the ten years following 1598 eight thousand Indians were converted and that by 1617 there were somewhere between eleven and fourteen thousand neophytes (Forrest 1965, p. 17). By the time Father Junípero Serra founded the first California mission, San Diego de Alcalá on July 6, 1769, forty-eight missions had been established in New Mexico, sixteen in Arizona, and over twenty in Texas (see Forrest 1965; Kessell 1976 and 1980; McCaleb, 1954; Burke, 1971).

Despite the erection of an elaborate mission system, however, pacification proved much more difficult than it had been in central Mexico. In New Mexico, for example, the pueblos resisted colonization and conversion. The missionaries exploited Indian labor, and this exploitation elicited great resentment. Moreover, the friars frequently found it difficult to preach the gospel, which according to one "is despised by these people on account of our great offenses and the harm we have done them" (Kessell 1980, p. 8). The truth is that the pueblo Indians never submitted, and in 1680 they revolted and drove the Spaniards from New Mexico. Colonization was also impeded by the fact that Spanish exploration extended over a vast area, and stable population centers were few and far between. Unlike central Mexico the Indian population of the Southwest was nomadic and mobile. Spanish colonization was also based on a *presidio*, mission, and *pueblo* system. The system depended on the exploitation of Indian labor, but because Indian labor had to be brought to the mission, it proved difficult to implement except among the more stable pueblos of New Mexico. Even the sedentary coastal tribes of California had to be brought to the missions because they did not live in villages. In Mexico, on the other hand, the Spanish used existing population centers and indigenous temples to effect their colonization and conversions.

Although the missions came late to California, it was here that the most elaborate and extensive settlements occurred. In all, twenty-one missions, four presidial towns (San Diego, Santa Barbara, Monterey, and San Francisco), and two pueblos (San Jose and Los Angeles) were established throughout the state. The success of the mission system was predicated on the assumption of a close symbiotic relation between the *presidio*, *pueblo*, and mission. Although the mission system was ostensibly established in order to Christianize and Hispanicize the heathen natives, these "sacred expeditions" also constituted an "aggressive defensive expansion" intended to strengthen Spain's control of New California against Russian southern expansion (Archibald 1978, p. xi). The *presidio* provided the military support necessary to secure these settlements against external attacks. The *pueblo* was foreseen as providing a civilian population and products that would supplement those produced by the mission. In reality, however, the relation between the three institutions was frequently characterized by competition and conflict. The problem of a labor shortage was intensified by the fact that the mission and the *presidio* competed for the labor of the military (ibid., p. 143). As the missions prospered, they assumed an increasingly important economic role, and it became difficult for civilians to compete with the cheap labor provided by Indian converts.

Although the missions ideally belonged to the Indian converts, and part of Hispanization was to provide Indians with the requisite skills necessary for survival in Spanish society, no mission was ever turned over to them (ibid., p. xi). The conflict between church and state intensified, for

> . . . As the efforts of the padres became increasingly successful, the mission powers expanded correspondingly. If they steadily enlarged their land holdings, crops, herds, workshops, churches, gardens, always in the interest of the natives, the military elements surveyed the wealth and influence with an envious eye of suspicion. As early as 1787 proposals were made for division of the properties, although even the authorities could not agree that the Indians were ready for freedom. (Berger 1941, pp. 99-100)

The death knell of the mission system came with the War of Mexican Independence from Spain. The Mexican insurrection cut off supply boats from San Blas (the only link between California and New Spain) and made California dependent upon its own resources. This, in turn, made the colonists more dependent on the missions for needed goods (ibid., p. 96). Punitive measures were also taken by the missions in order to secure badly needed Indian labor. The Spanish Cortes decreed in 1813 that all missions in America over ten years old be immediately secularized. The decree permitted any married Indian to leave if he could show that he had been a Christian for fifteen years and was able to support himself (ibid., p. 100). Some left, but others remained either out of loyalty or for fear of life outside the mission.

In 1818 the Frenchman Hippolyte de Bouchard, working on behalf of Mexican insurgents, launched an attack on Monterey and subsequent attacks on Refugio, San Buenaventura, San Juan Capistrano, and San Diego. Although Bouchard was repelled, his raid was unsettling to the colony, which remained loyal to Spain (ibid., pp. 96-97). Independence from Spain was effected with the signing of the Treaty of Cordova on August 24, 1821, and on April 11, 1822, the oath of allegiance was taken to Mexico. Several friars declined to take the oath, however (Geiger 1965, p. 103).

By 1834 partition was in full swing. This plan proposed dividing about one-half of mission properties among the Indians and leaving the remainder in the hands of secular administrators, who would use it for religious purposes (Berger 1941, p. 101). In 1834 ten missions were placed in the hands of civil trustees, six were turned over the following year, and the last five in 1836. The result, however, was not a smooth transition but a chaotic one:

> . . . Flocks were slaughtered, chattels were scattered and no one was responsible for the results. The worst sufferers were the Indians themselves, to whom the wealth really belonged. But they refused to work any longer and discipline entirely vanished. . . . The result was complete demoralization. When the war was impending between the United States and Mexico, Governor Micheltorena in 1844 authorized the sale of what was left of the missions to raise defense funds for the Mexican treasury. Within two years the mission collapse was complete. (Ibid.)

The American Take-over of Aztlán

By the time of the signing of the Treaty of Guadalupe-Hidalgo (1848), the mission system had collapsed. Yet, the impact of missionization and Mexicanization of the Southwest was to continue to the present day. Two hundred and fifty years of Spanish/Mexican influence would not be eradicated overnight.

E. C. Orozco argues that missionization of the *indio* in America entailed much more than the simple imposition of a foreign religious ideology, for there were strong elements within pre-Columbian religion and culture which predisposed the natives to accept and incorporate Christianity. The result was the successful creation of a new social order, Christian Mexicanism.

> . . . while the established and fundamental core of Mexican Catholicism was orthodox Christianity; the popular externals remained, as the missionaries had planned, indigenous Mexican American. As a consequence, many tribal groups in *Aztlán* were receptive to Mexican Christianity; there was an obvious racial and cultural affinity with the Spanish Mexican auxiliaries who migrated north. (Orozco 1980, p. 37)

The tendency of historians and other scholars to minimize or denigrate the Catholic and Mexican influence on the history and culture of the Southwest appears to be part of a more general anti-Catholic stance. Paul V. Murray (1965, p. 111) has noted that much of what we know about Mexican church history is drawn from American and English sources which reflect a strong anti-Catholic bias. According to Orozco "Anglo-American scholarship has generated considerable effort to negate the Christian influence on Mexican thought and culture" (1980, p. 38).

The anti-Catholic bias of such historians is not a random or whimsical attitude, but rather one deeply rooted in Anglo-American traditions. In the aforementioned work Orozco develops the thesis that the prevailing socioreligious foundation of the United States was *republican Protestantism*. Despite the popular myth of a "Christian America" the reality is that the United States was not founded by pious Christians but by men who were generally either nominally Christian or secular in their thought.

> In view of the neglected and impoverished spiritual condition of denominational Christian religion in the colonial and early republican period, the political ideology meshed with the deistic patterns of the country. That it eventually flowered and emerged as the uncontested major natural "religious" force in the body politic of the United States was not mere coincidence. (Ibid., p. 61)

But if there was a common denominator to Anglo-American Protestantism, it was a strong distrust and hatred of Catholicism. The American take-over of the Southwest was thus more than a political and military victory. It also signaled the imposition of *republican Protestantism* on Christian Mexicanism and was very much a racial/cultural victory. The violence and hatred directed at Chicanos in Aztlán during the nineteenth century was a manifestation of this deep-seeded conflict (ibid., p. 62). Manifest Destiny proved to be but a natural extension of these tendencies. The doctrine of *republican Protestantism* "mandated and compelled 'melting down' religious and ethnic differences for the presumed good of the whole" (ibid., p. 80).

Within this historical context it is perhaps not surprising to find that contemporary discussions of the Chicano and the church have tended to neglect, minimize, or to totally ignore our strong Mexican/Catholic heritage in the Southwest. Such accounts typically treat the Chicano not only as an immigrant group but as a late arrival who followed earlier waves of immigration by other Catholic groups such as the Irish and Italians. If there is a historical influence, it is a negative one which came via Mexico rather than Aztlán. According to the authors of the now classic work *The Mexican-American People*:

> . . . The historic conflict between the Church and government in Mexico had grave consequences for the Southwest Church. It resulted in a chronic shortage of priests in Mexico that became even more acute after the Revolution. Consequently, many of the nominally Catholic immigrants were ignorant about their religion, with only tenuous loyalties to the institutional Church and formal Catholicism. (Grebler, Moore, and Guzman 1970, pp. 449-50)

The authors add that as a result of government antipathy toward the church many Mexican immigrants brought anticlerical views with them. An additional obstacle to the Southwestern church was that the typical Mexican immigrant practiced a form of "folk Catholicism" which "combined some aspects of normal Catholic practice with pagan (Indian) rites" (ibid., p. 450). Thus, when poor resources were coupled with having to minister to a flock that was basically "uninstructed in the faith and deficient in their adherence to the general norms of Church practice" (ibid., p. 449), the task of the church became not only more difficult but overwhelming.

Grebler, Moore, and Guzman note that when the present Southwest was annexed, the Catholic Church had practically collapsed (ibid., p. 450). Church property was turned over to the bishops, who appointed priests to each parish. Although the mission system gave way to regular churches, many of these remained moribund. The basic thesis advanced is that the mission system left a poor legacy, making the church of the Southwest weak in comparison to the flourishing churches of the East and Midwest:

> . . . Institutionally, too, the Southwest Church differed significantly from the established Catholicism of the East. No firmly structured church existed to mediate the encounter of the Mexican and Anglo cultures. No equivalent of an Irish hierarchy was present to see to it that churches and schools were provided and foreign-language priests

appointed. The new American bishops were not ruling over large, relatively compact and populous urban centers. (Ibid., p. 452)

The priests are depicted as "*padres* on horseback" ministering to the pastoral needs of a "woefully uninstructed and non-practicing" Mexican clientele (ibid., p. 453). The result is that for much of the history of the Catholic Church in the Southwest, social action goals were subordinated to pastoral concerns. It is not until the 1920s that we see the emergence of a concern with "social action" on behalf of Mexican-Americans as a church goal.

While this may appear at first glance to be a reasonable and sympathetic position, closer examination suggests otherwise. The position is one which assumes that the Southwest church existed in isolation, independent of a sociopolitical context. In a subtle way it is a position that virtually blames Mexicans for their own oppression. The destruction of the mission system, for example, cannot be separated from the American take-over, for the two are very much intertwined. The hostility directed at the church and Chicanos is similarly part and parcel of the white Anglo-Saxon *republican Protestant* invasion. It is possible that the Southwest church did not flourish, not because of a shortage of priests and the absence of religious instruction among the Mexican clientele, but because anti-Catholic sentiment was inseparable from the racism which prevailed in the Southwest.

Chicanos were despised not only as Catholics but as members of a subhuman and despicable heathen race. Even Esteban Austin, who is generally portrayed as sympathetic to the Mexican, revealed the depth of his contempt in a letter to the honorable L. F. Linn.

> . . . A war of extermination is raging in Texas. . . . a war of barbarism and of despotic principles, waged by the mongrel Spanish-Indian and Negro race against civilization and the Anglo-American race.
>
> For fifteen years I have been laboring like a slave to Americanize Texas . . . to form a nucleous around which my native countrymen could collect and grow into a solid body that would forever be a barrier of safety to the southwestern frontier, and especially to the outlet of the western world . . . the mouth of the Mississippi . . . and which would be a beacon-light to the Mexicans in their search for liberty. . . . But the Anglo-American foundation, the nucleous of republicanism, is to be broken up, and its place supplied by a population of Indians, Mexicans and renegados, all mixed together, and all the natural enemies of white men and civilization. . . . Oh! Spirit of our fathers, where are you? Just and omnipotent God where is thy influence? Where is the fatherly care and protection of a wise and watchful government. (Orozco, p. 86)

The fact that most of the priests assigned to the Southwest were foreign (Spanish and French) is similarly dismissed as resulting from a "shortage of priests." What is ignored by Grebler, Moore, and Guzman, and others who take this position, is that the American annexation of the Southwest brought with it the colonization of all institutions, including the church. Insight into this process can be gained by looking at the infamous conflict between Padre Martínez and Bishop Lamy of New Mexico.

Martinez and Lamy are two colorful, historical figures whose conflict was more than one between two strong personalities: it was a conflict between two cultures. Jean Baptiste Lamy was French by birth but became a United States citizen in 1847. In the same year he was assigned to Covington, Kentucky (de Aragon 1978, p. 46). In May 1849 the American bishops met in Baltimore and discussed the newly acquired Mexican territory, believed to be in a "dormant" religious state.[5] A congressman from Connecticut had observed that the territory was

> . . . under the control of the clergy to an extraordinary degree. The standard of morals is exceedingly low . . . the Country is little better than a Sodom. . . . I am free to say that if all the vices which can corrupt the human heart, and all the qualities which reduce man to the level of a brute, are to be "annexed" to the virtue and intelligence of the American people, I DO NOT DESIRE TO BELONG TO ANY SUCH UNION. (Ibid., p. 47)

One of the recommendations of the bishops was the establishment of a vicar apostolic in New Mexico. In July 1850 Pope Pius IX established the vicariate apostolic of New Mexico with Father John Baptiste Lamy as its head.

The American take-over of the Southwest created a conflict between Mexican and American ecclesiastical and civil authority. After the war, Rome informed the Mexican bishops that it was their duty to maintain episcopal authority over the ceded territory (de Aragon 1978, p. 50). Bishop Zubiria of Durango asserted during an episcopal visitation to New Mexico in 1850 that "although the government had changed, his Diocesan authority had not" (ibid.). Undaunted by this knowledge, the American bishops proposed the founding by Rome of a new vicariate in New Mexico, citing the deplorable moral and spiritual state of the newly acquired territory and the immoral lifestyle of many of the priests as bases for its foundation. These accusations were buttressed by reports of American Army officers who wrote about "the supposed low morality, rampant prostitution, the drinking, gambling, dancing and every imaginable vice amongst the people and religious leaders" (ibid., p. 51).

Thus, when Lamy departed for New Mexico, he envisioned himself as a missionary with the formidable task of taming a misguided, fallen, and primitive people. This view was reinforced as he moved through Texas toward Santa Fe. He was shocked by the prevalence of violence and vice among the Mexicans and the spiritual and moral decay of the native clergy.

When Lamy arrived in Santa Fe on August 9, 1851, he found the Mexican clergy to be well entrenched. Bishop Antonio Laureano Zubiria headed the episcopal seat in Durango. Juan Felipe Ortiz was the vicar of Santa Fe, and second to Ortiz was Padre Antonio José Martínez. At least forty-one clergy had ministered to the needs of the people during the Mexican period of the church (ibid., p. 56). Padre Martínez headed our Lady of Guadalupe Seminary in Taos, which had enrolled thirty seminarians and was growing rapidly.

Unfortunately Rome had failed to notify the Diocese of Durango about the creation of the new vicariate apostolic, and Ortiz and the other priests demanded to see Lamy's papers. They refused, moreover, to acknowledge Lamy until they were officially authorized to do so by Bishop Zubiria. Lamy wrote to Zubiria, and when he did not receive an answer, he traveled to Durango in September 1851 to meet with the Mexican bishop. Zubiria informed him that Rome had not notified him of the change, but upon presentation of a papal document, he immediately recognized Lamy's authority and instructed Ortiz and other priests in Santa Fe to transfer their allegiance to him.

Although the native clergy acknowledged his authority, relations between them and the new vicar apostolic were strained. Lamy's contempt for them was clear. He hoped that the native clergy would either leave or "mend their ways," but when they did not, he began to take punitive action by reprimanding or suspending them (ibid., p. 61). In addition, Lamy ordered all pastors to collect tithes, which had previously been voluntary, and to keep one-fourth of what was collected and send the remainder to his office. Lamy's attack was not limited to the clergy but extended to the faithful, who were chastised for a number of things, including attending *fandangos*, which only encouraged immorality and vice. He further admonished them, "Be not deceived, neither fornicators, nor adulterers, nor highwaymen, nor those given to drinking nor blasphemers, nor thieves, shall inherit the kingdom of God" (ibid., p. 65). As Lamy continued to discipline and suspend priests and to exert tithes, resistance to him increased.

Padre Martínez joined this resistance, came to the aid of suspended priests, and spoke out against tithes. The "priest of Taos" was born in Rio Arriba County on January 7, 1793. Martínez had been married and was the father of a daughter prior to being ordained in 1820 after the death of his wife. Long before Lamy's arrival, Father Martínez had established a reputation as a leader and defender of human rights. In 1835 he also published a newspaper called *El Crepúsculo*. He opposed collecting tithes from the poor and favored the distribution of large land grants among the people (Acuña 1981, p. 55). Perhaps it was inevitable that Martínez's liberal and open philosophy would clash with that of Lamy. The issue that finally drew him into direct conflict with the vicar apostolic was suppression of the Holy Brotherhood of Penitents. The *Penitentes* consisted primarily of the poor of northern New Mexico. The Brotherhood was rooted in the Third Order of St. Francis of Assisi,[6] practiced public flagellation, and recreated the ordeal of Christ during Holy Week (ibid., p. 56). Lamy set out to restrict and disband the *Penitentes*. When Martínez came to their defense, Lamy attacked him and accused him of not being celibate. The priest of Taos was formally excommunicated, but he defied Lamy's mandate and continued to serve as a priest until his death on July 28, 1868.

As stated earlier, the conflict between Lamy and Martínez symbolizes a clash between Mexican and American cultures. Lamy extracted tithes from his flock to build churches and set up schools to educate them. But the parochial schools also sought to Americanize Mexican children and forbade the use of their Spanish mother tongue. Although New Mexico had traditionally and historically been a bilingual territory, the parochial schools made English the required language (de Aragon, p. 67). The Mexican church, on the other hand, was more sensitive to the needs of *la gente*. It was informal, people-oriented and had a clergy who was familiar with local customs and traditions, whereas the Anglo church was formal, bureaucratic, and insensitive to these needs. The Mexican clergy were not only more sensitive to pastoral concerns but became advocates for the rights of the people (Acuña 1981, p. 56).

The Need for a Chicano Liberation Theology

The history of *la raza* and religion is filled with paradoxes and contradictions. The conquest supposedly spelled the destruction of a native way of life and the imposition of an alien culture. Aztec gods and temples were destroyed and replaced with Christian symbols. Despite this devastation the conquest was never totally effected, however. The European Virgin, for example, was transformed into *La Virgen Morena, Guadalupe-Tonantzin*, the patron saint of the *indio* and *mestizo*, and in the process incorporated numerous elements of her Indian predecessor. *La Virgen* has consistently provided warmth and succorance for people of Mexican descent on both sides of the border. She has evolved into much more than a religious figure and has become at once a symbol of motherhood, womanhood, nationhood, and peoplehood. She embodies and integrates religion, family, and politics. In addition, her apparition before a poor *indio* proved that the *mexicano* was human and worthy of salvation.

It is appropriate that she would also emerge as an inspirational symbol for the *insurgentes* who revolted against Spanish rule in 1810 and that the call for independence came from a humble village priest, Miguel Hidalgo y Costilla. A century later Zapata's army of poor *campesinos* was to march once again behind the banner of *La Virgen*. More recently the farmworkers and César Chávez carried her banner on a "Pilgrimage to Sacramento." Such pilgrimages are part of our cultural tradition. They constitute "a trip made with sacrifice and hardship as an expression of penance and of commitment—and often involving a petition to the patron of the pilgrimage for some sincerely sought benefit of body or soul" (Chávez 1972, p. 385). Like the daily pilgrimages to the Basilica of Our Lady of *Guadalupe* in Mexico City, and the Lenten *penitente* processions in New Mexico, the pilgrimage of the California farmworkers is based on penance, sacrifice, and commitment. The farmworkers' struggle differs, however, in transforming the pilgrimage from an individual, private penance to a public demonstration of collective suffering and sacrifice. It is for this reason that the farmworkers' struggle is said to forge a unique link of pilgrimage, penance, and revolution (ibid., p. 386). Religion, culture, and politics for Chicanos are thus intertwined.

Despite this apparent coexistence, however, one of the most significant contradictions Chicanos face today is the disparity they see between the wealth of the church, on the one hand, and the poverty of their barrios, on the other. The church is a wealthy and powerful institution. In Los Angeles, for example, the Catholic church erected a 3.5-million-dollar church on Wilshire Boulevard, while ignoring the economic, political, and educational exploitation of its Chicano constituency. The Los Angeles church alone is said to have over one billion dollars in assets (Alurista 1972, p. 390). While Chicanos have always been faithful and supportive Catholics, the church until recently has opted not to use its wealth or influence to demand justice and equality for them. Not only are about 90 percent of all Chicanos Catholic, but they constitute about one-fourth of the total Catholic population in the United States and over two-thirds of the Catholic population in the Southwest. Chicanos, however, remain woefully underrepresented in the church structure. Chicano priests are few and far between, and until 1970 there was not a single bishop who was Chicano. Today there are but a handful of Chicano bishops, and less than 200 of the 58,301 priests in the United States are Chicano (Soto 1979, p. 50). In contrast, the Irish constitute only 17 percent of the Catholic population in the United States, but they make up 35 percent of the priests and 50 percent of the bishops (ibid.). Since the majority of Catholics in the Southwest are Chicano, one cannot escape the conclusion that the church in the Southwest persists as a colonial institution which is externally administered and controlled.

With lack of representation and input into critical policies and deci-

sions that affect them, it is not surprising that the Catholic hierarchy had remained impervious to the needs and concerns of its Mexican clientele (see
Isáis-A, 1979; Hurtado 1976 and 1979; and Soto 1979). Throughout the
nineteenth and well into the twentieth century the church traditionally
ministerd to pastoral concerns and neglected social action on behalf of
Chicanos. Even when the church began to go beyond pastoral care in the
1920s and 1930s, it did so largely in noncontroversial areas such as the
establishment of hospitals, clinics, and orphanages (Grebler, Moore, and Guzman 1970, p. 455). Another commonly expressed concern within the church
was fear of Protestant proselytizing. This concern was prompted by a view of
the Mexican as lacking in instruction and having only nominal commitment
to the faith, making him vulnerable to Protestant influence. Americanization
of the Mexican population was considered a worthy goal not only as a means
of thwarting Protestant proselytism but also a way of gaining legitimacy for
the church. (see Hurtado 1979, pp. 29-31). The Catholic Church was viewed
as "foreign," and itself existed within an alien and hostile environment.
Adherence to patriotism and Americanization would thus ultimately insure
its survival. Despite growing recognition of the economic and social exploitation of the Mexican, the solution of these problems was to be effected not
through basic changes in the social structure but through Americanization
and assimilation. It was the Mexican, not the social structure, that had to
change.

Throughout much of the present century the thrust of church goals
relative to Chicanos has been either strictly pastoral or linked to social action
in the service of pastoral concerns such as Americanization and charitable
work. Recognition of social action for social change as a worthwhile goal in
and of itself has come very slowly. According to Grebler, Moore, and Guzman
(1970, p. 461) it was not until World War II that the administrative hierarchy
of the church appears to have recognized social action on behalf of Chicanos
as a real concern. This redirection in goal orientation was undoubtedly influenced by the prevailing social and political climate. During the 1940s antiforeign sentiment was rampant, and racial divisions were exacerbated. The
zoot-suit riots and the Sleepy Lagoon case brought these tensions to the
forefront for Chicanos.

Concern with social problems experienced by the Mexican-American
community led in 1943 to the calling of a meeting in San Antonio by the
Social Action Department of the National Catholic Welfare Conference
(ibid.). The conference was historic in bringing together for the first time
church and civic leaders who worked with the Spanish-speaking population.
Archbishop Lucey acknowledged poverty and discrimination as key problems
faced by the Mexican-American and took a stand on social action. He saw
these problems as stemming from

A very general lack of labor organizations, the absence of good legislation and the greed of powerful employers have combined to create in Texas dreadful and widespread misery. The evil men who are driving tens of thousands of our people into a slow starvation will be held to strict accountability by the God of eternal justice. (Ibid., p. 462)

In 1945 the American Board of Catholic Missions underwrote a Bishops' Committee for the Spanish-Speaking. The formation of the bishops' committee officially signaled a change in orientation within the church toward social action on behalf of Chicanos (ibid.). A significant outgrowth of the bishops' committee was the creation in 1948 of the Spanish Mission Band, four priests who rather than being assigned to territorially based parishes were free to work with farm laborers and to travel from area to area throughout the state of California. Although initially ministering primarily to pastoral needs, the priests became increasingly politicized, and by 1959 they were involved in the issue of unionization for farmworkers. By the mid-60s Catholic clergymen were playing a key role in supporting the Delano strike and in organizing farm laborers in south Texas (ibid., p. 464).

Although a number of priests had begun to pursue social action on behalf of Chicanos, the church as a whole continued to be supportive of the status quo.[7] It was not until the latter part of the 60s that the neutrality of the church was challenged and tested (see Isáis-A. 1979, pp. 9-10; Soto 1979, pp. 60-65). The Chicano movement provided much of the impetus for this confrontation. As the movimiento unfolded, the church's role in either directly or indirectly perpetuating the status quo became increasingly apparent. One of the movement's basic goals was that Chicanos gain control over vital institutions that affected their daily lives. Chicanos had been quick to protest their lack of control and representation in education, politics, economy, and other institutions. Loyalty to the church was intense, however, and criticisms of this institution were slow to surface. The church was a sacred institution. When the church was finally scrutinized, however, it came under considerable attack. A number of contradictions emerged, including the gap between Christian ideals and church practice and the discrepancy between the wealth of the church and poverty in Chicano neighborhoods.

In the late 1960s groups such as Católicos por La Raza (CPLR) and PADRES, an organization of Spanish-speaking priests, emerged. Protests and boycotts were held in churches throughout the Southwest. Although termed an activist organization, CPLR simply called upon the Catholic Church to live up to Christian ideals. A Catholic education had taught them that Christ was a poor man who did everything possible to feed and help the poor (Católicos por La Raza 1972, p. 391). They also knew that in choosing to identify with the poor, Christ had gone to the established church one day and used a whip to drive out the money changers who exploited the poor (ibid.). *Católicos* understood from this example that

> . . . it is our fault if the Catholic Church in the Southwest is no longer a Church of blood, a Church of struggle, a Church of sacrifice. . . . We can't love our people without demanding better housing, education, health, and so many other needs we share in common.
>
> In a word, we are demanding that the Catholic Church practice what it preaches. Remember Padre Hidalgo. And remember that the history of our people is the history of the Catholic Church in America. We must return the Church to the poor. OR DID CHRIST DIE IN VAIN? (Ibid., p. 392)

These protests and their mandates served to dramatize differences between church, Christianity, and a real spiritual life. They revealed that the church had evolved into a corporation for profit that worked to maintain the status quo (del Grito 1972, p. 393). Christ himself was seen in a different light—as a radical and a revolutionary who challenged the established order.

While the Chicano movement was challenging the Southwest church in the 1960s, the church was also being challenged throughout most of Latin America. A movement to develop and implement what was termed the theology of liberation not only paralleled the efforts of Chicanos but placed the Chicano movement within a broader context of the liberation of Third World peoples. Like the Mexican and Southwest church, the church in Latin America was a colonial institution. In 1968, in the aftermath of Vatican II, bishops from throughout Latin America gathered in the city of Medellín, Colombia, for what proved to be a landmark conference. For the first time in church history a group of bishops took an unprecedented stand against oppression and for liberation. That this conference should take place in Latin America is in itself significant, for it is here that the church has most clearly functioned as an arm of colonization. The bishops recognized that the world is divided into rich and poor nations and that each nation is further divided into rich and poor. The bulk of the wealth in Latin America was recognized to be in the hands of a few, while the masses lived in dire poverty and starvation. The theology of liberation, on behalf of the poor, called for placing Christian ideals in the service of radical social change.

Cardinal Archbishop Juan Landázuri of Lima, Peru, captured the prevailing sentiment:

> No estamos reunidos aquí para conservar ni para defender lo que existe en nuestra iglesia. . . . Estamos para *saber escuchar y saber estar*. . . .

¿Quien, al *escuchar* las necesidades y las miserias de millones de hombres y mujeres Lationamericanos no siente que debe estar con ellos?

Saber *estar* significa . . . comprometernos en los esfuerzos de liberación, en las *luchas* de nuestros hermanos que buscan alcanzar condiciones de vida *más humanas*. . . . La salvación en America Latina es *hacer el reino de Dios* (El plan de Dios para con nosotros).

Esto abarca la *liberación* de todo el hombre, de condiciones de vida *menos* humanas a condiciones *más* humanas. . . . Esto es lo que queremos y es lo que *vamos a hacer*. (Centro de Reflexión Teológica, undated, p. 4)

We are gathered here neither to preserve nor to defend the existing state of our church. . . . We are here *to learn how to listen and to learn how to be*. . . .

Who, upon *listening* to the needs and the miseries of millions of Latin American men and women does not feel that he should be with them?

Learning to *be* means . . . committing ourselves to efforts for liberation, to the *struggles* of our brothers to attain a quality of life that is more *human*. . . . Salvation in Latin America is *to create the kingdom of God* (to make God's plan for ourselves).

This entails the liberation of the whole man from *subhuman* conditions of life to those that are suprahuman. . . . This is what we want and this is what we are going to do.

Participants at Medellín were concerned not only with poverty among individuals but with the poverty of nations as nations. Just as the poor were exploited by the rich within each nation, so did developed nations exploit underdeveloped ones. In the case of Latin America exploitation issued primarily from their dependent relation with the United States. Since the bishops opted to side with the poor in their struggle for freedom and the creation of a more just social order given that God created the world and everything therein for the use and enjoyment of all, not simply the rich, a theology of liberation was drafted. A basic tenet of the theology of liberation is that the impoverished condition in which the masses live is unjust.

While a natural link exists between the social and religious struggles of Chicanos and the liberation theology movements in Latin America, the theology of liberation has been slow to develop not only among Chicanos but in the United States as a whole. Much has been written about liberation theology, but few attempts have been made to apply it to Chicanos. Rather than dwell on these writings, it might perhaps be best to define briefly this concept and then identify obstacles to its implementation in Aztlán.[8]

A basic goal of the theology of liberation in Latin America and other oppressed countries is to "construct a just and fraternal society, where people can live with dignity and be the agents of their own destiny" (Gutiérrez 1973, p. x). Advocates of this view hold that the term *liberation* is a more accurate reflection of the aspirations of Third World people than *development*. Liberation "emphasizes that man transforms himself by conquering his liberty throughout his existence and his history" (ibid.). Liberation is thus a salvific process that unites without confusing man's relation to other men and with the Lord. The development of liberation theology is also an attempt to reconcile the traditional conflict between theology and Marxism and leans heavily on Marxist notions. To adopt this theological view is to recognize "that communion with the Lord inescapably means a Christian life centered around a concrete and creative commitment of service to others" (ibid., p. 11).

The theology of liberation is influenced not only by Marxism and external challenges to the church but by Vatican Council II under Pope John XXIII. In the early 1960s Vatican II "strongly reaffirmed the idea of a Church of service and not of power" (ibid., p. 8) and adopted a theological position which has been termed "signs of the times." This position called for pastoral activity, for commitment and service, but, most importantly, for going beyond spirituality alone to a concern with the "total man." Despite the significance of Vatican II the theology which emerged from Medellín went far beyond the signs of the times. Rather than speaking solely of liberation, Vatican II focused on processes such as dependence and underdevelopment. Gustavo Gutiérrez compared the two meetings.

> . . . Vatican II speaks of the underdevelopment of peoples, of the developed countries and what they can and should do about this underdevelopment; Medellín tried to deal with the problem from the standpoint of the poor countries, characterizing them as subjected to a new kind of colonialism. Vatican II talks about a Church in the world and describes the relationship in a way which tends to neutralize the conflicts; Medellín demonstrates that the world in which the Latin American Church ought to be present is in full revolution. Vatican II sketches a general outline for Church renewal; Medellín provides guidelines for a transformation of its presence on a continent of misery and injustice. (Ibid., p. 134)

The position developed at Medellín is similar to that taken by *Católicos por La Raza* and other Chicanos who have challenged the church. One important difference, however, is that at Medellín the bishops themselves called for liberation and social action on behalf of the poor and oppressed, whereas the southwestern hierarchy remains largely unresponsive to Chicanos.

Given a history of oppression of Chicanos, one might ask why liberation theology has not had a greater impact on the church in the Southwest.

A number of factors contribute to this. First, it is important to note that the United States is a Protestant nation and that Catholicism has been a minority religion in this country. The United States was founded by and for Protestants, and throughout the course of its history it has been ruled and controlled by them. Exploitation and discrimination against Chicanos has therefore occurred not only because of their race but because of their religious affiliation. Second, Chicanos have been subjected to a subordinate and dependent relation within the southwestern Anglo church, serving as a minority within a minority institution. Third, racial, cultural, religious, and linguistic diversity within the United States generally makes solidarity and mobilization difficult. Could Chicanos unite with other Catholics, or is such unity precluded by racial, ethnic, and class differences?

The internal homogeneity of Latin American nations, on the other hand, has facilitated unity, as has their economic dependence on the United States. Most Latin American nations are basically characterized by groups with a common cultural, racial, and national heritage and with a shared language, along with a division of people into rich and poor. Since wealth is heavily concentrated in the hands of a few, contradictions within the society are largely manifested along class lines. It is precisely because of this disparity and these contradictions that liberation theology has gained momentum and that the church in Latin America has taken the side of the oppressed over the oppressor. The church has come to recognize that it can no longer plead neutrality without recognizing its complicity in the exploitation of the masses.

A basic lesson to be learned from the Latin American experience is that for Chicanos gaining power within the church is a prerequisite for the development of a theology of liberation. Much of the impetus for liberation theology in Latin America has come from the clergy themselves, not from the masses. As long as Chicanos are underrepresented among the clergy and the hierarchy of the church, they will lack the requisite leadership to effect significant change. The paradox, of course, is that gaining control of the church will be difficult until Chicanos attain liberation in other spheres. Religion has the potential to play a significant role in the liberation of Chicanos, for it is a basic unifying force across educational, economic, geographical, and generational lines.

Despite the importance of religion and the promise held by liberation theology, we must not forget that liberation is an organic process that must emerge from within a people. It cannot be imposed or imported. T. Richard Shaull observes, "If we want to think theologically about liberation, then it is *our own liberation* that must concern us" (1975, p. 76). Shaull is not addressing the issue of Chicano liberation, but his observation applies, nonetheless. We should be sensitive and responsive to parallel movements both within the United States and in the Third World. But we should be leary of those who would provide us with ready-made formulas for liberation. Recognizing parallels between our situation and that of Third World countries is not sufficient unless we also begin to recognize that we *are* the Third World. The fact that we are internally colonized within the territorial boundaries of the United States and surrounded by affluence does not minimize the importance of our struggle; it only makes it that much more difficult. In the last analysis, like other groups seeking liberation, it is incumbent upon us to chart our own course and determine our own destiny. Rather than import a liberation theology, we must develop one from within our own rich culture and history: a theology of liberation that not only builds on but traverses this rich legacy.

7

La Familia Chicana

While there has been a proliferation of research and writing on the American family, studies have tended to focus on the dominant family type, and little is known about family forms that vary from the modal middle-class, white Protestant ideal (Mindel and Habenstein 1976, p. vii). In their quest to generalize about "the family," researchers have tended to neglect or minimize internal social class and ethnic variations. When ethnic variations have been considered, the dominant family system typically has served as a yardstick against which to measure such deviations. Analyses of ethnic families thus tend to be pathological and pejorative evaluations conducted by researchers who are insensitive to the nuances of the sociocultural systems they are studying.

In recent years minority scholars have begun to question such generalizations. Social scientists have shown an inordinate concern with the black family, for example, but historically this interest has been problem-oriented (Staples 1976a, p. 221). Under the guise of objectivity and the value-free ethic one finds that social scientists are frequently asking, "What is wrong with the black family and why is it different from the white middle-class norm?" As the largest ethnic minority, blacks have made significant inroads and have been able not only to set aside many erroneous beliefs about the black family but to present a more accurate view of the organization and functions of the family in the black community.

Behavioral scientists have similarly shown great interest in the Mexican-American family, and generalizations concerning the Mexican-American family abound. Such generalizations tend to be based on meager, if not nonexistent, empirical evidence, however. A number of Chicano writers have sought to counter the mythical and stereotypical social-science characterization of the Mexican-American family (Montiel 1970; Murillo 1971), but Chicanos lack power and influence and their protests have typically been either muted or ignored. Also, while Chicano perspectives on *la familia* have served as a badly needed corrective for the negative and stultifying social-science view, they have not been without their own pitfalls. In their eagerness to counter the pejorative social-science view, they have tended to overcompensate and present an idealized and romanticized image of the family.

Thus two polar and contradictory views of the family have emerged. Detractors of the family see it as a "tangle of pathology" which impedes the advancement and acculturation of Chicanos, whereas supporters see it as a warm and nurturing institution that provides succorance in an otherwise hostile and unrewarding environment. This chapter seeks to present an overview and evaluation of these polar perspectives, along with a new, more balanced framework for studying the Chicano family. It will attempt more specifically to (1) discuss and evaluate both traditionally pejorative social-science depictions of the family as well as more sympathetic views of the family and (2) reassess the structure, functions, and values of the Chicano family in light of these earlier perspectives. It is hoped that this revised and more complete perspective will supersede both the traditional, pejorative, social-science view and the newer, romanticized and idealized internal view of the family, thereby advancing a Chicano perspective and at the same time enhancing our understanding of the contemporary *familia.*

The Social-Science Myth of the Mexican-American Family

An examination of social-science literature on the Mexican-American family reveals a consistently pathological and pejorative view. These negative depictions have resulted from the tendency of social scientists to see the Mexican-American family as a radical departure or deviation from the dominant, egalitarian, Anglo-American family; Mexican and Mexican-American families appear rigid and authoritarian by comparison.

A prevailing feature of these studies is that they uncritically accept the concept of *machismo* as an explanation for all that is wrong with the Mexican and the Mexican-American family (Montiel 1970). Infused with psychoanalytic concepts and paradigms, they attempt to establish a modal Mexican personality type that is characterized by a pervasive feeling of inferiority and a rejection of authority. An added assumption is that the Mexican family and the Mexican-American family are isomorphic, so that one can extrapolate findings from one setting to another. Despite the obvious hazards involved in applying psychoanalytically based Mexican national character studies to the United States, these explorations "have been accepted as the 'true' description of the Mexican character, the Mexican male, and ultimately the Mexican and Mexican American family" (Montiel 1970, p. 58).

Among the most influential studies of Mexican national character and the Mexican family are Maria Bermúdez's *La vida familiar del mexicano*, Díaz-Guerrero's *Psychology of the Mexican*, and G. M. Gilbert's study of mental health in a Mexican village. Bermúdez argues that Mexicans are locked into rigid conceptions of masculinity and femininity which make it difficult for

men to be "candid and humane" and for women to be "dignified and independent" (1955, p. 101). Díaz-Guerrero similarly concludes from eleven
structured questions that the male and the female are unable to fulfill their
rigid role expectations and consequently tend toward neurosis (1975, p. 10).
Despite the careful use of psychoanalytic jargon and pseudoscientific dis-
claimers these studies inevitably conclude that *machismo* produces maladap-
tive pathological responses. They adopt a simple psychoanalytic model in
which *machismo* becomes a malady and Mexican cultural traits are symptomatic of illness or disease. This pathological view is then used to perpetuate
deeply ingrained, though unsupported, assumptions about Mexican culture.
G. M. Gilbert, for example, asserts on the basis of interviews with nine older
males that there was

> . . . a prounounced tendency to either severely constricted affect
> or to morbid-depressed-hypochondriacal types of responses among the
> older males . . . this may be indicative of increasing impotence and
> "castration anxiety" as the males fail in the lifelong struggle to live up
> to the demands of *machismo*. (Gilbert 1959, p. 212)

The pathological model of the family has in turn been applied by
American social scientists to Chicanos. Researcher after researcher, without
the benefit of empirical evidence, depicts a *macho*-dominated, authoritarian
Mexican-American family (see Humphrey 1944; Jones 1948; Peñalosa 1968;
Madsen 1973; and Carroll 1980). Marriage, according to this view, does not
encumber the freedom of the male, as he is allowed to pursue the same pattern of social life after marriage that he did as a bachelor. He comes and goes
as he pleases, stays out all night (engages in *parrandas*), drinks, fights, and may
even establish a second household (*casa chica*). Life for the male is characterized by an incessant preoccupation with sex. Although all women are sexual
objects to be pursued and conquered, an important distinction is made between good and bad women. Bad women are considered fair game, while good
women are to be respected and revered. Mothers, wives, and daughters are
saintly, virginal creatures who do not enjoy sex and are to be shielded and
protected from male predators. Good women are not only virtuous but self-
sacrificing and enduring figures as well. Whereas the man retains much of his
autonomy after marriage, women are completely circumscribed by marital
and familial roles (Peñalosa 1968, p. 683). Women who do not accept their
subordinate position or who question the authority of the male typically are
subjected to physical punishment or abuse (Hayden 1966, p. 20). Wives,
moreover, "should accept this punishment as deserved," and they may even
be "grateful for punishment at the hands of their husbands for such concern
with shortcomings indicates profound love" (Madsen 1973, p. 22).

The *macho* demands complete deference, respect, and obedience not only from the wife but from children as well. In fact, social scientists maintain that this rigid, male-dominated family structure has negative consequences for the personality development of Mexican-American children. It fails to engender achievement, independence, self-reliance, or self-worth, values which are highly esteemed in American society. Celia Heller (1966, pp. 34-35) observes:

> The kind of socialization that Mexican-American children gen-
> erally receive at home is not conducive to the development of the
> capacities needed for advancement . . . by stressing values that hinder
> mobility—family ties, honor, masculinity, and living in the present—
> and by neglecting the values that are conducive to it—achievement, in-
> dependence, and deferred gratification.

The authoritarian Mexican-American family constellation then produces dependence and subordination and reinforces a present-time orientation which impedes advancement. Chicanos live in a perpetual "mañana land." It happens, then, that while Anglo culture stresses achievement and control of the environment, Chicano culture stresses fatalism and resignation (Samora and Lamanna 1967, p. 135). Alvin Rudoff's categorical condemnation of the family and culture is also illustrative of this view of Mexican-Americans.

> . . . The family constellation is an unstable one as the father is
> seen as withdrawn and the mother as a self-sacrificing and saintly figure.
> The Mexican-American has little concern for the future, perceives
> himself as predestined to be poor and subordinate, is still influenced by
> magic, is gang-minded, distrusts women, sees authority as arbitrary,
> tends to be passive and dependent, and is alienated from the Anglo
> culture (1971, pp. 236-37).

In comparison to the Anglo-American family, then, the Mexican-American family is perceived by many social scientists as a tangle of pathology. It propagates the subordination of women, impedes individual achievement, engenders passivity and dependence, stifles normal personality development, and on occasion can even give rise to incestuous feelings among siblings.

> . . . It may very well be that this type of family structure also in-
> creases the incestuous attraction between brothers and sisters. In
> middle-class families this attraction may become accentuated by the
> family being partly closed off from the outside world and in poor fam-
> ilies by the cramped living quarters. This theme of incestuous feelings
> between brothers and sisters is significantly a fairly common one in
> Mexican novels, movies, and plays. (Peñalosa 1968, p. 688)

The stereotypical view of the family is so deeply ingrained that social scientists are reluctant to abandon it even in the face of evidence to the contrary. When research findings indicate that the Chicano family is less rigid than was previously assumed, there has been a tendency to either dismiss such findings or suggest that they reflect greater acculturation and assimilation to the dominant pattern. Hawkes and Taylor (1975, p. 807), for example, were struck by the finding that the prevailing pattern of decision-making and action-taking among husbands and wives in Chicano migrant farm families was egalitarian rather than male-dominated as hypothesized. Faced with these unexpected results, they turned to factors that might explain them, such as increasing acculturation, urbanization, and "the decreasing dependence of women upon their husbands in *this country*" (1975, p. 810, emphasis mine). Only after unsuccessful attempts to account for these results do the authors reluctantly suggest that

> . . . many of the traditional stereotypes of groups such as ethnic minorities noted in the literature and in public assumptions need more adequate verification. It is possible that more sophisticated methods of research may negate many of our previous assumptions. (Hawkes and Taylor 1975, p. 811)

Sympathetic Views of La Familia

Some Chicano social scientists have sought to reexamine social-science depictions of the Mexican-American family and in the process to dispel the many myths and stereotypes that surround it. Miguel Montiel (1970; 1973) has written incisive critiques of Mexican-American family studies. He argues that such studies have perpetuated erroneous stereotypes as a result of their unquestioned reliance on a pathological psychoanalytic model that sees *machismo* as the root of all the problems encountered by Mexican-Americans. "This formulation is inherently incapable of defining normal behavior and thus automatically labels all Mexican and Mexican American people as sick—*only in degree of sickness do they vary*" (Montiel 1970, p. 62). Despite the cogency of his remarks Montiel presents neither a revised view of the family nor an alternative framework for future studies to follow. In other words, while Montiel clearly refutes prevailing stereotypes about the family, he fails to offer new insights into the dynamics of Chicano family life.

Octavio Romano (1968b) has similarly criticized social-science accounts of Mexican-American culture and family life. After reviewing the works of Tuck, Heller, and Samora and Lamanna, he concludes that these works constitute an exercise in social-science fiction which present a distorted picture of Mexican-Americans as passive, masochistic vegetables, controlled by a traditional culture. With respect to the family Romano notes that social scientists would have us believe that Mexican-American parents "are their children's own worst enemies" (1968, p. 19) and that they potentially threaten the American way of life. Romano uses Madsen as exemplary of this view. According to Madsen (Romano 1968b, pp. 19-20) "Anglos believe that equality in the home and self-advancement are necessary to maintain the American ideals of freedom, democracy, and progress. Mexican-Americans believe that putting family above self is necessary to fulfill the will of God." The emphasis on familism not only impedes advancement and acculturation but threatens the very foundations of our democratic form of government. The work of Romano is an important corrective for mythical social-science depictions, but, like that of Montiel, it does not offer a substitute view of the family.

A number of other Chicano writers have offered an alternative view of the family. They argue that *la familia* is not the cold and unstable constellation social scientists depict, but a warm and nurturing institution. Parents are not their children's own worst enemies: "only a person who has never experienced the warmth of the Mexican American family would tend to see it primarily from a negative perspective" (Alvirez and Bean, 1976, p. 277). The family, according to this new perspective, is the most important unit in life, and the individual is likely to place the needs of the family above his own (Murillo 1971, p. 102). Thus, if there is a conflict between the family and school or work, the individual will usually be more sensitive to familial demands. The concept of *machismo* is important, but it is defined more in terms of family pride and respect than in terms of male dominance. As the ultimate authority in the family the father is responsible to the outside world for the behavior of family members. "An important part of his concept of machismo or maleness, however, is that of using his authority within the family in a just and fair manner. Should he misuse his authority, he will lose respect" (Murillo 1971, p. 103) not only within the family but in the community at large. *Machismo* is not a pathological force or a tool for protecting male prerogatives, but a mechanism for upholding family pride and honor.

What was previously described as a rigid and authoritarian family is now redefined as a stable structure where the individual's place is more clearly established and secure. The family "seems to provide more emotional security and sense of belonging to its members" (Murillo 1971, p. 99). Roles and expectations are largely determined by a member's age and gender. The father is granted deference and respect as head of the household, but other adults such as grandparents (*abuelitos* and *abuelitas*) are also accorded respect.

The family is thus seen as a warm and nurturing unit that provides support throughout the lifetime of the individual. In times of stress or when problems arise one typically turns to the family for help rather than to outside agencies. Sharing and cooperation are encouraged and valued not only among children but among adult family members. Anglo-controlled agencies find it difficult to understand why Chicanos are leary of outside help (Ramos 1973) or why badly needed resources are distributed to more needy family members. Help patterns are clearly established, and it is not uncommon for family members to pool resources to purchase large or expensive items such as a house or a car (Alvirez and Bean 1976, p. 277).

A Reassessment of the Chicano Family

Thus we have two views of the Chicano family that are at variance with one another—the traditional social-science view of the Chicano family as rigid, cold, and unstable, and a more sympathetic view of it as warm, nurturing, and cohesive. Although these two views would appear at first glance to be polar and irreconcilable, they are not totally dissimilar. They are in agreement over a number of characteristics of the Chicano family. Both hold that the Chicano family is characterized by (1) male dominance, (2) rigid sex-age grading so that "the older order the younger, and the men the women," (3) clearly established patterns of help and mutual aid among family members, and (4) a strong familistic orientation whereby individual needs are subordinated to collective needs.

The basic difference between the two views, then, is not to be found in their substantive characterization of the family, since there is much overlap between them, but in their interpretation and evaluation of these characteristics. While the familistic orientation of Chicanos is universally recognized, critics see it as undemocratic, un-American, and impeding individual achievement and advancement; sympathizers, as a source of emotional and material support in a hostile and unrewarding world. These polar depictions of the family are important not so much for what they reveal about the family but for what they reveal about those who study the family.

Though the more positive view of the Chicano family emerged as a response to stereotypical characterizations, it too has demonstrated a strong tendency to make sweeping generalizations about the family that neglect or minimize its internal diversity. In their quest to negate pejorative depictions, defenders of the family have substituted a series of positive and idealized stereotypes which, ironically, incorporate many of the same beliefs they sought to supplant. Thus, negative stereotypes have been discarded in favor of positive and romanticized characterizations that result in polar caricatures of the Chicano family.

The task at hand now is to present a more balanced view that captures the reality of Chicano family life without exaggerating or distorting that reality. It is therefore important to note that the family system to be depicted is an ideal type that may not correspond to any real family. Just as there is no one uniform Anglo-American family, so there is no one Chicano family but a number of family types that vary according to region, recentness of migration to the United States, education, social class, age, and urban-rural locale. Given this internal diversity, it is necessary to extrapolate key features found among Chicano families across various settings and situations. The traits attributed to the Chicano family are not true of all families, but they are more likely to characterize the Chicano than the Anglo family.

Probably the most significant characteristic of the Chicano family is its strong emphasis on familism. While the impact of the family may have been eroded somewhat by urbanization and acculturation, it is still a central institution for the individual. The family is a basic source of emotional support for the child as he develops close bonds not only with members of the immediate family but with grandparents, aunts and uncles, cousins, and family friends. A study of young children, age seven to thirteen, in a Houston *barrio* concluded that "in the child's-eye-view the central feature is home, and the people at home" (Goodman and Beman 1971, p. 111). Significantly, in response to the question "Who do you love?" none of the *barrio* children included anyone but relatives in their responses, whereas Anglo children and black children included many nonfamily members, and friends also played a prominent part in their listing of persons loved (Goodman and Beman 1971, p. 112). Grandparents (*abuelitos* and *abuelitas*) are also important in the lives of children, but they are likely to be seen as warm and affectionate rather than as authority figures. "Grandparents appear to be highly influential, as distinguished from being powerful" (Goodman and Beman 1971, p. 111). Like parents in the kibbutz, they are free of the responsibilities of parenthood, and their relationships with grandchildren can be warm and nurturing (Talmon 1961). In addition to being loved, however, grandparents are respected because they are considered to be older and wiser.

The emphasis on familism is such that extended kinship ties assume a prominent place within the culture. In a classic study of Chicanos in San Bernardino, California, Ruth Tuck noted that there is a stronger value on familism in Latin America than in the United States.

> In Latin America, the family includes not only parents and children, but an extended circle of friends as well. Several generations are likely to live under the same rooftree. Grandparents, uncles, aunts, and cousins are considered part of the intimate family circle. . . . They visit back and forth frequently; they form a common council in crisis or times of decision. (Tuck 1946, p. 122)

Visiting and help and mutual aid among extended kin are said to provide strength and support for the individual. Grebler, Moore, and Guzman
maintain that

> In addition to emotional relationships, kinship ties among Mex-
> ican Americans are described as avenues of exchanges of a more in-
> strumental nature, as they are in American society as a whole. Mutual
> financial assistance, exchange of work and other skills, and advice and
> support in solving personal problems are ideally available within the ex-
> tended kin network of most Americans, reliance on kin is carried to an
> extreme in the traditional Mexican-American family system. (1970, p.
> 352)

M. Jean Gilbert also found a high level of extended-family participation
among Chicano respondents, although the frequency of interaction and exchange was influenced by the availability of kin. Persons living in barrios
were most likely to exchange with a larger number and a higher percentage
of kin (Gilbert 1978, p. 43).

The strong familistic orientation of Chicano families has often been
linked to their rural background, since it is assumed that extended-kin relations are attenuated in urban locales. Grebler, Moore, and Guzman, on the
basis of data obtained in Los Angeles and San Antonio, concluded:

> To judge from the limited data on living arrangements and visit-
> ing patterns, then, relationships within the extended kinship group
> among Mexican Americans have declined in importance with increased
> urbanization, acculturation, and contact with the dominant system. A
> similar decline has been found in many societies. (1970, p. 354)

More recent research, however, seriously questions the assumption that
urbanization inevitably weakens kin networks. Maxine Baca Zinn, in fact, rejects this view, arguing that much of the research and writing relative to the
Mexican-American family has been based on a model of "an outmoded traditional patriarchal institution" (1979a, p. 59). This model sees the decline in
patriarchal authority and the weakening of kin ties as a natural evolutionary
process.

> . . . Chicano family research has been guided by an ideal con-
> struct, postulating, on the one hand, the "traditional" Mexican patriar-
> chal type, and on the other, a "modern" egalitarian family type. The
> concept of modernization has not been made explicit in Chicano family
> literature, but many of its underlying assumptions have guided thinking
> in this area, most notably the idea that universal evolutionary changes
> in family structure occur with urbanization and industrialization.

Projected changes centered on the inevitable decline of the kinship unit and the decline of traditional patriarchy. (Ibid.)

Baca Zinn is also critical of the strong tendency in the literature to attribute
Chicano family patterns to cultural values rather than to structural forces
(1979a, p. 67; 1982b, p. 263). Another way of viewing Chicano kinship patterns is as a structural adaptation "to the lack of external support systems
available to Chicanos in American society" (1979a, p. 67). From this perspective kin networks should become more, rather than less, important in urban-
industrial society. There is evidence, for example, that kinship ties among urban Chicanos in the Midwest have not declined (see Baca Zinn 1982c, pp.
88-89; Sena-Rivera 1979).

Another characteristic of the Chicano family is that relatives are frequently included as friends. There is no sharp distinction made between
relatives and friends, as they are often one and the same. Not only are
relatives included as friends but friends are symbolically incorporated into the
family. The institution of *compadrazgo* (godparentage) dates back to the early
postconquest period in Mexico. This Spanish custom was apparently adopted
by the Indians during the colonial period (1550-1650), as widespread epi-
demics led to massive native depopulation, leaving many orphaned children
(Gibson 1966, p. 142). *Compadres* (godparents) thus originally functioned as
parent substitutes. Over the centuries the original meaning of *compadrazgo*
has been modified, so that *compadres* have more of a social function than one
of parent substitutes. Nonetheless the custom remains intact.[1] One study
found that nearly all the adult respondents reported at least one such relationship, and in many instances, two, three, or more (Goodman and Beman 1971,
p. 111).

Both pejorative and positive accounts of the Chicano family, as has
been noted, see the male as the ultimate and unquestioned authority in the
family. Such characterizations have focused on the formal aspects of Chicano
culture, neglecting its more subtle and informal nuances. The father is formally accorded much deference and respect, but he is not the all-powerful
lord and master of the household, as has been suggested. There is, in fact,
an implicit contradiction in the stereotypical view of the *macho* who comes
and goes as he pleases and the view of him as the all-powerful authority and
arbitrator in the family. The male may officially be the ultimate authority,
but he is frequently aloof or uninvolved in family matters. The father tends
to be warm and affectionate when children are little, but as they enter pu-
berty, relations between him and the children become more tenuous (Rubel
1966, p. 66).

The expectation of women, on the other hand, is one of almost total
devotion to the family (Murillo 1971, p. 104). She should be warm, nurturing,
and minister to the needs of her husband and children. Ministering mothers

are respected, revered, and recognized as important figures, despite their alleged low status in the family. Indeed, for children their importance appears to take precedence over the father. A study of Chicano children found that the father is seen as a somewhat distant authority who is frequently slighted, especially by boys. "Few say they go to him with questions, either for information or for permission to do something" (Goodman and Beman 1971, p. 112). Significantly, few want to be "like father when they grow up" or to have a job like his. This remoteness may result from his frequent absence from home. He may leave home before the children are awake and not return until late in the evening (Goodman and Beman 1971, p. 112). Mothers, however, play a critical part in the lives of children. They perform many domestic tasks like preparing breakfast, fixing lunches, cooking dinner, washing dishes, and various other household chores. Mothers are also responsible for setting parameters on the children's behavior. They determine when one gets up or goes to bed and when one comes in from playing (Goodman and Beman 1971, p.112). "She scolds, she sometimes slaps or spanks for disobeying small rules, and she stops sibling squabbles" (Goodman and Beman 1971, p.112). Thus, while the woman does not have the formal prestige or status of the man, she has great informal influence in the home.

Other research also seriously questions the extent to which the ideal of male dominance in conjugal roles is actually observed (see Cromwell and Cromwell 1978; Mirandé 1979). It suggests that the prevailing pattern of decision-making and action-taking among husbands and wives is not authoritarian and male dominant but relatively egalitarian. Hawkes and Taylor (1975) found that decision-making and action-taking among California migrant farm families was basically egalitarian. An in-depth analysis of one hundred married couples in Fresno, California, by Leonarda Ybarra (1977 and 1982a and b), representing a broad cross section of the Chicano population, revealed a wide range of conjugal role patterns, but most couples shared in decision-making. The Mexican-American Study Project surveyed respondents in Los Angeles and San Antonio. Grebler, Moore, and Guzman found that sex, age, and income differences in conjugal roles were not significant and concluded, "The most striking finding relates not to internal variations in the departure from traditional sex specialization, but rather to the conspicuous presence of a basically *egalitarian* division of household tasks" (1970, pp. 362-63).

Similarly, Cromwell and Ruiz (1979) concluded on the basis of an intensive analysis of four major studies on decision-making within Mexican and Chicano families that the data did not support the hypothesis of male dominance. After an extensive review of literature on conjugal role relationships, Maxine Baca Zinn (1975b, p. 26) concluded that although the Chicano family is ostensibly patriarchal, it is in fact mother-centered. While the pattern may appear contradictory, it is not when one considers that each sex has primary responsibility in its respective sphere (Baca Zinn 1976, p 27). Men are generally delegated more power and authority relative to outside institutions, and women are primarily responsible for the daily affairs of the family.

The strong familistic orientation of the Chicano family has led some observers to conclude that it is an extended family much like the traditional Chinese family system. While Chicanos are familistic, the Chicano family is not a functioning extended system like the Chinese. (For a discussion of the traditional Chinese family see Levy 1968; Leslie 1973, pp. 80-122; Ho 1965; Lee 1953; and Huang 1976). In fact, for Chicanos the distinction between *casa* (household) and *familia* (relatives) is significant (Sena-Rivera 1977 and 1979). The father is formally head of the household, but as has been noted, much of the authority is more apparent than real. The concept that the oldest surviving male be recognized as the patriarchal head of the household is also not found in Chicano culture. Grandparents are more important as sources of warmth and support than as authority figures. While patterns of mutual aid and support are clearly established, nuclear families should ideally function as relatively autonomous and independent units. One may choose to live near parents and other relatives, or perhaps even with them out of economic necessity, but the norm is that the nuclear family remains autonomous in a separate residence (Grebler, Moore, and Guzman 1970, p. 355).

Though the mother has been depicted as a lowly and insignificant figure, she is extremely important in intrafamily relationships. Her relationships with children are characterized by warmth and affection. Whereas the father-son relationship is somewhat distant, the mother's relation with her daughter is more intimate. Early participation in the domestic realm often produced identification with the mother and her maternal role. "Little girls learn early to assume responsibilities and tasks, especially those that are particularly maternal in character, such as taking care of smaller siblings" (Peñalosa 1968, p. 687). In addition, "The confinement of females within the home gives rise to a closely knit group of a mother and her daughters, a relationship which perdures throughout the lifetime of the individuals" (Rubel 1966, p. 100). The same close environment gives rise to enduring relationships between sisters.

Although the mother-son relationship does not appear to be as strong as the mother-daughter relationship, it is nonetheless a close bond. During childhood she is more likely to be pampering and indulgent with her son than with a daughter. Especially during adolescence mothers are permissive with their sons. These socialization practices are indicative of a somewhat dualistic conception of appropriate behavior of males and females. Adolescent girls tend to be much more restricted and sheltered than adolescent boys (Rubel 1966, p. 77). The boy is frequently seen as a fledgling *macho* who must be allowed to venture out of the home so he may "test his wings" and establish a masculine identity. Peers contribute significantly to the process of socialization into manhood. He begins to hang out with other boys, or *la palomilla*, and peer relations may begin to rival family ties in importance. These associations are prominent for the man and are retained even after marriage.

Despite the persistence of social roles which severely circumscribe the behavior of the female there is evidence that these roles are undergoing change and modification (see Mirandé and Enríquez 1979). Many women, especially of the younger generation, are challenging their traditional roles. In urban areas Chicanitas are venturing beyond the protective confines of the home and joining social clubs or gangs, while others are pursuing higher education and professional careers. Thus the *palomilla*, or peer group, is no longer the exclusive domain of the male. Few contemporary Chicanas are willing to accept their traditional role, moreover. Many are seeking greater equality not only in the society at large but also within the Chicano community. Traditional male-female relations are undergoing change particularly among younger and better educated urban Chicanos. Many Chicanas are advocating changes that incorporate positive cultural values and permit "more flexibility in carrying out a greater variety of activities that traditionally have been denied her" (Murillo 1971, p. 106).

The Chicano family has thus been subjected to many of the same forces of change as the Anglo-American family. It has had to adapt to alterations resulting from increasing urbanization, industrialization, and acculturation. Middle-class urban Chicano families appear to be more equalitarian and to have discarded some of the more traditional features of the family, for example. Similarly, as the influence of the church declines, so may the importance of the institution of *compadrazgo*.

Recent research, however, suggests that changes within the Chicano family are not simply the result of assimilation and acculturation into American society. Mexican society, after all, is also undergoing urbanization and industrialization, and most people who migrate to the United States originated in urban areas and occupied nonagricultural occupations in Mexico (Barrera 1979, pp. 67-68). We have seen, moreover, that kinship patterns remain strong for Chicanos despite urbanization and industrialization.

There is also overwhelming evidence which challenges the myth of a monolithic patriarchy. "Virtually every systematic study of conjugal roles in the Chicano family has found egalitarianism to be the predominant pattern across socioeconomic groups, educational levels, urban-rural residence, and region of the country" (Staples and Mirandé 1980, p. 894).

The Chicano Family: Social and Demographic Characteristics

There are a number of structural and demographic features which distinguish the Chicano family from the dominant American form (U.S. Bureau of the Census 1984b). One distinctive feature is its high fertility relative not only to white but to black families (Alvirez and Bean 1976, pp. 280-81). "Ever-married Spanish-origin women in the United States have proportionately more children than non-Spanish origin women do, although the proportion having five or more children was greater in 1970 than in 1978 for both groups" (U.S. Bureau of the Census 1980, p. 8). In 1970 18 percent of the Spanish-origin women and 11 percent of the non-Spanish-origin women reported having five or more children, whereas in 1978 the figures were only 11 percent and 7 percent, respectively (ibid., p. 8). There has also been a corresponding increase in the proportion of married women of Spanish and non-Spanish origin who are childless. In 1978 the proportion of non-Spanish women who were childless was 19 and the proportion of Spanish-orgin childless women was 15, compared to 17 and 13 percent respectively in 1970 (ibid., p. 6). Thus, although Hispanic women still have more children, they are clearly having smaller families today than in the past. Largely because of higher fertility and lower life expectancy the Chicano population is a youthful one, with a median age of about 21 compared to a median of 31 for the rest of the population (U.S. Bureau of the Census 1981, p. 5). Chicanos average about four persons per family; other families average three (U.S. Bureau of the Census 1980, p. 12). Mexican-origin families are also larger than those of other Spanish-origin groups. Yet Hispanic women as a whole have more children than other women. The rate of births per 1,000 over the past year for women 18-44 was 83.6 for black, 68.1 for white, and 97.9 for Hispanic women (U.S. Bureau of the Census 1984a, p.6).

The vast majority of Chicano children under 18 years of age (80.2 percent) live with parents in intact families, 14.5 percent live with the mother, and only 1.8 percent live with the father (U.S. Bureau of the Census 1980, p. 46). Among black families 42 percent of the children under 18 lived with both parents, 47 percent lived with the mother, and 2 percent with the father (U.S. Bureau of the Census 1983b, p. 4). For white children 81 percent lived with both parents, 15 percent with the mother, and 2 percent with the father (ibid., pp. 4, 7). Chicano families are about as likely to be maintained by a woman (15 percent) as other Spanish-origin families (17 percent) or Anglo families, but they are far less likely to be maintained by a woman than black or Puerto Rican families (40 percent) (U.S. Bureau of the Census 1980, p. 12).

Not surprisingly, family income is substantially lower for Chicano families than for other families. The median income in 1982 for Mexican-origin families was $16,399. This was substantially lower than the median family income for Cuban families ($18,883) and families not of Spanish origin ($23,907), but higher than the income for Puerto Rican families ($11,148) (U.S. Bureau of the Census 1984b, p. 13). Twenty-two percent of all Mexican-origin families fell below the poverty level, whereas only 9 percent of families not of Spanish origin are classified as poor[2] (U.S. Bureau of the Census

1978b, p. 15). Spanish-origin families maintained by women were especially likely to be under the poverty level. Fifty-three percent of such families were poor, compared to only 12 percent of those with both husband and wife present (U.S. Bureau of the Census 1980, p. 16). Spanish-origin families below the poverty level were mostly larger families (4.05 persons per family) and those in which the person maintaining the family was not a high school graduate (78 percent) (ibid.).

The marital status of Chicanos does not differ significantly from the general population, with approximately 60 percent of the population in each group classified as married, but Chicanos have a higher proportion of single and a lower proportion of widowed or divorced persons (U.S. Bureau of the Census 1980, pp. 1-2). Thirty-four percent of all women of Mexican origin 14 years and over are single (never married), 60.9 percent married, 1.6 percent widowed, and 3.5 percent divorced (ibid., p. 2). The corresponding figures for men of Mexican origin are 28.2 percent single, 61.5 percent married, 5.8 percent widowed, and 4.5 percent divorced. Persons not of Spanish origin are somewhat more likely to be divorced (4.3 percent of the women and 6.0 percent of the men) than those of Spanish origin. Thus, while Chicanos are about as likely to be married as the general population, they are less likely to be divorced.

Although the growth in the divorce rate in the United States over the last decade or so has been striking, "there are no significant differences between the ratio increases for Black, White or Spanish origin" (U.S. Bureau of the Census 1983b, p. 3). For every 1,000 married spouse-present couples, black persons had 220 divorced persons and whites had 107. This represented a 165 percent increase for blacks since 1970 and a 143 percent increase for whites. For Spanish-origin persons the ratio was 118 per 1,000 in 1982 and only 61 per 1,000 in 1970 (ibid.). Thus, the divorce rate has increased dramatically for all groups, including Hispanics.

Since intermarriage has been presumed to be an important index of assimilation, there has been much interest in the outmarriage rates of Chicanos. The conclusions of earlier studies that intermarriage rates of Chicanos suggested a "breakdown of ethnic solidarity in an increasingly open system" (Grebler, Moore, and Guzman 1970, p. 471) have been called into question by more recent research. While the overall trend during the present century has been toward intermarriage in the Southwest (Bean and Bradshaw 1970, p. 393), the trend appears to have stabilized and, perhaps, reversed in recent years. Murguía and Frisbie (1977, p. 387) concluded after examining recent trends in intermarriage:

> . . . If the level of Spanish-surname intermarriage is conceived as the most conclusive, objective indicator of the degree of assimila-

tion. . . . it seems probable that the Mexican American population will continue to represent a distinct sociocultural entity for some time to come.

Even a cursory examination of history reveals that outmarriage between Mexicans and Anglos is not a new or recent phenomenon. Marriages between Anglo men and Mexican women were common even before 1848. Outmarriage was motivated by two principle forces. One was the sex ratio, given that there was a preponderance of Anglo men and a scarcity of white women. Intermarriage was also a mechanism used by Anglo males to marry into wealthy Mexican families and to acquire land. According to Carey McWilliams,

> . . . American, British, Scottish, German, and French adventurers . . . had infiltrated the province prior to 1846. There were only a hundred or so of these adventurers but they played a role of crucial importance at the time of the conquest. With scarcely a single exception, these curiously assorted characters had married daughters of the *gente de razón* after first joining the Catholic Church and accepting Mexican citizenship. Once related to the "best families" by marriage, they became eligible for land grants and were permitted to engage in trade. Embracing the daughters of the land, they also made a pretense of embracing its customs, adopting the prevailing style of dress and Hispanizing their surnames. At the time of the conquest, of course, they went over to the American side en masse, and in many cases, induced their in-laws to collaborate with those who were directing the American invasion. (McWilliams 1968, p. 90)

Interestingly, then, prior to the American take-over of the Southwest Anglo intermarriage often symbolized assimilation into Spanish and Mexican culture (Pitt 1966, p. 19). Some Anglos, such as Stephen Austin, even assumed Mexican first names (i.e., Esteban).

Patterns of intermarriage were not random or arbitrary, but selective. Intermarriage generally took place with Mexican women who were light-skinned and belonged to the upper classes (Acuña 1981, p. 41). Although most Mexican women did not intermarry, many in the elite social classes married Anglos. In San Antonio, for example, between 1837 and 1860

> . . . 906 Mexican women wed Mexican men, while only 88 chose to marry Anglos. But of those Anglo-Mexican unions almost half, or 42, involved women from high status families. The significance of those interracial marriages goes far beyond their numbers, since at least one daughter from every *rico* family in San Antonio married an Anglo. (Dysart 1976, p. 370)

While it is commonly asserted that mixed marriages created ethnic alliances, tensions among such families were not unusual. There was constant friction, for example, between Juan Bandini, his sons and daughters, and his three Anglo sons-in-law—Abel Stearns, Charles H. Johnson, and J. Cave Couts (see Pitt 1966, pp. 110-16).

Richard Griswold del Castillo found that prior to 1848 most of the foreigners who settled in Los Angeles married Mexican women and were incorporated into the California elite (1979, p. 74). Prior to the American takeover a large number of Anglos adopted local customs and became "Mexicanized gringos," but after the Gold Rush many of them held racist attitudes and were opposed to anything Mexican. Despite such antipathy intermarriage became increasingly more common after the war with Mexico. In the 1850s only one out of ten marriages was mixed, but by the early 1860s one out of three marriages was exogamous (Griswold del Castillo 1979, pp. 74-75). The rate of intermarriage increased considerably after 1864 and peaked in 1870, when 64.0 percent of the marriages were mixed. By 1875 only 11.2 percent of the marriages in Los Angeles were mixed (ibid., p. 76). Significantly, very few Mexican men married Anglo women; almost all exogamous marriages were between Anglo men and Mexican women.

Griswold del Castillo's findings must be interpreted with caution, however, for rates of intermarriage have traditionally been higher in Los Angeles than in other areas. Available data from 1850 to the present in three states suggest that the highest rates of exogamy are found in California and the lowest in Texas, with New Mexico occupying an intermediate position (Murguía 1982, p. 87). In Texas the highest recorded rate was 16 percent in Bexar County in 1973. "In New Mexico, the highest rate was 31 percent in Bernalillo County in 1967; in California, the highest rate was 38 percent for the entire state in 1962" (ibid.). This suggests that rates of exogamy may be higher in areas where there has been less isolation of the Chicano population and less open interethnic hostility. According to Grebler, Moore, and Guzman (1970, p. 407) "Contemporary Los Angeles is far less hostile to Mexican Americans and offers much greater economic opportunity than do most of the other large Southwest metropolitan communities." Although there has been a gradual trend toward increasing rates of exogamy, there was stabilization in the 1960s and 1970s, perhaps as an outgrowth of the Chicano movement.

Murguía introduces a "breaking of ties" theoretical framework which proposes that intermarriage is an indicator of assimilation into American life.

> . . . In this way of looking at majority and minority contacts, both minority and majority individuals are seen as being bound by sub-communal ties to generally homogeneous subsystems. The extent to which individuals of each group outmarry will depend on individual

characteristics encouraging contact with outgroups. (Murguía 1982, p. 60)

He found, for example, that several variables such as type of ceremony, sex, and generation are strongly related to exogamy (ibid., p. 105). Spanish-surnamed persons who marry in a Protestant or civilian ceremony, for example, are more likely to outmarry than those who marry in the Catholic Church. Spanish-surnamed women are more likely to be exogamous than Spanish-surnamed men, and second- or later-generation persons are more apt to be exogamous than those of the first generation. While metropolitan place of birth was significantly related to exogamy for women, it was not for men (ibid., p. 84).

The Chicano Family in Historical Context

Social scientists have approached the study of ethnic families with a melting-pot, immigrant-group model of American society. According to this model American society is composed of diverse ethnic groups who migrate freely to the United States. New arrivals may bring in different cultural values, but they inevitably are integrated into the melting pot. Recent immigrants also tend to be economically disadvantaged, but their position improves with time, according to this view. Ultimately, then, ethnic minorities are incorporated into the dominant culture and society.

Armed as they were with this assimilationist paradigm, it is not surprising that social scientists would see Chicanos as a curious anomaly. Chicanos did not join the melting pot but clung to their traditional culture and familial values. The Chicano family structure was thus seen as rigid and authoritarian in comparison to the egalitarian Anglo ideal, and parents were often considered their children's worst enemies because they hindered their achievement and advancement: in other words, because they were obstacles to assimilation and acculturation. The authors of the classic Mexican-American Study project, for instance, remarked that *machismo* inhibits the achievement of Chicano men (Grebler, Moore, and Guzman, p. 351). Familism, similarly, "deters collective and individual progress, however defined" (ibid.).

Traditional social scientists failed to recognize that Chicanos are native to the Southwest. They are not recent immigrants; their arrival in this region predates not only the founding of the United States as a nation but the landing of the Pilgrims at Plymouth Rock. Their initial entrance into the society, moreover, unlike other immigrant groups, was not voluntary.

Chicanos, however, have actively opposed the insidious oppressive conditions of internal colonialism, and the family has been a critical force in this opposition. In an environment where Chicano institutions have been rendered subordinate and dependent, the family has been the only institution to escape colonial intrusion. Whereas the black family was controlled and manipulated by slavery, the Chicano family has been relatively free of direct manipulation and control. The *macho* as titular head of the family is usually seen as actively combating acculturation and assimilation, but the woman is no less resistant. As the center of the family and the mainstay of the culture and its traditions, the Chicana has helped to counter the encroachment of colonialism. She prepetuates the language and values of Chicanos.

Another factor that has helped to stem the tide of colonialism is the proximity of Mexico to the United States. Chicano patterns of migration are not random or arbitrary. People tend to migrate to areas where they anticipate work or where relatives, friends, or acquaintances reside. This continual influx of new arrivals maintains and reinforces cultural bonds that resist the push toward integration and Americanization. Unlike European immigrants who found themselves isolated from a distant homeland, Chicanos are not far from their native roots. The influence of Mexican culture and the Spanish language are therefore ongoing. This is not to suggest that the Chicano family has been oblivious to change. The Chicano family is not a transplanted, traditional patriarchal Mexican family, but a dynamic and evolving unit. The family has changed and adapted to external conditions and structural forces in the United States, but such change has not simply resulted from assimilation and acculturation to American life.

In sum, it appears that the Chicano family has often been viewed as an impediment to democratic ideals and a counter force to the "American Way of Life" because it has resisted acculturation and assimilation. Thus, attacks on the family by social scientists and the public at large indicate that it has not been a "tangle of pathology," as we have been led to believe, but an institution that has worked only too well.

8

Machismo

The concept of *machismo*, once the almost exclusive domain of Mexican or Latino culture, has recently come into popular usage in American society. Though frequently mispronounced as "mako" or as "makizmo," it has undeniably penetrated American mass culture. Songs extolling the virtues of *machismo* have been written, and it is not uncommon for rock groups, movie stars, athletes, or other Anglo males to be ascribed *macho* qualities or termed "very *macho*". There is even a men's cologne called *Macho*, and *macho burritos* are available at local fast-food restaurants. In its contemporary usage *machismo* connotes masculinity, physical prowess, or male chauvinism, and its incorporation into mass culture suggests that these qualities are not without substantial market appeal.

The popular usage of *machismo* might appear to be an extension of traditional *mexicano*-Chicano usage, but a more careful examination suggests that these are not only disparate but completely incongruous terms. This chapter examines various meanings and connotations of *machismo* and focuses especially on differences between Anglo and Chicano conceptions. It also seeks to dispel numerous myths and misconceptions about the term and to articulate a perspective on *machismo* that is consistent not only with the equalization of sex roles in the Chicano community but with the liberation of all Chicanos from cultural oppression. In the process the association of *machismo* with Latino male dominance, violence, and criminality will hopefully be called into question.

The Pathological View of *Machismo*

Traditional social-science depictions of *machismo*, as previously noted, typically equate this concept with irresponsibility, inferiority, and ineptitude (Montiel 1970; Baca Zinn 1975a). Beyond being a cultural trait, *machismo* is viewed as a pathological force that pervades and colors all aspects of social life, especially relations between the sexes.

If it is not the prototype of pathological studies, then certainly Octavio Paz's *The Labyrinth of Solitude* (1961) is one of the most influential discussions

165

of *machismo*. In this classic treatise on Mexican national character Paz traces the Mexican's feeling of inferiority to the spiritual rape and Conquest of Mexico. According to Paz (1961, p. 74) "All of our anxious tensions express themselves in a phrase we use when anger, joy or enthusiasm cause us to exalt our condition as Mexicans: ¡*Viva México, hijos de la chingada!*" The battle cry is shouted on September 15, Independence Day, as an affirmation of ourselves to anonymous "others"; the sons of the Great Whore. The phrase is at once self-affirmation and self-deprecation in that all Mexicans are acknowledged as sons of a mythical mother, *La Chingada*.

La Chingada is the violated mother who was forcibly penetrated by the conquering Spaniard. The *macho* is the *Gran Chingón* who rips open and violates the woman. The verb *chingar* is emotionally charged and imbued with multiple meanings and nuances. It can refer to an aggressive form of sexual intercourse, but the term may also denote failure. Despite its multiple meanings *chingar* always connotes violence—"an emergence from oneself to penetrate another by force" (Paz 1961, p. 76). It may imply ripping someone open by force, violation, or deception. Accordingly, all women, even when they give themselves willingly, are torn open by the man. The aggressiveness, insensitivity, and unpredictability of the *macho* is best symbolized by the word power. He is not only powerful but unpredictable as he goes about committing *chingaderas* and in so doing rips up the world.

The *Chingada* is symbolized in Mexican folklore by *La Malinche*, or Doña Marina, a young Indian woman who served as Hernan Cortés' translator and concubine during the conquest and who persists in Mexican and Chicano culture as an infamous emblem of female transgression and treachery (see Mirandé and Enríquez 1979, pp. 24–31). The historical facts are that she was given to Cortés as a slave at the tender age of fourteen and that she proved to be a brilliant and articulate woman who played a crucial role in the shaping of history, having won the respect of Spaniards and Indians alike. Yet popular Mexican and Chicano folklore has labeled her a traitress, a whore, and the mother of a bastard *mestizo* race. She is called a traitress because she gave herself to the conqueror, thereby humiliating and emasculating the male. *La Malinche* also represents the many Indian women who were fascinated, seduced, or otherwise violated by the Spaniards. Even today *malinchistas* are persons who betray their people or who advocate Mexico's opening itself to foreigners.

The cult of *machismo*, according to this tradition, has its origin in the Conquest of Mexico (for a discussion of this theme see Paredes 1967). Unable to protect women from the raping and plundering which ensued after the conquest, Mexican men developed an overly masculine and aggressive response to suppression. The cult of *machismo* is thus seen as a compensation for powerlessness and weakness which becomes manifest as the impotent, powerless, colonized man turns his frustration and aggression inward toward his wife and family. Ultimately *machismo* is but a futile attempt to prove one's masculinity.

Social scientists have assumed that the pathological psychoanalytic model described by Paz, Ramos, and others also holds for Chicanos. Depictions of a *macho*-dominated, authoritarian Mexican-American family prevail in the literature, although, as noted in the foregoing chapter, such depictions typically lack empirical support.

William Madsen's classic study *The Mexican-American of South Texas* (1973) is representative of pathological views of Chicano culture and *machismo*. According to Madsen (1973, pp. 20–25) *machismo* ranks second in importance in Chicano culture only to devotion to family. Mexican-American men are subjected to a continual drive to live up to the demands of *machismo*, which entails demonstrating that men are stronger, smarter, and vastly superior to women in all spheres of life. Before he is considered a "real man," the male must command respect from others for himself and his family. Honor and respect are thus critical components of *machismo*, as are drinking capacity, physical prowess, and virility. The male is also likened to a rooster so that "the better man is the one who has the most girl friends; if married, the one who deceives his wife most" (Madsen 1973, p. 22). The *macho's* counterpart is the quiet and submissive Mexican-American woman. "Where he is strong, she is weak. Where he is aggressive, she is submissive. While he is condescending toward her, she is respectful toward him" (Madsen 1973, p. 22). The Latin woman is so awed by her husband that she always honors, respects, and obeys him, despite his extramarital transgressions.

The *macho* demands complete allegiance, respect, and obedience not only from his wife but from his children as well. A child's relationship with the father, especially in the case of male children, is said to be characterized by formality, deference, and respect. There is perhaps no greater sin than showing disrespect toward one's father. Madsen (1973) asserts that "ideally, the Latin male acknowledges only the authority of his father and God. In case of conflict between these two sources of authority, he should side with his father" (p. 20). Although fathers are imbued with power and authority, theirs is a distant authority, and the relationship between parents and children is described as formal and distant. The authoritarian, father-dominant Chicano family structure presumably creates dependence, stifles normal personality development, and discourages achievement in children.

Grebler, Moore, and Guzman (1970) come to essentially the same conclusion. After examining the adverse effects of both the black matriarchy and the Chicano patriarchy, the authors conclude, "There may be a process common to lower-class and especially minority lower-class families—whether they are traditionally patriarchal or matriarchal, clannish or disorganized, weak or strong—that presses toward the emergence of a basically similar low-achieving man" (p. 369).

At the same time that many social scientists assert that the cult of *machismo* engenders passivity and dependence within the family, they also assert that it leads to aggressive, violent behavior outside the family. The adolescent male continually needs to prove or validate his masculinity outside of the home—to test his wings so to speak. The peer group becomes crucial to the process of asserting or demonstrating one's masculinity. A premium is placed, for example, on proving one's toughness and manhood by drinking, fighting, and demonstrating sexual prowess. Given this emphasis on violence and aggression, social scientists conclude that it is not surprising that Mexican-American males frequently run afoul of the law.

Rudoff has explained that the preponderance of delinquency among Chicano youth stems from familial and cultural values which are endemic to Chicanos. Cultural emphasis on *envidia* (envy), *falso* (hypocrisy), and *machismo* (manliness), for example, impede both the more normative acculturation process or treatment processes for incarcerated delinquents. With respect to *machismo* Rudoff (1971) asserts:

> The Mexican-American subculture maintains a sharp delineation in sex roles. Beginning with adolescence and throughout the life of the male, he is socialized to be a *macho*. *Machismo* (manliness) is measured primarily by sexual prowess and secondarily by physical strength and courage (p. 226)

Chicano criminality is thus a natural by-product of the cultural emphasis on aggressive and violent behavior among males. According to Heller (1966), in acting out his role as protector and guardian for younger siblings, the Mexican-American boy tends to "commit acts which bring him to the attention of the police" (p. 35). Going a step further, she suggests that delinquent Mexican-Americans are actually overconforming to a cultural pattern (p. 76).

Although carefully cloaked in the jargon of social science, a more recent study (Stumphauzer, Aiken, and Veloz 1977) further develops the theme of criminality as inherent to Chicano culture and the Chicano community. Commenting on earlier analyses, the authors observe:

> . . . What we believe is being missed, and what we hope to focus on is the whole behavioral ecology of a high juvenile crime community. We find it necessary, after attempting to work in one such area, to first understand how delinquent behavior is being taught and learned throughout a community. (p. 76)

Without focusing on *machismo* per se, many of its classic and stereotypical components are revealed in their use of *"mi vida loca"* ("my crazy life"). This gang concept becomes the key explanatory variable for what are termed "behavioral excesses" among youth in the community. The *vato*, or street dude, sees himself as crazy and willing to do practically anything to gain acceptance from peers regardless of risks involved. There is an emphasis on fatalism, danger, and getting maximum excitement and enjoyment out of life today. " 'Mi Vida Loca' usually has a violent connotation, meaning that the individual conducting his life accordingly is willing to put himself in maximum risk situations such as risks of personal freedom (as with conflict with the police), or those situations in which the risk may involve the potential loss of his life (drug abuse, gang violence, etc.)" (p. 81).

Nowhere is the association of Chicano cultural values, especially *machismo*, and adult criminality made more explicit than in R. Theodore Davidson's *Chicano Prisoners: The Key to San Quentin* (1974). The major thesis of Davidson's book, as suggested by the title, is that Chicano prisoners hold the "key" to a full understanding of prisoner culture throughout California because the third and deepest level of that culture is controlled by Chicanos, particularly the Mexican Mafia, or *Familia*. Undergirding the strength, integrity, and organizational success of Family is a cultural emphasis on *machismo*.

> . . . Family actions accord with the highest ideals of *machismo*; they are honest and moral when viewed from within the prisoner culture. . . . Chicanos have a firmly established reputation for their willingness and ability to engage in violence. With its strong emphasis on the ideals of *machismo*, the seriousness of most of its activities, and the necessity to maintain secrecy, Family has increased that reputation. . . . With Family, the pattern of violence is even more extreme than among Chicano prisoners. . . . Family violence does not stop halfway—with the knifing of an opponent; it goes all the way—to the death of the non-family individual. (pp. 82–83)

Potential members must demonstrate their *machismo* beyond doubt. A prerequisite to membership in Family, according to Davidson, is to have killed, or "hit," someone and to have done so in a *macho* manner (p. 86).

While the thesis that Chicano prisoners are honorable, honest, powerful, righteous, and manly has considerable appeal in that it presents a romanticized and idealized conception of valued cultural traits, a more careful examination reveals a view of Chicano culture that is negative, if not openly pejorative. Davidson (1974), for example, sees drug use as endemic to the culture when he asserts "Marijuana is culturally accepted by the majority of Chicanos—much like the teen-age and later use of cigarettes are in the Anglo culture" (p. 66). While acknowledging that heroin is not as widely approved in the Chicano community, use of heavy drugs is accepted by many Chicanos, and within the peer group it is defined as very *macho*. The use and sale of drugs, moreover, becomes a way of maintaining one's *machismo* in an Anglo-dominated society; "And, if they should be caught, doing time in prison as a real convict, although an unpleasant experience, is a very *macho* thing" (p. 68). Thus, Davidson would have us believe that being in prison is not really all that bad and that, by implication, some Chicanos might even prefer to be incarcerated, since they obviously have much more power and prestige within prison and can more readily retain their *machismo* than on the outside.

In a more recent work, *Homeboys: Gangs, Drugs, and Prison in the Barrios of Los Angeles*, Joan Moore (1978), unlike Davidson, de-emphasizes the role of *machismo* as a key explanatory variable, noting that while "both machismo and the convict code have long been cited to explain Chicano convict behavior . . . neither idea is necessary for the sociological understanding of prison norms as they affect men from the barrio" (1978, p. 218). Although not openly pejorative, Moore likewise links Chicano gangs, drugs, and prison behavior to one another and to the sociocultural context of the barrio, thereby implying that gang life is endemic to Chicano culture. Commenting on early studies of rural communities, she notes that,

> There is some hint about the precursors of Chicano urban gangs in the portrayals of young male sociability groups in the small rural towns of South Texas (Madsen 1964; Rubel 1966). The *palomilla* (literally, "flock of doves") are a group of young men who cheerfully go from one village to another, drinking, dating, and raiding. Fights are a considerable part of the fun. (1978, p. 42)

While Moore cautions against the suggestion that urban gangs "are a simple importation of such cultural items" (1978, p. 42), activities such as drinking and fighting do seem to be culturally determined.

Moore identifies three distinctive features shared in common by Chicano gangs in Los Angeles, El Paso, and other large cities: (1) a territorial base, so that the word for gang and for neighborhood is identical, (2) age grading, so that a new "Klika," or cohort, emerges about every two years, and (3) fighting and the use of drugs. She states unequivocally, "all Chicano gangs are fighting gangs—and most, if not all, use drugs" (1978, p. 36). The gang is also seen as a specialized structure of the barrio (like the neighborhood church) that "cannot be understood outside the whole barrio and the ethnic context" (1978, p. 36). Perhaps what is most sorely lacking in Moore's analysis is the identification of large segments within the barrio that eschew gang violence and decry barrio warfare. Moore does offer a fourfold typology of career types which consist of one "deviant" and three types of "squares." The first two types are squares who live in the barrios of Los Angeles: one is the new immigrant to East Los Angeles, and the other is the native who cannot make it in the Anglo system. The third type is the barrio-oriented deviant whose primary reference group is the gang during adolescence and the *pinto-tecato* (prisoner-junkie) network in adulthood. Finally, there is the square who leaves the barrio and enters the dominant Anglo society, who could be termed "the successful Chicano," or noncolonized non-Chicano. The point is that there is no room in Moore's typology for a Chicano to be "normal" (i.e., neither square nor deviant).

Since pathological views associate *machismo* with aggression, violence, and proneness to criminality, it is not surprising to find that the concept is also linked to rape. The *macho*, after all, has little regard for women; he treats them with disdain and contempt, disregarding their needs and concerns as human beings. Women are objects to be used for the gratification of the male. In one of the most complete, comprehensive, and influential compilations of information on the topic of rape, Susan Brownmiller (1975) develops the thesis that rape is the outgrowth of *macho* attitudes which are prevalent among the lower socioeconomic classes and among racial minorities. Brownmiller argues that there is a "subculture of violence" among the disadvantaged. Despite the protestations of more liberal or radical theorists

> . . . there is no getting around the fact that most of those who engage in antisocial, criminal violence (murder, assault, rape and robbery) come from the lower socioeconomic classes. . . .
> We are not talking about Jean Valjean, who stole a loaf of bread in *Les Misérables*, but about physical aggression as "a demonstration of masculinity and toughness" . . . the prime tenet of the subculture of violence. Or, to use a current phrase, the *machismo* factor. Allegiance or conformity to *machismo*, particularly in a group or gang, is the *sine qua non* of status, reputation and identity for lower-class male youth. Sexual aggression, of course, is a major part of *machismo*. (p. 181).

A less extreme, but equally stereotypical, view of *machismo* is articulated by Janet Saltzman Chafetz. She points out that gender-role stereotypes vary by class position, region, and race and ethnicity.

> . . . more than most other Americans, the various Spanish-speaking groups in this country (Mexican-American, Puerto Rican, Cuban) stress domesticity, passivity, and other stereotypical feminine traits, and dominance, aggressiveness, physical prowess, and other stereotypical masculine traits. Indeed, the masculine gender role for this group is generally described by reference to the highly stereotyped notion of *machismo*. In fact, a strong emphasis on masculine aggressiveness and dominance may be characteristic of most groups in the lower ranges of the socioeconomic ladder. (1978, p. 47)

A Reassessment of Machismo

The negative, pejorative views of Chicano culture and *machismo* which prevail in much of social-science literature suggest that there is a definite need for a reevaluation and reinterpretation of the term from a Chicano perspective. This is particularly true when one observes a marked contrast in its application to Anglo males in the mass media. Without discarding the concept or denying its existence in Mexican-Chicano culture, such a reinterpretation would hopefully provide a more undistorted and sympathetic view which is consistent with the sociohistorical realities of the Chicano experience in U.S. society. In fact, it appears both ironic and fitting that much of the push to redefine *machismo* should come, not from men, but from the alleged victim of male oppression, the Mexican-American woman. Perhaps it was inevitable that a more contemporary and serious reexamination and reevaluation of the traditional role of *la mujer* would also necessitate a new look at the male role. The quiet, submissive, saintly, chaste Chicana has, after all, been the stereotypical analogue to the all-powerful, domineering, insensitive, and sexually permissive male.

Adaljiza Sosa Riddell's (1974) reexamination of sex roles in the Chicano community adopts a colonial model, but not one that is pathological or condescending as is the case in traditional views of *machismo*. She observes that as a colonized people, in Mexico and the United States, Chicanos as well as Mexicans have had very little control over their self-images or cultural definitions and that male-female relations have been distorted and stereotyped by social scientists. Even more disturbing, she argues, is that many Chicanos and Chicanas have in turn internalized these negative self-images and cultural stereotypes. Contemporary *machismo*, accordingly, is a myth perpetrated on Chicanos by the Anglo colonizer who first emasculates the colonized man and then takes pleasure in watching him try to prove his masculinity. Our own experiences, however, contradict such stereotypical views:

> . . . Within each of our memories there is the image of a father who worked long hours, suffered to keep his family alive, united, and who struggled to maintain his dignity. Such a man had little time for concern over his "masculinity." Certainly he did not have ten children because of his machismo, but because he was a human being, poor, and without "access" to birth control. We certainly remember mothers and sisters who worked in the fields or at menial labor in addition to doing the work required at home to survive. (p. 156)

Such positive and nontraditional depictions as these are found not only in Chicana research but in Chicana literature as well. In a poem, "Eulogy

For A Man From Jalostitlan," Rita Gutierrez-Christensen (1976) describes her father's death during a trip to Mexico. He had failed to take medicine for a heart condition. The poem unveils a warm relationship between a father and his four daughters, a man who was undoubtedly *macho* in the best sense of the word.

> He returned three weeks later
> In a Mexican coffin,
> Dressed in an elegant Mexican suit
> (He always liked nice clothes.)
> A trace of a smile on his face
> And the bottle of pills unopened . . .
>
> Our girlfriends complained of whippings,
> Spying by older brothers.
> Our father never touched us.
> He talked instead and if that failed,
> He could always rely on his tsz, tsz,
> A sound he made with his tongue
> And the roof of his mouth.
> And so we were brought to reason. . . .

Recent social-science research also questions the view of the father as being cold, insensitive, and unfeeling (see Mejia 1976; Luzod and Arce 1979; Baca Zinn 1982a; Burrows 1980).

Other poems suggest that warmth and compassion can pervade relations not only between father and daughter but between a man and woman. Angela de Hoyos' short poem "Words Unspoken" addresses the issue of male dominance directly and reveals considerable insight into male-female relations among colonized people. The poem suggests that if the colonized woman appears conquered, her "submission" may be more knowing and willing than one would surmise from more unidimensional and stereotypical accounts.

> You may boast that in your prison
> You have locked me for no reason
> Save the fact that in your house
> there shouts a man
>
> and I'll stay—NOT to add glory,
> O my conqueror, to your story—
> but because my instinct tells me
> that perhaps

> underneath all that bravado
> quakes a hopeless desperado
> who longs to win a battle
> now and then.
> (1977, p. 3)

Virginia Granado is more direct in her praise and admiration of the *macho*; the *vato* or *pachuco* of the *barrio*. Her positive view of *machismo* focuses more on attributes such as cultural pride, dignity, and integrity than on violence or the subordination of women. *Machismo*, moreover, is used to connote resistance to cultural oppression and subordination.

> El es uno de los pachucos that have refused to fall—. . . .
> His shoulders, they carry that pride, wisdom,
> that machismo that we of "La Nueva Raza" are
> discovering now . . . his was always there. . . .
> He was there the time of the "zoot suits," he was
> there when they weren't allowed to eat in restaurants . . .
> He's here now that we're trying to change things.
>
> I know he's glad . . . but if only I had listened,
> if only I had listened, I would've heard
> him teach me of my gente long ago.
> For the beauty of my culture which he has kept alive
> in me. . . .   (1974, p. 37)

Attempts to redefine *machismo* have not been limited to poetic expression but also extend to Chicano social scientists who are making efforts to cast it in a more positive light. Some Chicano social scientists suggest, for example, that it is not a pathological force that rules the actions of an impotent and powerless colonized man, but rather an active expression of resistance to oppression. Maxine Baca Zinn (1975a, p. 23) argues "that aggressive behavior of Chicano males has been both an affirmation of Mexican cultural identity and an expression of their conscious rejection of the dominant society's definition of Mexicans as passive, lazy, and indifferent." The view of *machismo* as a compensation for inferiority, whether its ulitmate cause is seen as external or internal to the oppressed, is consistent with a colonial mentality in that it blames Chicanos for their own subordination (Baca Zinn 1975a, p. 25). She further suggests that the positive dimensions of *machismo* will be unearthed only when social scientists begin to examine the way Chicanos themselves define the concept.

Another reinterpretation contends that for Chicanos *machismo* is not so much the expression of male pride as it is the political expression of an ethnic identity that transcends gender. Armando Rendon, for example, perceives it as symbolic of peoplehood or nationalism:

... The essence of machismo, of being macho, is as much a symbolic principle of the Chicano revolt as it is a guideline for the conduct of family life, male-female relationships, and personal self-esteem. ... The Chicano revolt is a manifestation of Mexican Americans exerting their manhood and womanhood against the Anglo society. Macho, in other words, can no longer relate merely to manhood but must relate to nationhood as well. (1972, p. 104)

Baca Zinn (1975a) has sought to develop the concept of "political familism," arguing that the Chicano cultural emphasis on familism is consistent with political activism and that the Chicano movement holds the potential not only for decolonizing Anglo-Chicano relations but for bringing about an end to sexual domination within the culture. Political familism entails the fusion of cultural and political resistance into "a process of cultural and political activism which involves the participation of total family units in movements for liberation" (p. 16). Other writers lend further support to the thesis that familism is a critical element in Chicano political participation. After analyzing Chicano political organizations, Tirado found that one of the keys to the success and longevity of such groups has been a provision for total family involvement, either by establishing women's or youth auxiliaries or by having regular social functions in which all members could take part (1970, p. 74). The more recent successes of the farmworkers in California and La Raza Unida Party in Texas are attributable, at least in part, to total family participation in these movements.

In "Chicano Men and Masculinity" Baca Zinn presents an extensive review of the literature on *machismo* and Chicano male roles. Perhaps its most significant contribution is to seriously question "the assumption that male dominance among Chicanos is exclusively a cultural phenomenon" (1982a, p. 40). Although she agrees that the concept of *machismo* has been maligned and stereotyped in traditional social-science research, positive refutations of such stereotypical characterization have tended to focus exclusively on cultural interpretations of the phenomenon and have neglected structural explanations. They therefore are unable to explain changes in sex roles over time or ethnic differences in definitions of masculinity. Baca Zinn (1982a, pp. 34–35) poses the following questions:

1. What specific social conditions are associated with variation in gender roles among Chicanos?
2. If there are ethnic differences in gender roles, to what extent are these a function of shared beliefs and orientations (culture) and to what extent are they a function of men's and women's place in the network of social relationships (structure)?
3. To what extent are gender roles among Chicanos more segregated and male dominated than among other social groups?

4. How does ethnicity contribute to the subjective meaning of masculinity (and femininity)?

Baca Zinn suggests, moreover, "That masculine roles and masculine identity may be shaped by a wide range of variables having less to do with culture than with common structural position" (ibid., p. 35). The class position of Chicanos has had a significant impact on normative and behavioral components of masculinity. Rather than viewing *machismo* in exclusively cultural terms, it is possible to see it as a response to the position of Chicanos in the stratification system and their exclusion from public roles within the dominant society. White males, she argues, have generally had more roles open to them and, hence, more sources of identity.

> . . . However, this has not been the case for Chicanos or other men of color. Perhaps manhood takes on greater importance for those who do not have access to socially valued roles. Being male is one sure way to acquire status when other roles are systematically denied by the workings of society. This suggests that an emphasis on masculinity is not due to a collective internalized inferiority, noted in a subcultural orientation. To be "hombre" may be a reflection of both ethnic and gender components and may take on greater significance when other roles and sources of masculine identity are structurally blocked. Chicanos have been excluded from participation in the dominant society's political-economic system. Therefore, they have been denied resources and the accompanying authority accorded men in other social categories. (Baca Zinn 1982a, p. 39)

While Baca Zinn has made a valuable contribution by pointing to structural forces and conditions that shape gender roles, her conceptualization is not without its own pitfalls. Her emphasis on structural variables, specifically class, is such that it virtually negates the impact of culture. How, for example, would one explain the pervasiveness of the ideology of *machismo* across social classes in Mexico and the United States? How also would a class analysis account for the prevalence of male dominance among white middle- and upper-class males? An additional conceptual difficulty is the use of male dominance, masculinity, gender segregation and stratification, masculine roles, and *machismo* interchangeably without defining these terms. Her perspective appears to be based on a negative conception which equates *machismo* with male dominance and the subordination and exploitation of women. But to see it simply as male dominance is to fail to grasp the significance of this cultural phenomenon. Such a conceptualization is incapable of recognizing that *machismo* is a value that transcends both gender and national boundaries. The value persists among *raza* on both sides of the border, and it is found among women as well. *Hembrismo* ("femaleness") is the female equivalent of *machismo*, and *la hembra* (the "female") is the feminine counterpart of *el macho* (Delgado 1974–75, p. 6).

This critique is intended neither to justify male dominance nor to minimize its prevalence. Male dominance is present in the Chicano community, but it is not peculiar to that community. Male dominance, moreover, has little, if anything, to do with *machismo* or masculinity. One can be dominant over women and not be *macho*, and one can certainly be *muy hombre* without abusing or controlling them. Mahatma Gandhi, as a case in point, exemplified positive *macho* qualities such as courage, honor, and integrity without dominating women and while remaining celibate for at least part of his life. Abelardo Delgado stated it well.

> It is only fair that I proceed to counter gringo interpretations (and those of some mixed-up Chicano carnales and carnalas as well) about machismo. A man who beats up his wife is not a macho, but a coward and an abuzon. A man who steps out on his old lady and has extramarital affairs is not a macho but a sinverguenza, two-timing bato. A man who gets plastered, stoned or pulls a knife on his compas for no reason at all is not a macho but a drunk and troublemaker. These and other such attributes have been erroneously labeled as displays of Machismo . . . it is time we correct false stereotypes which eventually are believd even by us. (Delgado 1974–75, p. 6)

Vicente T. Mendoza would label such behavior as "false" manifestations of *machismo*. Genuine *machismo* is characterized by true bravery or valor, courage, generosity, and ferocity, while false *machismo* uses the appearance or semblance of these traits to mask cowardliness and fear (1962, pp. 75–86).

While male dominance is virtually a universal trait, what may be unique to Mexican and Chicano culture is the division of the universe into masculine and feminine components and the elevation of *machismo* to the level of a national character trait or cultural world view. According to Américo Paredes

> Los ingredientes del machismo se encuentran en muchas culturas. Sin embargo, lo que se ha observado en México es todo un patrón de conducta, una filosofía popular se podría decir. ¿Será México único en este respeto? (1967, 72–73)

> The ingredients of machismo are found in many cultures. Nonetheless, what has been observed in Mexico is a whole code of conduct, a popular philosophy, one might say. Is Mexico unique in this respect?

Abelardo Delgado contends, moreover, that perhaps the most positive of the *macho* characteristics is a noncompromising nature. "This does not mean a macho does not change his mind or that he doesn't bargain on a trade or issue, but he does this before arriving at a noncompromising level from which he is immovable even if it costs his life" (1974–75, p. 6)

Conclusion: *Machismo* and Decolonization

Traditional social science has viewed *machismo* as a pathological force that controls the behavior and culture of Mexicans and Chicanos, an attempt by the colonized man to compensate for feelings of inferiority by trying to prove his masculinity via excessive demonstration of force and violence (see Delgado 1974–75; Mirandé 1982a; Baca Zinn 1982a). While such characterizations oftentimes appear sympathetic, especially when the source of oppression is viewed as external to the colonized, they ultimately advance the interests of the dominant group by shifting emphasis away from external oppression to deficiencies within the culture and psyche of the conquered group (Baca Zinn 1975a, p. 25).

A well-established principle of colonization, both the classic and internal variety, is that the process involves much more than physical, political, and economic exploitation and subordination; it involves cultural control as well. Internally colonized groups lack power and control over institutions which are vital to their existence (see Moore 1970; Acuña 1972; Barrera, Muñoz, and Ornelas 1972; Blauner 1969, 1972; and Almaguer 1971). The church, the school, the economy, and the political system are subject to external control and administration. Even more important, the mass media and publishing outlets are also externally controlled. This becomes especially critical for Chicanos, since in an internally colonized setting, as compared to classic colonialism, there is less emphasis on direct physical control and manipulation and more on indirect symbolic control. While force remains an important mechanism of control, more sophisticated and indirect methods have evolved. One such mechanism, the mobilization of bias, was discussed previously. Through it the manipulation of symbols in the media and the schools perpetuate myths concerning the inferiority of Chicanos (Barrera et al. 1972, p. 490).

The inherent danger in this process is that Chicanos have to function in Anglo-controlled institutions, are surrounded by externally manipulated symbols, and are inevitably pressured to internalize negative images of themselves and their culture. They are, moreover, pressured to seek Anglo approval for their actions. This creates a vicious cycle when the colonized adopts the world view of the colonizer and may even become a suboppressor of his own people.

The major point of all this is that not only Anglo but even Chicano conceptions of *machismo* must be understood within a colonial context.[1] The traditional social-science view of *machismo* is necessarily negative and condescending, for, despite its trappings, its ultimate aim is to blame the problems of the colonized on defects or shortcomings in their own culture. Attempts to describe Chicanos as dominant, controlling, violent, or prone to criminality are dangerous even when presented as positive and romanticized cultural traits by Chicanos themselves. They are, in fact, more dangerous precisely because they appear benign or even positive and are therefore more likely to be internalized. When Chicanos internalize and espouse negative and stultifying views of *machismo*, the mobilization of bias has come full circle as negative caricatures of Chicanos give way to positive ones. What greater testimony could be given for the veracity of externally induced stereotypes than to have them internalized and articulated as positive cultural attributes by the group in question.

But surely *machismo* must be more than an Anglo stereotype. Is there not a real process in Chicano culture that can be described as *machismo* without being caricatured or stereotyped? In a very real sense *machismo* is both a stereotype and a real cultural process; or stated another way, it has both authentic and stereotypical components. Yet the components are totally separable only in an analytic sense, because to the extent that stereotypes are defined as real and internalized they are incorporated into the culture. Cultural processes, on the other hand, are not immutable or irreversible. To the contrary, if colonized people are to be decolonized, it becomes imperative that they take an active part in demythicizing their experiences and in redefining themselves and their culture.

Part of this process entails recognition of *machismo* as an important component of the culture, not simply a negative and pathological force, as many social scientists would have us believe, but as a positive force that has served to resist cultural genocide. *Machismo* is ultimately a symbol of the resistance of Chicanos to colonial control, both cultural and physical. It symbolizes the pride, dignity, and tenacity of the Chicano people as they have resisted the onslaught of economic, political, and cultural control. It symbolizes, most importantly, resistance to acculturation and assimilation into Anglo society. If the term is associated with the male and with masculinity, it is not because he has more actively resisted acculturation and assimilation, but perhaps because his resistance has been more visible and manifest.

The *pachuco* has been an especially visible symbol of cultural autonomy and resistance. His distinctive dress, demeanor, mannerisms, and language not only express his manhood but set him off culturally from the dominant society. To be a *chuco* is to be proud, dignified, and to uphold one's personal integrity as well as the honor and integrity of the group. It is at once an affirmation of one's manhood and one's culture.

Critics might counter, however, that this is nothing more than a glorified and romantic position that veils or begs the question of Chicano violence. Can we ignore the daily violence in the barrios of the Southwest or minimize its importance? While violence should not be ignored, neither should we blindly accept the stereotype of Chicanos as an inherently violent people. No conclusive evidence has been advanced supporting the position that Chicanos are more prone to violence than other groups. The position, moreover, is essentially a racist one reminiscent of nineteenth-century evolutionist theories which saw violence and criminality as biologically inherited traits.

The alleged violence and criminality of Chicanos should be reexamined from a colonial perspective. Colonized people are typically victims of direct and indirect forms of violence, and what is perceived as violence by Chicanos is frequently a response to such victimization.

Chicanos are no more prone to violence than Anglo-Americans. Violence takes different forms for different groups, and perceptions of the proclivity to violence also vary. Chicanos are not more violent, but they are perceived as more violent because they lack the power to fashion and control the symbols that shape public opinion. It is the Anglo-controlled media which manipulates, shapes, and colors many of our views and attitudes on issues such as gang violence, Chicano criminality, and the Mexican Mafia. Even when the issue of Chicano violence is not directly addressed, the media can reinforce the belief that Chicanos are violent by focusing on stories that feature violent or disruptive activities (e.g., gang violence, protests, confrontations with police). Chicanos do kill one another, and gang violence is a persistent feature of barrio life; but so do other groups in the society, and Anglo violence is no less persistent. The difference, then, lies not in Chicanos being more violent, but in public perceptions and conceptions of violence. Not only is there more media interest and coverage of Chicanos' presumed criminality but such activities are defined as a group or collective phenomenon; the same activities by Anglos are defined as isolated individual acts. Anglo violence may be as rampant in the media, but it is not defined as Anglo violence; it is simply violence.

Just as violence and criminality among Chicanos have been exaggerated and distorted in the media, so has the extent of male dominance. While male dominance is undoubtedly a persistent cultural trait, the real issue is not whether Chicano culture has been male dominant, but whether male dominance is peculiar to Latino culture or, instead, is an almost universal feature of human societies. A related issue is the extent to which male dominance has been transformed from an idealized cultural trait to a pathological force or malady.

The view of the Chicano male as powerful, assertive, and dominant, and of the woman as weak, docile, and submissive, is now being challenged (see chapter seven). Few persons who have grown up in a Chicano family would see the woman as weak, quiet, or submissive, for if there is a persistent image of *la mujer* in the culture, it is that she is strong, enduring, and integral to the functioning of *la familia*. The father may formally be accorded respect and importance, but his power may also be more apparent than real.

This chapter has sought to redefine *machismo* and to suggest a perspective on the concept that is not only positive and consistent with the nuances and complexities of Chicano culture but that captures the essence of the oppressive relationship which exists between Chicanos and the dominant society. Such a redefinition is essential given the prevalence of negative and pathological views of *machismo* and the mobilization of bias which places Chicanos in a defensive posture and leads us to internalize negative images about ourselves and our culture. While the discussion is not intended to be definitive or conclusive, the rejection and redefinition of negative self-images of a people is an important first step in the process of decolonization and liberation.

PART III

Theoretical Perspectives

9

Critique and Synthesis

Much of the social-science literature on Mexican-Americans, especially prior to 1970, has been based, overtly or covertly, on an assimilationist model of race and ethnic relations. This prevailing model is now being challenged not only by the colonial perspective which rejects the view of Chicanos as an immigrant group in favor of a conquest model but, more recently, by a Marxist perspective which sees the subordination of Chicanos and other racial-ethnic groups as resulting from the oppressive nature of capitalism. Although the models were discussed in earlier chapters, this chapter presents a more detailed review and evaluation of them. In addition to discussing the relevance of each for understanding the experience of persons of Mexican descent residing in the United States, the thesis is advanced that the models are not completely antagonistic and that some assumed differences among them may be more apparent than real. Finally, it is argued that theoretical advances in Chicano sociology will be made not only when such similarities and differences are recognized but greater conceptual clarity and specificity is attained.

Overview of the Models

Prior to discussing each of the models some general comments are in order. First, because the models emerged in a rough chronological order, one could say that the assimilationist model prevailed in the social sciences through the 1950s and into the 1960s. One could also say that this model was challenged, and to some extent supplanted, by more radical nationalistic perspectives in the late 1960s and early 1970s, and that from the mid 1970s forward nationalistic perspectives have been challenged by Marxist models. Thus, the internal colonial model rejected the view of Chicanos as an immigrant group in favor of a conquest perspective; Marxism traced the subordination of Chicanos and other racial-ethnic groups to the oppressive nature of capitalism.

While the emergence of the models has followed this chronological order, it would be inappropriate to assume that one has been superseded by the other. In fact, it would be fairer to say that most colonial and Marxist

185

theorists would agree that mainstream social science is still heavily infused with assimilationist assumptions. This is precisely why the need for alternative sociologies is as great today as ever. It is also important to note that because the models have been assumed to be competing and conflicting, there has been a persistent preoccupation with identifying differences among them. This, unfortunately, has obscured possible similarities among the three models. Finally, it is not always clear whether the models are intended to be theoretical explanations of existing empirical patterns, ideological justifications for either maintaining or changing the status quo, or as scenarios of the future.

The Assimilationist Model

Perhaps the most basic premise of the assimilationist perspective is that racial and ethnic minorities are immigrant groups who entered American society voluntarily. Their ultimate fate is therefore assimilation into the so-called melting pot. Concepts such as assimilation, consensus, cooperation, and integration are thus integral to the model.

Not surprisingly, social scientists who subscribed to the assimilationist perspective have tended to be inordinately concerned with the malfunctioning of the Chicano family (see chapter seven), for the family was typically perceived as the root of all the evils encountered by Mexican-Americans (see Humphrey 1944; Jones 1948; Peñalosa 1968; Heller 1966; and Madsen 1973). According to this view other "immigrant" groups also brought different cultural values with them, but these values were discarded as they assimilated into the great melting pot. Chicanos, however, refused to be melted down and adhered to their traditional cultural and familial values. Thus, from this perspective the key to success for Mexican-Americans was acculturation and assimilation.

The essential elements of the assimilationist model can be seen when the model is first presented as an ideal type and is then contrasted with an ideal type of the colonial model (for a discussion of the assimilationist perspective see Glazer and Moynihan 1963; Gordon 1964; Murguía 1975; Blauner 1972, ch. 2). According to the assimilationist model

1. American society is composed of diverse racial-ethnic groups integrated into an orderly, cohesive "melting pot" of diverse interests.
2. The entrance of these diverse groups into American society is on an individual and voluntary basis.
3. Immigrant groups generally come from less industrialized and less-developed nations and are lacking the skills necessary to compete effectively in modern society.

4. Immigrants enter the society at the bottom of the socioeconomic ladder, but their economic position is markedly better than it was in their country of origin.
5. New arrivals are initially at a disadvantage economically, socially, and politically, but their ultimate fate is assimilation and integration into the host society.
6. The keys to gaining parity for immigrant groups are education and acculturation to the values and culture of the dominant group and rejection of more traditional cultural and familial values.
7. Groups who do not attain parity are those that for one reason or another have failed to assimilate and to take advantage of the opportunities afforded in our open, pluralistic society.

The assimilationist model can thus be classified as a cultural deficiency theory of race and ethnic relations (for a discussion of such theories see Barrera 1979, pp. 176-79). Given that most groups have been upwardly mobile after entering the society at a disadvantaged position, the continued subordination of others is ultimately ascribed, not to external structural forces, but to internal defects within the group itself, especially deficiencies in the family structure and in cultural values. Based on an individualistic and volitional view, the model ultimately blames oppressed people for their oppression by suggesting that any group that wants to is able to "pull itself up by its own bootstraps," so to speak. Chicanos have not made it, according to this view, because they have been unable or unwilling to assimilate. Chicano culture, and the Chicano family, moreover, are viewed as impediments to assimilation and acculturation.

At least three variants of the assimilation model have been identified: (1) Anglo conformity, (2) melting pot, and (3) cultural pluralism (Gordon 1964; Murguía 1975, pp. 18-21). Put simply, the Anglo-conformity model states that new immigrant groups automatically take on the values and language of the Anglo-Saxon Protestant host group. The melting-pot, or amalgam, model rejects the view that any one group is dominant and suggests, instead, that all groups contribute to the formation of a new hybrid society that results from the mixing of many cultures. The cultural-pluralist model pays lip service to the preservation of culturally distinct groups within American society. These groups are said to maintain cultural, linguistic, and religious autonomy, while being held "equal under the law" and integrated into the political and economic system.

At first glance these models appear to show internal diversity within the assimilation perspective, but upon closer examination such diversity seems more apparent than real. The three can be seen as slight variations of a single model. In a very real sense the ideology of the "melting pot" and of "cultural pluralism" mask the subordination of certain racial-ethnic groups by creating the illusion of equality. The Anglo-conformity model similarly suggests that Anglo domination is limited to the cultural arena and does not extend to the political or socioeconomic level. Their basic point of commonality, and their basic flaw, is the assumption that groups will automatically attain economic and political parity. The difference in the three variants, then, lies only in the degree of cultural assimilation emphasized by each.

The Internal-Colony Model

The internal-colony model arose in response to and sought to refute the basic underlying assumptions of the assimilation model, noting that American society has not readily integrated people of color and that the image of the United States as a melting pot is essentially mythical (for a discussion of this model see Fanon 1963, 1967; Memmi 1965; Blauner 1969, 1972; Moore 1970; Almaguer 1971: Acuña 1972; Barrera, Muñoz, and Ornelas 1972; and Barrera 1979). It holds, moreover, that the initial introduction of Chicanos, blacks, and native Americans into American society was forced and involuntary. Like Third-World peoples colonized by European powers, these groups entered into a forced and dependent relationship with the dominant group, but their colonization took place within the territorial boundaries of the United States. They are, therefore, internally colonized. According to the internal-colony model

1. American society is composed of diverse racial-ethnic groups, but rather than being integrated into an orderly and cohesive "melting pot," the society is characterized by the subordination of some groups by others who benefit from their subordinate status.
2. While Europeans immigrated individually and freely, the entrance of certain racial-ethnic minorities was not only forced and involuntary but in mass.
3. Although it is frequently asserted that internally colonized groups come from less-advanced underdeveloped nations, some groups have in fact come from older, advanced civilizations which in many ways were superior.
4. Internally colonized people enter the society at the bottom of the socioeconomic and political ladder, and their subordination is maintained through a variety of mechanisms.
5. Internally colonized groups make up a dependent and secondary colonial labor force that receives lower wages and few, if any, of the benefits received by workers in the primary labor force. They are dependent rather than free labor.
6. The subordination of internally colonized groups is not only economic

and political but cultural as well. The dominant group seeks to render their culture dependent and to eradicate their language, thereby facilitating control of the colonized group.

7. Although the cultures of internally colonized people have been rendered dependent, they have not been eradicated, and such groups have not been assimilated or integrated into the dominant society.

8. The dominant group permits a certain amount of upward mobility for individual members of internally colonized groups who are either more Caucasian in appearance and/or willing to adopt the values and culture of the dominant group. Ironically, such individuals are accepted largely to the extent that they are perceived as *not* identifying with or representing the interests of the colonized group.

When applied to the Chicano, the model holds that Chicanos are a colonized people who were conquered militarily, forcefully incorportated into the United States, and had a foreign language and culture imposed upon them.

The Marxist Model

Although the Marxist model has been present for well over a century, its application to Chicanos and other racial-ethnic minorities has been limited. A commom criticism of Marxism has been its inability or unwillingness to deal with issues of race or ethnicity. Yet of late there has been a resurgence of interest in the application of Marxist and neo-Marxist perspectives to Chicanos and other racial-ethnic groups.

Marxist critics of the internal-colony model argue that such a perspective is limited, nonprogressive, and that by focusing on racial and cultural oppression attention is diverted from the root causes of racism and inequality—capitalism. The model is held to be not only misguided but counterrevolutionary. Its focus on race and culture turns attention away from the oppression of working-class people of all colors. Marxism holds instead that

1. Capitalism is inevitably oppressive and based on the exploitation of some groups by others.

2. Racial minorities constitute an exploited underclass within American society.

3. The basic cause of the exploitation of racial-ethnic minorities is economic rather than racial or cultural.

4. Racism will end only when capitalism is destroyed and a classless society is established.

5. Paradigms which focus on racial-cultural exploitation are misguided be-

cause they are dealing with the effects rather than the root causes of such exploitation.

6. By assuming that all whites are oppressors and all people of color oppressed, one is blinded to the fact that the white proletariat are oppressed and some people of color are oppressors or would-be oppressors.

7. The issue is ultimately not one of race or culture but one between the oppressors (capitalists) and the oppressed (proletariat).

Marxists and neo-Marxists have thus been critical of the application of the internal-colony model to Chicanos and other racial-ethnic minorities, arguing that such applications at best are wrong or misguided, and at worst, dangerous and counterrevolutionary (see González 1974; Almaguer 1975; Fernandez 1977). The model, if carried to its logical extreme they argue, would lead to a race war between whites and internally colonized people. Decolonization will come only as a result of the unification of all Chicanos regardless of economic status or political ideology. When extended to a Third-World perspective, the colonial model calls for the mobilization of all people of color against white oppression. In either case the implied result is a race war (see González 1974, p. 157).

An additional criticism of internal colonialism is that it is said to presume that Chicanos are a nation, or a nation within a nation (for a critique of the national question see Gómez-Quiñones 1982). Gilbert González holds:

> . . . A nation according to historical materialist theory, would be a group of people having in common a single history, language, culture, territory, and economy (different from a nation-state in that the latter has political control over its territory). (1974, p. 156)

Chicanos would thus be a national minority rather than a nation according to this definition. Rather than having a separate economy, Chicanos are a dependent labor force within the American economy. Although concentrated in the Southwest, we are geographically dispersed throughout the United States. The linguistic, historical, and cultural diversity of Chicanos is also used to argue that we are not a nation.

Raul Fernandez also questions the idea that Chicanos constitute a nation, or even a culture. He argues instead that

> The border region is to be defined neither as a culturally homogeneous area nor as a nation. The bases upon which it is permissible to speak of the area as possessing a degree of cohesiveness are twofold— geographic and economic. (Fernandez 1977, p. 155)

The geographic features which enhance the area's homogeneity are well known. The economic unity of the border region is to some extent also tied to this natural geographical base, but its basis is ultimately ascribed to the uneven economic development of the United States and Mexico. The border region, according to Fernandez, reflects this uneven development which results from the emergence of monopoly capitalism in more economically advanced nations.

> The relations of economic domination and dependence which exist between the United States and Mexico are but one concrete example of the general principle about the relationship of domination and dependence which exist between advanced countries and poor countries. As such, the basis of the economic unity of the border is founded on inequality, uneven development, and domination. (Fernandez 1977, p. 156)

The key to economic independence for the region and, implicitly for Chicanos, lies with the elimination of imperialism and uneven economic development.

Although Fernandez's treatment of the border as an economic region is unique, a basic flaw in his conceptualization is the failure to distinguish differences in the experiences of persons of Mexican descent living north and south of the border. That the economic status of both *mexicanos* and Chicanos has been profoundly affected, if not determined, by the economic dependency of Mexico on the United States is irrefutable, but this in no way obviates the unique economic, cultural, and political experiences of the Chicano people. Fernandez's conceptual framework may enhance our understanding of the border region, but it does not advance our understanding of Chicanos.

Critique and Evaluation of the Models

This review of the foregoing theoretical models suggests at least three interrelated patterns. First, the literature is antagonistic, so that proponents of a particular model generally argue for the superiority of that model over the others. Second, the predominant focus has therefore been on differences rather than on possible similarities among them. Finally, it has generally been assumed a priori that the models are inherently incompatible and/or mutually exclusive. As a result few writers have looked for similarities, commonalities, or possible points of reconciliation among them.

An additional point of confusion exists in the literature relative to the level of analysis employed. It is not clear, for example, whether the assimilationist perspective is arguing that Chicanos *are* or *should be* assimilated. Edward Murguía sets out to see how well the assimilationist and colonial models fare with the realities of the Chicano experience today. He also attempts to assess the conceptual adequacy and theoretical consistency of each model and the extent to which each is ideologically biased (Murguía 1975, p. 1). In asking how well each "fits" the reality of the Chicano experience, Murguía is ostensibly focusing on the real rather than the ideal dimension, yet even a cursory reading of his treatment of the models suggests that there is a strong prescriptive component both to the assimilationist and colony models. In the end Murguía concludes that both models are lacking and opts for a third model—cultural pluralism—which he sees as lying on "a continuum" between the two polar choices. Murguía comments on the three models:

> The unique aspects of the study that follows are that the assimilation and colonial models, their ideologies and the relationship between them are described in this one work, not only theoretically but also in relation to the Mexican American people. Also, uniquely, a third model, cultural pluralism, will be introduced as being the result of either incomplete assimilation or incomplete decolonization, depending on one's perspective. Ultimately, however, an argument will be made to the effect that cultural pluralism in its classic form does not seem to be attainable given current socioeconomic conditions in the United States. (Ibid. p. 2)

Murguía's choice of words here is unfortunate and suggests a lack of conceptual clarity. To say that cultural pluralism in its classic form does not seem "attainable" indicates that "cultural pluralism" is being advanced not as a model but rather as a desirable or more palatable ideology. In fact, since the three models are presented by Murguía as "ideal types," they are by definition logical constructs rather than descriptions of empirical reality. They are, in other words, not attainable by design. An additional problem with his conceptualization is that the criteria for assessing whether one model is superior to another is never clearly stated. Thus, one gets the distinct impression that each of the ideal types is, in a sense, a "straw man." The models are presented in such an ideal and extreme form that they are doomed to fall short when gauged against the complex reality of the contemporary Chicano experience. When one finally sifts through his analysis, what Murguía appears to be saying is that while Chicanos have never been totally conquered or assimilated, neither do they live in an equal pluralistic relation with Anglo Americans.

Perhaps the most comprehensive review of recent theoretical developments in Chicano sociology is presented by Maxine Baca Zinn. Although her analysis does not focus on the three models per se, much of her review is relevant to this discussion. Baca Zinn concludes that earlier works which relied heavily on cultural-deficiency theories (i.e., assimilationist) have gradually been supplanted by more sophisticated structural theories of social inequality (i.e., internal colonial and Marxist). While she applauds the emergence of these less pejorative macrolevel theories, she feels that not enough attention has been given to microlevel explanations of social inequality. Rather than opting for one theory or model over another, Baca Zinn holds that, ultimately,

> . . . Sociology is a pluralistic discipline characterized by numerous alternative conceptions of theory, explanations and data; that is, by different approaches or perspectives. Different kinds of social phenomena require separate theories. Like sociology generally, the sociology of Chicanos can be carved up in many different ways, from the interpersonal to the institutional and societal levels. Analyzing these different levels and types of social phenomena calls for alternative and selected application of sociological theories. (Baca Zinn 1981, p. 257)

Her review of theoretical developments concludes with a critique of my paradigm of Chicano sociology.[1] Specifically, she isolates two basic problems. First, what I propose is *not* a paradigm, since a paradigm "is the broadest unit of consensus within a science and serves to differentiate one scientific community (or sub-community) from another" (Ritzer 1975, p. 156). Second, "Mirandé treats colonial theory as an integral component of a Chicano paradigm, but ignores the potential contributions of other theories. It must be emphasized that the study of Chicanos will require the adoption of multiple theoretical perspectives" (Baca Zinn 1981, p. 268).

These are potentially incisive criticisms, but a basic pitfall in her analysis is the treatment of colonialism as a theory. To say that I treat colonial theory as integral to the paradigm while ignoring the potential contribution of other theories is to distort not only the paradigm but Chicano history. My inclusion of the colonization of Chicanos came in response to those assimilationist theories which saw us negatively from a cultural perspective and as a volunteer immigrant group. Its inclusion is called for not so much because colonialism is a more "adequate theory" but because it is a very basic and significant historical process. Colonization is not a theory but rather a historical fact and a way of life. It is a component of the paradigm but is not the paradigm. In a very real sense colonization is also the broadest unit within Chicano sociology which differentiates it from mainstream sociology.

My position essentially is that *any* theory of Chicanos, whether on a macro- or microlevel, Marxist or culturalist, must recognize the colonization of the Chicano. To do otherwise is to ignore history. In the same way that any theory of black oppression must consider the legacy of slavery, so must Chicano sociology take into account our legacy of conquest. I am opposed to assimilationist perspectives precisely because they choose to minimize or ignore this basic historical fact. To recognize the colonization of Chicanos is not, however, to deny that Chicanos are subjected to forces of assimilation, or to be closed to other models or theories which might enhance our understanding of the Chicano experience. To the contrary, if there is a point of convergence between the assimilationist and colonial perspectives, it is that both hold that Chicanos are subjected to assimilative processes. One perspective (assimilationist) applauds and welcomes these processes; the other (colonial) resists them. The difference between the models is not so much in their treatment of assimilation, then, as it is in their response to it. An additional point of convergence is that both models acknowledge the fact that Chicanos have resisted assimilation, but the assimilationist perspective sees us as a curious anomaly or as pathological for *not* joining the melting pot, whereas the colonial model romanticizes and idealizes this resistance.

One might do well, then, to view assimilationist and nationalistic perspectives more as ideological statements relative to the appropriateness of the response of Chicanos and other racial/ethnic groups to the larger society. In fact, when one begins to focus on behavioral descriptions of the Chicano experience, there is considerable overlap between the perspectives. Both agree that (1) American society is made up of diverse ethnic groups, (2) racial and ethnic minorities entered the society at the bottom of the socioeconomic and political ladder, (3) the key to gaining equality for subordinate groups has been education and acculturation to the values and culture of the dominant society and rejection of their own culture, and (4) groups and individuals who have not attained parity are those who have failed to assimilate. Both perspectives, as was noted earlier, argue that assimilation has been held out by the dominant society as prerequisite to achievement and upward mobility. The assimilationist perspective views this positively; the colonial, negatively. Despite these apparent similarities a crucial difference is that according to the colonial model the dominant society permits a limited amount of social mobility of internally colonized groups, but only for the select few who are perceived as rejecting identification and loyalty to the colonized group (i.e., noncolonized non-Chicanos). It does not, in other words, generally permit mobility for the groups as a whole or for persons as members of colonized groups. The choice for internally colonized groups is thus largely between individual achievement and cultural genocide.

An additional difficulty is that assimilation is frequently treated as a unidimensional rather than a multidimensional phenomenon. A distinction often blurred is that between cultural and economic or political assimilation. Proponents of the colonial model readily admit that Chicanos are subject to cultural assimilation. In fact, a major component of the colonial model is that native cultures are rendered subordinate and dependent. A basic paradox, however, is that, contrary to the assimilationist model, such cultural assimilation does not necessarily guarantee economic or political power for the group. Racial and ethnic minorities can be culturally assimilated without being integrated into the American melting pot. The whole thrust of decolonization movements is to devise mechanisms for retaining cultural autonomy, while attaining economic and political parity.

A related problem has been a tendency to put undue emphasis on cultural assimilation. Milton Gordon (1964, p. 71), for example, breaks the process of assimilation down into seven components:

1. cultural assimilation—change of cultural patterns to those of the host society,
2. structural assimilation—large-scale entrance into cliques, clubs, and institutions of the host society,
3. marital assimilation or amalgamation—large-scale intermarriage,
4. identificational assimilation—development of a sense of peoplehood based exclusively on the host society,
5. attitude receptional assimilation—absence of prejudice,
6. behavioral receptional assimilation—absence of discrimination, and
7. civic assimilation—absence of value and power conflict.

Although only the first is termed "cultural," in reality all seven dimensions are cultural. With the possible exception of the last category economic and political assimilation are ignored. Gordon views economic mobility as a factor that can divide an ethnic or racial group along class lines. The two variables of ethnicity and class are handled via the introduction of the concept of ethclass. Since class has primacy over ethnicity in this model, ethclasses are subgroupings of members of an ethnic group within a particular class. If one forms primary relations outside one's ethclass, one is more likely to do so with persons of *different* ethnic background within one's class than with members of one's ethnic group who are in a different class. Such a conceptualization ignores the very issue of economic integration of racial/ethnic people as a group by assuming that (1) ethnic groups are in fact represented within each social class, (2) class has primacy over race or ethnicity, and (3) interethnic conflict is minimal or nonexistent.

Although Marxism is generally seen as being in conflict with both the internal colonial and assimilationist perspectives, it shares commonalities with each. Like the assimilationist model, Marxism gives primacy to social class over ethnicity. It differs from the assimilationist model in seeing oppression as a structural or group, rather than individual, phenomenon, however. Marxism recognizes the subordination of racial minorities, but it sees the root of racism as being economic rather than racial or cultural. Racism, accordingly, will end only when capitalism ends. The issue is really one not of race but of class, as capitalists regardless of race will exploit and oppress the proletariat. Racial and ethnic minorities are overrepresented among the proletariat because they have served as a cheap and dependent labor force.

In recent years several scholars have sought to merge, or at least integrate, Marxist and colonial models. One of the first authors to present such a synthesis was Robert Blauner. In *Racial Oppression in America* (1972) he recognized the need for a theory that links racial oppression and racial conflict to the capitalistic structure, while noting that no contemporary theory has done this effectively:

> This suggests a major defect of my study. It lacks a conception of American society as a total structure beyond the central significance that I attribute to racism. . . . racial oppression and racial conflict are not satisfactorily linked to the dominant economic relations nor to the overall distribution of political power in America. The failure of Marxism to appreciate the significance of racial groups and racial conflict is in part responsible for this vacuum, since no other existing framework is able to relate race to a comprehensive theory of capitalist development. (1972, p. 13)

Blauner envisions, but does not actually propose, a new theoretical model that merges racial and capitalist class realities, and he concludes that neither Marxist nor colonial models capture the complexity of racial oppression in advanced capitalistic societies. He cautions, however, that "it will be no simple mechanical task to merge these two frameworks into a theory that is integrated and convincing" (ibid, p. 14).

Although Blauner does not effectively merge the two models and is generally classified as a proponent of the colonial model, he sees colonialism as being inextricably linked to capitalistic development. According to Blauner "Labor and its exploitation must be viewed as the first cause of modern race relations; as we have seen, the main outlines of this division of labor are still reflected in the privileged position of whites within the occupational distribution and economic stratification of present-day multiracial societies" (ibid., p. 29). He argues further that colonial labor was crucial to the development of capitalism in the Western Hemisphere:

> . . . capitalism and free labor as Western institutions were not developed for people of color; they were reserved for white people and white societies. In the colonies European powers organized other systems of work that were noncapitalist and unfree. (Ibid. p. 58)

Blauner is critical of orthodox Marxist theory for obscuring the internal diversity of the working class and patterns of labor status. Specifically, he is critical of their failure to recognize that white European immigrants worked within the relatively free capitalistic wage system, whereas people of color were a dependent and unfree labor force. Although the position of white immigrants was essentially low, they worked largely within the industrialized modern sectors and had the opportunity to be upwardly mobile, economically, politically, and socially (ibid. p. 62). Perhaps Blauner's most important contribution is identifying the material basis of racism.

A more recent work by Tomás Almaguer seeks to expand upon and further delineate the interrelationship between race and class exploitation. According to Almaguer "the racism and racial oppression faced by colonized people has been more than just part of an 'ideological superstructure,' for it has a very real structural basis in the organization of production" (1975, p. 72). Racism is thus much more than epiphenomena or a manifestation of false consciousness. Almaguer's work and that of Blauner are significant in representing genuine attempts to integrate Marxist and colonial theory.

For Almaguer racism is much more than part of the ideological superstructure, which serves not only to justify racial domination but economic, political, and cultural control. After tracing the historical roots of Chicano oppression in both Mexico and the United States, he concludes that "race was not only to provide the central source of ideological justification of the colonial situation, but it also became the central factor upon which classes in colonial society were to develop outwardly and take their form" (1975, p. 74). Although Chicanos served as an exploited subproletariat that was unfree labor and helped to develop American capitalism, after 1940 we were gradually incorporated into the lowest segments of the working class.

Almaguer is critical of those Marxists who hold that racism will end automatically by doing away with the class basis of this oppression. If racism is to be eliminated, we must recognize that members of the white working class receive short-term benefits from racial exploitation and that racism is not a simple manifestation of false consciousness. Almaguer suggests:

> What is needed now is an honest appraisal of the many ways in which the working class has become segmented and divided. An assessment of racial minorities within the working class is but one step in this direction. It is only when oppressed peoples begin to seek out the commonalities—as well as differences—in their oppression that we can hope to build those political alliances that will be both meaningful and ultimately effective. (Ibid. p. 95)

The most comprehensive and ambitious attempt to integrate Marxist and colonial theories is Mario Barrera's *Race and Class in the Southwest*. Like Blauner and Almaguer, Barrera contends that Chicanos were a dependent colonial labor force during the nineteenth and well into the twentieth century, but today many are part of the working class, while others have joined the middle and professional classes. The situation faced by Chicanos is thus more complex today than in the past.

> . . . Chicanos have been incorporated into the United States' political economy as subordinate ascriptive class segments, and . . . they have historically been found occupying such a structural position at all class levels. (1979, p. 212)

In seeking to synthesize the two models Barrera proposes a modified version of the internal colonial model which retains the concept of class segmentation. Social classes are the most general structural elements in society. Chicanos, according to this model, are members of all classes, but they constitute a subordinate segment within each. They share certain interests with other members of their class, but because they suffer institutional discrimination, they also have interests in common with all Chicanos regardless of class position.

Barrera's concept of class segmentation is similar to Gordon's ethclass, but it differs in the sense that Barrera recognizes that members of a Chicano subordinate segment (ethclass) share both common class and colonial interests. In a sense, by giving primacy to ethnicity and recognizing that even Chicano capitalists occupy a subordinate position within this class, Barrera has turned Gordon on his head.

Although Barrera's theory of class segmentation is more complex and sophisticated, his conceptualization is not without problems. By trying to integrate and synthesize colonial and class theories Barrera may not do justice to either. One problem is his tendency to define class in terms of income, education, and occupational categories rather than in terms of one's relation to the means of production. A second, related problem is the treatment of classes as aggregates of individuals who occupy a broad occupational category (i.e., census data), not as distinct sociological entities. To view some Chicanos as "capitalists" may distort reality, for most who are upwardly mobile are, at best, professionals or petty bourgeois. It is imperative that Marxist class analysis be linked to ownership and the relationship of social classes to the means of production.

On the other hand, from a colonial perspective it is difficult to accept his definition of Chicanos as a colony simply because they have contact with one another. Barrera's greatest failing may be that he has a "top-to-down" view of social inequality. He therefore starts with the assumption that classes are the "broadest units" in society and then sets about trying to see how Chicanos "fit in" these broader units. How one could see classes as the broadest units and subscribe to a colonial model is puzzling indeed.

I propose that if Chicano sociology is to serve the interests of oppressed groups, it must examine the position of Chicanos from the perspective of Chicanos: in other words, from the bottom up. Colonization entails the subordination of one group by another. To be colonized is to be powerless: to lack control over vital institutions such as the economy, polity, religion, education, and, even one's culture. Since colonization is a process whereby one group subordinates another, its effectiveness cannot adequately be gauged through census data on occupational categories.[2] Such a methodology is wanting not only from a colonial but from a Marxist perspective.

Summary and Conclusion

Having critically reviewed and evaluated these three models, I will now attempt to summarize and integrate the major conclusions of this chapter. I hope, in the process, to isolate those elements that are critical to the development of a Chicano sociology and to build on my earlier paradigm.

(1) The assimilationist, colonial, and Marxist models have generally been assumed to be antagonistic, if not mutually exclusive.

(2) Because proponents of one model have sought to demonstrate that their model is superior to other models, they have ignored possible commonalities or similarities among them.

(3) It is often unclear whether the models are proposed as theories designed to explain the experiences of oppressed groups or as ideological justifications either for the status quo or for radical social change.

(4) Under careful scrutiny it becomes clear that the models are not always in conflict and that differences among them are sometimes more apparent than real.

(5) The assimilationist and colonial models both recognize that minorities are subject to assimilation and cultural control, but the former views assimilation positively and the latter, negatively. The basic differences between the perspectives are thus as much ideological as they are theoretical or empirical.

(6) The ideological quality of the assimilationist model has led its proponents to (a) view assimilation as an individual rather than as a collective phenomena, (b) focus on cultural assimilation, and (c) look for defects in the culture and values of oppressed groups to explain their subordination.

(7) Marxism is similar to the assimilation theory in that it gives primacy to social class over ethnicity, but it differs in recognizing racial and class oppression as a structural, rather than individual, phenomena. It is also similar to the assimilationist model in that it holds that over time racial minorities have become more integrated into the economy.

(8) Both Marxism and colonialism are structural models, but they differ in the primacy given to race and class. In a sense Marxism sees capitalism as the basis for racism, while colonialism sees racism as the basis for advanced capitalism.

(9) Although Marxism and colonialism are often treated as conflicting or opposing theories, for Chicanos class and colonial oppression are largely inseparable. (In the same way that racism and sexism are inseparable for Chicanas.) They can only be separated analytically or conceptually.

(10) For Chicanos colonial and class exploitation are much more than academic theories. They are part of an historical experience and a way of life.

(11) If a theory is to grasp adequately the Chicano experience, it must consider not only the economic and occupational oppression of the Chicano but political, educational, religious, and cultural oppression as well.

(12) It must also recognize that the oppression of Chicanos and other racial/ethnic groups should be viewed as a group or collective process.

(13) Finally, theories of Chicano sociology should take into account how the proximity of Mexico and its history of neocolonial dependence on the United States contributes to the exploitation of Chicanos, without at the same time obviating differences between the Chicano and Mexican experience.

10

Epilogue: Toward a Chicano Paradigm

From the preceding chapters it is clear that the need for a Chicano social science springs not so much from the absence of literature on the topic as it does from the absence of works that reflect a Chicano world view or are sensitive to our culture. In fact, over the years social scientists have demonstrated an inordinate concern with the Mexican/Chicano people, particularly with their cultural and familial values. *Raza*, however, has not fared very well in social-science depictions. When compared to middle-class, Anglo Protestant and Judaic values, Chicano cultural, familial, and religious values have been found wanting. Relative to these external perspectives, the Chicano people have been viewed as inferior and as lacking those characteristics essential to success in modern, urban, American society. A persistent theme is that Anglo culture is modern, individualistic, futuristic, and achievement oriented; in contrast, Chicano culture is traditional, collectivistic, backward, and lacking in achievement.

Perhaps it was Celia Heller who stated it most unabashedly when she asserted:

> . . . The kind of socialization that Mexican American children generally receive at home is not conducive to the development of the capacities needed for advancement . . . by stressing values that hinder mobility—family ties, masculinity, and living in the present—and by neglecting the values that are conducive to it—achievement, independence, and deferred gratification. (1966, pp. 34-35)

The limited upward mobility of Mexican-Americans cannot be seen simply as the result of prejudice and discrimination, then, for other racial and ethnic groups have been more successful in overcoming these same obstacles (e.g., East European Jew and Japanese). Eastern European Jewish culture, for example, gives impetus to success by providing excuses for failure.

> . . . In contrast, among Mexican Americans, not to try when there are obstacles is to avoid failure which would blemish one's manliness and honor. . . . This fear of risking failure, of risking rejection . . . figures prominently in the Mexican-American orientation. (Heller 1971, pp. 233-34)

201

Other studies have similarly identified the cultural emphasis on *machismo* as an impediment to success and upward mobility. Alvin Rudoff, as previously noted, has said that the Mexican-American

> . . . has little concern for the future, perceives himself as predestined to be poor and subordinate, is still influenced by magic, is gang-minded, distrusts women, sees authority as arbitrary, tends to be passive and dependent, and is alienated from the Anglo culture. (1971, pp. 236-37)

Not surprisingly, a closed and authoritarian family structure inevitably leads to a high level of family violence. Carroll (1980) contends that values and norms which are endemic to Chicanos result in excessive family violence. The democratic Jewish-American family, on the other hand, is believed to generate a very low level of violence. Whereas the Chicano family emphasizes severe discipline and coercion as a mechanism for conflict resolution, the Jewish-American family emphasizes

> . . . the pursuit of knowledge and the use of the mind rather than the body. The value of intellectuality resulting from these values was proposed to lead to the favoring of articulateness, argumentativeness, and bargaining as a way to solve family disputes. (Ibid. p. 80)

The implication of this type of social-science research is clear—economic, political, and cultural oppression is the result not of external forces such as racism and class exploitation but of deficiencies within the culture and values of Chicanos themselves. Octavio Romano, one of the pioneers of Chicano scholarship, has commented on the tendency of traditional social scientists to blame Chicanos for their own oppression. He felt that the rationalizations developed by these social scientists were ingenious.

> . . . Although recitations of the rhetoric vary in emphasis and degree of sophistication, the essential message is the same: Mexican-Americans are simple-minded but lovable and colorful children who because of their rustic naiveté, limited mentality, and inferior, backward "traditional culture," choose poverty and isolation instead of assimilating into the American mainstream and accepting its material riches and superior culture. (Romano 1968a, p. 2)

After an extensive critical review of the literature Nick Vaca similarly argued that the prevailing social-science paradigm was one of cultural determinism, "based on a definition of Mexican-American culture as composed of values detrimental to success in the American way of life" (1970b, p. 45). The model was accepted because it explained the problems of Chicanos in the United States without blaming the dominant society or Anglo institutions. Vaca (1970b, p. 45) summarizes Mexican-American and Anglo value systems as put forth in social-science literature.

Mexican-American Value System	Anglo Value System
subjugation to nature	mastery over nature
present oriented	future oriented
immediate gratification	deferred gratification
complacent	aggressive
nonintellectual	intellectual
fatalistic	nonfatalistic
nongoal oriented	goal oriented
nonsuccess oriented	success oriented
emotional	rational
dependent	individualistic
machismo	effeminency[1]
superstitious	nonsuperstitious
traditional	progressive

While contemporary works tend to be less openly pejorative and more sophisticated, the theme that many of the problems of acculturation and assimilation of Mexican-Americans into the melting pot are a result of adherence to a rural, agricultural, and less modern value system is alive and well today. The persistent preoccupation with the Chicano family is not surprising, for the family is the primary vehicle for the transmission of culture. As Maxine Baca Zinn observed, however, the family is typically seen in a negative and stereotyped manner.

> . . . The negative stereotype of the Chicano family found throughout the literature is that of an outmoded traditional patriarchal institution. This stereotype which has been labeled "the social science myth of the Mexican American Family" by Montiel is rooted in two sociological frameworks: modernization and acculturation. Chicano family research has been guided by an ideal construct, postulating on the one hand, the "traditional" patriarchal type, and on the other, a "modern" egalitarian family type. The concept of modernization has not been made explicit in Chicano family literature, but many of its underlying assumptions have guided thinking in this area, most notably the idea that universal evolutionary changes in family structure occur with urbanization and industrialization. (1979b, p.59)

Interestingly, at the same time that many social scientists have depicted the family as traditional and Chicanos as controlled by a monolithic culture, such social scientists have been remarkably resistant to change or to modifying their own traditional views about Chicanos. Referring to those who would reject the introduction of a Chicano self-image into social-science thought, Octavio Romano remarked,

> . . . In doing so, wittingly or unwittingly, it matters not, they will have opted to join the ranks of the traditionalists in social science who have passively accepted the traditional view of the totally non-rational Mexican-American as handed down from social science generation to social science generation since the early 1900's, and before, down to the present day. (1970, p. 12)

It would be simplistic to blame these general failings on the attitudes of individual social scientists. Some have undoubtedly been prejudiced or, at least, insensitive; others have not; and a few have proven sensitive and concerned. Upon closer examination the problem appears much more insidious and complex. It is not, after all, a problem of individuals, but one of institutions and ideas. It may, in other words, be endemic to the scientific enterprise. The issue is not between "insiders" and "outsiders" as we have often been told, but between traditional dominant societal perspectives and emergent minority world views. A basic assertion of this work is that not only sociology but science itself reflects a majority world view. Such a world view is evident not only in the problems identified but in the manner in which they have been pursued. The pattern is so pervasive that minority scholars have often become engulfed by it, pressured to adopt prevailing perspectives and to reject, directly or indirectly, their cultural heritage.

In retrospect, the late 1960s and early 1970s proved to be a significant period in Chicano scholarship as works by Octavio Romano, Nick Vaca, Deluvina Hernandez, and others appeared. This era was significant not only in marking the "entrance" of Chicanos into the discipline but in challenging "the legitimacy of both existing societal practices and values" (Baca Zinn 1981, p. 256). Some have been critical of this "protest" literature for not going far enough or for not offering alternative theoretical frameworks and reformulations. With the benefit of hindsight it is now easy to find fault, but the contribution of these early works to the development of Chicano sociology was significant and should not be obscured. Their basic contribution is not so much that they rejected prevailing social-science depictions, but that they called for alternative Chicano paradigms. If realized, the objectives these pioneers envisioned would be revolutionary, for they promised to revamp completely social-science perspectives. In fact, Octavio Romano felt:

> . . . This situation is unique in the annals of American social science. It is unique because a population heretofore studied is now studying the studiers. The final outcome of this venture is yet to be revealed. Nevertheless, it promises to introduce perspectives that are

unique in social science, perspectives which have their origin within a previously studied population [Mexican-Americans] whose objectifications in the past have not been an accepted, explicit, and integral part of traditional social science thought. As such, these perspectives will introduce a self-image into the arena of rational thought. If this self-image is rejected by non-Chicano social scientists, then, in effect, they will have rejected summarily the rationality of the Chicano. (1970, p. 12)

Subsequent to the 1960s new generations of Chicano scholars might be faulted for failing to develop and advance these early formulations. Whereas a number of black scholars have developed significant works on black sociology, the two available sociological treatises on Mexican-Americans are written by Anglos (Moore 1976 and Stoddard 1973). In addition, the widely acclaimed The Mexican-American People (Grebler, Moore, and Guzman 1970) had two Anglos as senior authors and a Chicano as a junior author. Although both Moore and Stoddard acknowledge the need for "insider" views, a comprehensive Chicano statement on sociology or social science has yet to appear.[2]

Despite theoretical and methodological advancements a common pitfall found among more recent formulations, as we have seen, has been the failure to distinguish between the sociology of Chicanos and Chicano sociology. The frame of reference in these works is typically sociology, not Chicanos. This distinction is not simply a semantic one, for the sociology of Chicanos seeks to apply existing sociological theories and paradigms to Chicanos. A Chicano sociology needs to be developed, with its own distinctive theories, methods, exemplars, and paradigms: in other words, a Chicano perspective.

Of more contemporary interest to a growing number of scholars has been Marxism and its relevance for Chicanos. While some researchers have discarded an earlier colonial perspective altogether, others like Mario Barrera and Tomás Almaguer have made attempts to integrate colonial and Marxist models. Works like theirs are becoming increasingly more sophisticated theoretically and have done much to enhance our understanding of how Chicanos have been rendered and maintained in an economically subordinate position. Yet they share two basic failings. First, there is an inordinate concern with political economy to the neglect of other significant aspects of the Chicano experience. The result is a unidimensional and somewhat limiting view of Chicanos. Barrera (1979), Acuña (1981), Fernandez (1977), Camarillo (1979), and Almaguer (1974 and 1975), for example, focus almost exclusively on political economy. I contend that a full understanding of Chicanos can only come through an examination of all vital institutions that impinge on our people. That economic exploitation is significant goes without saying. If we focus only on political economy, however, and neglect other areas such as religion, education, immigration, the legal and judicial system, and the family and sex roles, our knowledge and understanding of the Chicano experience remains incomplete. If we focus exclusively on culture, on the other hand, we will ignore structural forces that impinge on Chicanos.

There is thus a need not only to examine these institutions individually but to look at interrelationships among them along with the interaction between culture and political economy. What, for example, is the relationship between the economy and religion? How have religious theodicies functioned to perpetuate the subordination of the Chicano? What is the relationship between the economy and the family and sex roles? The tendency to view institutions in isolation is consistent with an Anglo world view; Anglos tend to segmentalize life experiences, Chicanos to integrate them. Family, religion, and politics for Anglos are separate, if not antithetical, institutions, whereas within our Mexican heritage they are very much intertwined. *La Virgen de Guadalupe*, for instance, is at once a familial, religious, and political symbol. A related premise of the present work is that the contemporary situation cannot and should not be divorced from its historical context. Hence much of the book has been devoted to outlining this historical background.

The second shortcoming in Marxist analysis is perhaps more serious than the first. Like those who subscribe to the "sociology of Chicanos," Chicano Marxists in effect simply take existing perspectives and apply them to Chicanos rather then develop perspectives that spring from a Chicano world view. For a Chicano it makes very little difference whether he is exploited because he is a member of the proletariat or because he is a Chicano; what matters is that he is exploited and that race and class oppression have been inextricably linked.

We should bear in mind that Marx was European. Not only did he fail to address adequately the issue of racial exploitation, but there is evidence which suggests that he may not have been free of racist sentiments. He defended American imperialism, for example. Marx approved the annexation of Texas and wondered whether "it was such a misfortune that glorious California has been wrenched from the lazy Mexicans who did not know what to do with it?" (cited in Nomad 1961, p. 103).

My ultimate intent, however, is not to denigrate Marxist analysis or conventional sociology, but to point out that there is a need in Chicano scholarship seriously to question traditional Western/European perspectives and to work for the development and application of a uniquely Chicano world view. Marxism is vital and must be considered a critical component of a Chicano perspective. However, a basic premise of this work is that a full understanding of Chicanos lies within rather than outside of our rich cultural heritage. Hence we must go beyond existing perspectives if we are to develop a Chicano paradigm.

Is a Chicano Paradigm Possible?

One of the first scholars to propose a Chicano paradigm for the social sciences was Dr. Octavio Romano. In "Social Science, Objectivity, and the Chicanos" (1970) he pointed to the need for a Chicano social science that would serve as an important corrective for traditional pathological depictions of Chicano culture and history. He cautioned, however, against simply selecting "from the present array of sociological and anthropological theories, dress them up in up-to-date Space Age terminology, apply them to Chicanos and thus assume the mantle of contemporaneity before the uninitiated in social science theory" (1970, p. 11). A crucial component of this paradigm was rejection of the separation of mind and body and the introduction of a rational Chicano self-image which would supplant the traditional view of Chicanos as *"only passive receptors and retainers"* (p.13) of culture. Romano (ibid., pp. 13-14) proposed an eight-point paradigm.

> *First,* from the standpoint of self-image. Chicanos do not view themselves as traditionally unchanging social vegetables (traditional culture), but rather as creators of systems in their own right, for they have created cooperatives, mutualist societies, political blocks, international networks of communications, and social networks, to name a few examples.
>
> *Second,* Chicanos view themselves as participants in the historical process, for they are inseparable from history.
>
> *Third,* this population has been the creator and generator of social forms such as dialects, music, personal networks, creators of communities where none existed before, and they proclaim their Mestizaje and, as such, constitute a pluralistic people.
>
> *Fourth,* Chicanos see in their historical existence a continuous engaging in social issues, the spurious concepts of "resignation" and "fatalism" notwithstanding. Two examples are the pioneering of the labor movement in the West, and the fifty-year or more struggle for bilingual education (not bilingual acculturation theory).
>
> *Fifth,* the concept of the illiterate Mexican American must go, for it is true that this population has published well over 500 newspapers in the Southwest from 1848 to 1950, to say nothing of countless posters, signs, newsletters, and the like.

Sixth, the Chicano must be viewed as capable of his own system of rationality, for without this faculty he could not have survived, established philosophies of economics, politics, Chicano studies programs, and philosophies of human existence.

Seventh, intellectual activity has been part and parcel of Chicano existence as evidenced by speech patterns, bilingualism, and a highly sophisticated humor that relies heavily upon metaphors and satire. This activity requires of the participants a mastery of language in order to engage in this common practice.

And *Eighth*, as a population whose antecedents are Mexican, the bulk of Chicano existence has been oriented to a symbiotic residence within ecosystems. . . . In other words, what in ignorance and crudeness has been called the Mexican *traditional subjugation to nature* by Saunders, Edmunson, Kluckhohn, Heller, Samora, and many other social scientists, in reality has been a conscious philosophy for the maintenance of ecological balance in an ecosystem.

Romano's intent was clearly to identify key elements of a Chicano paradigm or philosophic world view. One might disagree with some of these components or fault him for not including others such as political economy, but he should be recognized for blazing the trail in identifying the need for a Chicano paradigm. He recognized that the paradigm was tentative and that others, undoubtedly, would follow (ibid, p. 13).

Another pioneer in Chicano social science was Deluvina Hernández (1970). In *Mexican American Challenge to a Sacred Cow* Hernández also presents a critical evaluation of traditional social-science literature. Like Romano, she found that such literature is often steeped in assimilationist assumptions and tends to blame Chicanos for their own failure. Although she did not propose a paradigm, Hernández implicitly argued for the creation of Chicano social science when she stated:

. . . Social science research has been sold out relative to objective and meaningful study of the Mexican American minority group in the United States and in the Southwest. The researchers of the past and those of the present . . . are the tools of agencies of social control and of the sponsoring centers of power which need to solve "dilemmas" or "problems" which threatened prevailing social patterns. Further, it is suggested that for not entirely unselfish reasons, these researchers have sought to provide the stamp of objective expertise on that which they have desired to do. . . . These researchers have sold out social science research in this instance by maintaining their "objective" veneer and not recognizing that their work has been as much a response to their

institutional environment as the response of Mexican Americans has
been to theirs. (1970, pp. 48-49)

In addition to Romano in anthropology and Hernández and Vaca in
sociology there was during the 1960s and 1970s a parallel movement by
scholars who questioned traditional perspectives on Chicanos in their respective fields: social work (Montiel 1970 and 1973); political science (Muñoz
1970 and 1983; Barrera, Muñoz, and Ornelas 1972; Rocco 1977); history
(Acuña 1972; Gómez-Quiñones and Arroyo 1976); psychology (Martinez
1977), and philosophy (Carranza 1978).

This proved to be a revolutionary period, as Chicanos challenged traditional perspectives in virtually every academic discipline. It was, in a sense,
an intellectual Chicano renaissance. Despite the promise of these early works
they have been criticized for not really offering alternative theoretical frameworks or perspectives. Baca Zinn (1981), for example, says that the protest
literature did not go far enough and put undue emphasis on culture as the
primary determinant of Chicano behavior, while ignoring the contribution
of social organization or social structure.

Following the tradition of these earlier works, I proposed a tentative
Chicano paradigm for the social sciences in 1978 (see chapter nine). Baca
Zinn, however, contends that what I proposed was not really a paradigm.
Following Ritzer's definition, she argues that a "Paradigm is the broadest unit
of consensus within a science and serves to differentiate one scientific community (or subcommunity) from another" (Ritzer 1975, p. 157). According
to Baca Zinn

> . . . What most needs to be clarified is the difference between
> theories and paradigms. . . . It is clear that we must work toward the
> development of a Chicano paradigm that can incorporate theories now
> being developed in the discipline. (1981, p. 268)

What I proposed was limited, at best a theory or perspective, but certainly not a paradigm. An additional problem was that I only focused on one
theory (colonialism) and ignored the potential contribution of others. A genuine paradigm would have to incorporate cultural as well as micro- and
macrolevel explanations. In a sense Baca Zinn is correct because I perceived
the paradigm as emergent or tentative and not as a full-blown one and noted
that "although it is admittedly tentative and suggestive, hopefully it will
serve as a model or starting point for future research and theorizing on Chicanos" (1978, p. 306). As Romano, I anticipated that other Chicano scholars
would refine and further develop the paradigm. The paradigm did, however,
emerge from dissatisfaction with social-science perspectives and from the
deeply held conviction that prevailing paradigms and the ethos of scientism

worked to maintain Chicanos in a subordinate position. As Kuhn (1962), I argued not only that paradigm choice was polemical and beyond the scope of science but that Chicano sociology and similar approaches would be resisted by establishment science because they questioned prevailing paradigms. Despite its tentativeness, acceptance of a Chicano paradigm could potentially signal the onset of a scientific revolution that would seriously call into question and challenge prevailing paradigms and world views.

Ritzer maintains that sociology is a multiple-paradigm science and identifies three basic sociological paradigms: social facts, social definitions, and social behavior. These qualify as paradigms in that they are much broader than theories and serve to organize, integrate, and guide theories. "It subsumes, defines, and interrelates the exemplars, theories, methods, and instruments that exist within it" (Ritzer 1975, p. 157). The exemplar for the social-facts paradigm, for instance, is Emile Durkheim, especially his *Rules of Sociological Method*, in which he introduced and expanded on the concept of a social fact. "Durkheim argued that social facts were to be *treated* as things . . . for purposes of sociological analysis" (1975, p. 158). The two most important theories to be included within this paradigm are structural functionalism and conflict theory. The exemplar for the social-definition paradigm is Max Weber, and the dominant theories are action theory, symbolic interactionism, and phenomenology. The contemporary exemplar of the social-behavior paradigm is B. F. Skinner, and the dominant theories are behavioral sociology and exchange theory. Ritzer holds:

> . . . The three paradigms discussed in this paper explain much of contemporary sociology, but it is important to point out that there are things that do *not* fit. Two good examples of this are critical theory and biologism. Both of these perspectives may well form the bases of new sociological paradigms in the future. . . . However they lack, at least now, the political clout needed to rally a large number of adherents. (Ibid., p. 164)

The implication of Ritzer's position for the development of a Chicano paradigm are not only clear but profound. First, if political clout, rather than logic or theoretical parsimony, is the ultimate criterion for gaining paradigmatic acceptance and legitimation, nontraditional perspectives are, almost by definition, doomed to failure. Second, since sociology is a multiple-paradigm science, there is no logical or theoretical reason to preclude the emergence of alternative paradigms such as the one I proposed. And most significantly, none of the paradigms identified by Ritzer, even the would-be paradigms, reflect the perspective or world view of oppressed racial and ethnic groups. Despite their avowed differences, all are based on Euro-American world views and subscribe to the basic tenets of scientism. Thus, although Ritzer's and

Baca Zinn's conceptions of sociology as a multiple-paradigm science makes Chicano paradigms at least theoretically possible, the recognition that political clout rather than logic is the ultimate condition for acceptance makes their emergence highly improbable. The problem with such conceptualization is that it fails to recognize that the fundamental cleavage between the dominant society and oppressed groups virtually precludes the acceptance of our paradigms. Their acceptance, after all, would mean rejection not only of prevailing paradigms but of the dominant order.

A basic tenet of my initial paradigm, it will be recalled, was that the ethos of scientism works to perpetuate the subordination of Chicanos and other groups through its undue emphasis on objectivity, value neutrality, and universalism. I argued, in effect, that these norms "discourage the emergence and incorporation of minority paradigms and neutralize attempts by minority scholars to modify prevailing world views" (1978, p. 302). I further contended that if sociology is to be a vehicle for liberation and for eliminating rather than perpetuating oppression, it must take the side of the oppressed. I called, in other words, for an advocatory sociology, while at the same time recognizing that its acceptance would be resisted by establishment sociology for being "political, partisan and otherwise incongruous with the norms of science" (1978, p. 307).

My intent in advocating a new paradigm of Chicano sociology was to reject prevailing conceptions of Chicanos that emerged from the field of study which I termed the sociology of Mexican-Americans and saw as being in direct opposition to Chicano sociology. The sociology of Mexican-Americans simply took existing perspectives and applied them to Chicanos, while it failed to "develop new paradigms or theoretical frameworks consistent with a Chicano world view or responsive to the nuances of Chicano culture" (ibid., p. 295). Recent works by Baca Zinn, Moore (1978), and other contemporary sociologists are less pejorative, more insightful and sophisticated analyses of Chicanos. Although these works tend to refer to us as Chicanos rather than Mexican-Americans, they are still largely exercises in the sociology of Chicanos rather than in Chicano sociology. The distinction is fundamental to the development of a Chicano paradigm.

A basic problem with Baca Zinn is her failure to distinguish between the sociology of Chicanos and Chicano sociology. Except when referring to my paradigm, she does not use "Chicano sociology" but terms like the "sociology of Chicanos," "sociological writing about Chicanos," "sociological treatments of Chicanos," and "the study of Chicanos." For Baca Zinn "what most needs to be clarified is the difference between theories and paradigms" (1981, p. 286); for me the distinction between Chicano sociology and the sociology of Chicanos is even more critical. Baca Zinn's ultimate frame of reference appears to be sociology, not Chicanos. She sees sociology as "a pluralistic discipline characterized by numerous alternative conceptions of theory, explanations, and data—that is, by different approaches or perspectives" (1981, p 257). The study of Chicanos, thus, "will require the adoption of multiple theoretical perspectives" (ibid., p. 268). Her intent clearly is to apply existing sociological theories and paradigms to Chicanos. My intent, on the other hand, is to develop a Chicano sociology with its own distinctive theories, methods, exemplars, and paradigms: that is, a Chicano perspective not only on Chicanos but on sociology and science. The first approach sees sociology as the center of the universe and seeks to make Chicanos fit its theories and paradigms; the second sees Chicanos as the center and seeks to make sociology conform to a Chicano world view. It is significant that rather than calling for an alternative sociology, Baca Zinn wants to work toward the development of "a Chicano paradigm that *incorporates theories* now being *developed in the discipline*" (1981, p. 268, emphasis mine).

The Roots of a Chicano Paradigm

Despite recent trends and theoretical developments, and the growing sophistication of the sociology of Chicanos, the need for Chicano sociology seems as great today as ever. The fundamental issue for Chicano sociologists is whether to make the study of Chicanos fit into prevailing social-science paradigms or to develop new paradigms that emanate from within Chicano culture and the Chicano experience.

According to Ritzer the four basic components of a paradigm are an exemplar, image of the subject matter, theories, and methods. Let us examine each of the four components to see if a tentative Chicano paradigm can be identified.

Exemplar

Although a number of proponents of the protest literature could be seen as exemplars (e.g., Vaca 1970; Hernández 1970; and Montiel, 1970), the primary exemplar of the Chicano paradigm is clearly Octavio Romano, not only in his writing but in his journal, *El Grito*, which sought to expound and develop a Chicano world view. In "Anthropology and Sociology of the Mexican-Americans" Romano (1968b) argued that social scientists have distorted Chicano history in their depictions of Mexican-Americans as passive and controlled by a monolithic traditional culture. Rather than being objective, social-science accounts have been "pernicious, vicious, misleading, degrading, and brain-washing in that they obliterate history and then rewrite it in such a way as to eliminate the historical significance of Mexican-Americans" (1968b, p. 24).

Romano (1970) further develops the implications of the cult of objectivity for Chicanos in "Social Science, Objectivity, and the Chicanos." For Romano, that objectivity is an essential component of the scientific enterprise is a central tenet of scientism. But such emphasis on objectivity is based on a dualistic conception of man, a belief in the separation of mind and body. This dualism can be traced to Greek Orphic mysticism. "Western man.. . . in his quest for a pure objective reality (that is, to be objective) began to consider events, phenomena, and ideas as apart from personal self-consciousness, to be dealt with ideally in a detached, impersonal, and unprejudiced manner" (1970, p. 5). Although social science continues to be guided by the cult of objectivity, a belief in the necessity of separating oneself and one's beliefs from external objective reality, this belief has gradually been called into question by Chicano social scientists. Romano, therefore, felt that social science was entering a new revolutionary era. The situation was unique not only because "the studied were now studying the studiers" but because social science would be grounded in a Chicano world view (1970, p. 12).

Image of the Subject Matter

The basic image of the subject matter is one where the Chicano is viewed as creator of culture and as actively resisting oppression rather than as being passive and dependent. The yardstick for evaluating Chicanos is not Anglo culture and values but Chicanos themselves. Chicano culture and family are not pathological but adaptive, coping mechanisms that provide warmth and succor in an otherwise hostile environment. Whereas Western culture is based on objectivity and the separation of truth and feeling, Chicano culture is based on subjectivity, particularism, and the merging of truth and feeling. We must therefore look within our *indio-mestizo* cultural heritage for truth and knowledge.

Theories

Internal colonialism and Marxism are generally recognized as the two dominant theories of Chicano sociology today (see chapter nine), although colonialism should more properly be viewed as a description of a historical process than as a theory. Also, a number of contemporary social scientists have attempted to integrate and synthesize the two perspectives (see Blauner 1972; Almaguer 1975; Barrera 1979). They have sought, in other words, to identify both the racial and class basis of Chicano oppression. Although these works are significant contributions, and they have advanced our knowledge of Chicanos far beyond cultural deficiency theories, they are still based primarily on Western models of truth and reality. Both are structural theories and fit well within what Ritzer terms the social-facts paradigm. Theories that are truly organic to Chicano culture and world views have yet to be developed.

Methods

Chicano methodology is even less well developed than Chicano theory.[3] To date there has not been a systematic statement on Chicano methodology. Yet some of the early protest literature did point the way toward possible future methodological developments. Certainly any method that separates the individual from his social milieu is unacceptable from a Chicano perspective. Field research and participant observation appear most consonant with a Chicano paradigm, but it must be a methodology that does not draw a dichotomy between participation and observation or between truth and feeling. It must be a methodology, in other words, that permits the Chicano sociologist to advance our understanding of the Chicano experience without in any way neutralizing or compromising his or her position as an advocate for Chicano issues: a methodology that permits one to be both researcher and Chicano.

Chicano methodology would certainly challenge the basic tenets of scientism—objectivity, value neutrality, and universalism. Instead it would promote subjectivity, value commitment, and particularism. Its primary referent in identifying problems for research and in utilizing the results would be the Chicano community rather than the academic community. Some of the primary exemplars of Chicano methodology are Ernesto Galarza (1964, 1970, and 1977), George I. Sánchez (1940), Manuel Gamio (1930 and 1931), and Américo Paredes (1958).

In *"With His Pistol in His Hand"*: *A Border Ballad and Its Hero,* for example, Dr. Américo Paredes (1958), noted Chicano folklorist, skillfully, if not brilliantly, researched the story of the Chicano social bandit Gregorio Cortez (see chapter four). The basic contribution of this pioneering work is that it demonstrated how one could carry out ethnographic research that is scholarly and, at the same time, socially committed and sensitive to Chicano culture. Paredes, for example, shows how an interpreter's ignorance of the subtleties of the Spanish language contributed to the shoot-out with Sheriff Morris and to Cortez becoming a fugitive from justice. The sheriff attempted to arrest Cortez after he denied buying a horse (*caballo*) because he had bought a mare (*yegua*) (ibid, p. 61). His statement "you can't arrest me for nothing" was probably translated as "no white man can arrest me" (ibid., p. 62). Sheriff Morris was subsequently "interpreted to death." This is clearly an impressive scholarly work, but one imbued with a Chicano world view, nonetheless. In fact, in reading Paredes one cannot help but wonder whether it is possible to do valid ethnographic research without being knowledgeable of and sensitive to the nuance of the culture under study.

In a more recent work Paredes (1977, p. 2) indirectly argues for a Chicano social science, but he cautions against the tendency of Chicano scholars to be overly critical of traditional social scientists. The problem with Anglo ethnographers like William Madsen and Arthur Rubel is not that they are racist but that they are ignorant of Chicano language and culture. They may, however, have an unconscious bias which forces data to fit "preconceived notions and stereotypes" (ibid.). A second problem is that, unlike anthropologists who studied so-called "primitive" cultures, the work of contemporary ethnographers is subjected to more critical review.

> . . . It was one thing to publish ethnographies about Trobrianders or Kwakiutls half a century ago; it is another to study people who read what you write and are more than willing to talk back. The present-day anthropologist writing about minority groups in the United States faces problems undreamed of by Malinowski or Boas. (Ibid.)

The issue of whether to use "ethnics" as ethnographers may not be that relevant, especially if they "receive the same kind of training that has been received by their mentors in the past" (ibid.).

One possible remedy is the use of better sampling techniques that reflect the internal diversity of the Chicano people. Even more central, however, is the issue of language. Many anthropologists who purport to be fluent in Spanish are often only minimally fluent, and they fail to appreciate the nuance and complexity of the Chicano language.

> . . . As a matter of fact, some of us less-gifted verbalists are not particularly fluent speakers even in our native tongue. We may console ourselves, however, with the thought that parrots and very small children are terrifically fluent without knowing much of what they say. (Ibid., p. 3)

Paredes presents an interesting example from Rubel's *Across the Tracks.* Rubel recorded the following conversation at the headquarters of a Chicano political candidate:

> . . . Sometimes the conversation of the campaigners focused on strategy. At such times there was much talk of *hacienda* [sic] *movida, hay mucha movida,* and "moving the people." Such phrases implied that the Mexican-American electorate—the *chicanazgo* [sic]—was a dormant mass, which had to be stirred into activity. (1977, p. 4)

Rubel's ignorance of Chicano speech patterns is amazing. He confuses *hacienda* for *haciendo* (moving) and *chicanazgo* for *chicanada* (the people). What the campaign workers were actually saying is that they wanted to "make a move." "Not knowing the significance of *movida*, Rubel misinterprets the conversation, drawing unwarranted, stereotyped conclusions about Chicano behavior from what he thought he heard, seeing Chicanos as passive, apolitical, and incapable of organizing much of anything" (ibid., p. 4).

Another very common error results from the failure to understand or appreciate Chicano humor and our capable and subtle use of verbal art. In doing research social scientists would do well to "Keep in mind that Chicanos and Mexicans do have a sense of humor, and that they love to put strangers on" (ibid., p. 8).

One of the most provocative statements on Chicano methodology has come from Baca Zinn (1979b) in her article "Field Research in Minority Communities: Ethical, Methodological and Political Observations by an Insider." She extends the insider-outsider controversy by applying it to minority researchers and showing that while they hold certain advantages in carrying out field research in minority communities, they face ethical, methodological, and personal concerns that are unique. One of the problems insiders who research their own communities have is that they often become emotionally and socially involved with the people they study. In leaving the field the researcher may become keenly aware of the uneven, perhaps exploitative, nature of the relationship (1979b, p. 217). This is presumably a heavier burden for an insider than it is for an outsider.

Baca Zinn concludes:

> . . . The creation of a social science which has liberating rather than oppressive ramifications will require fundamental alterations in the relationships between minority peoples and conditions of research. Gestures of reciprocity do not, by themselves, alter the unequal nature of research relationships. Nor is having research conducted by insiders sufficient to alter the inequality that has characterized past research. Field research conducted by committed minority scholars may provide a corrective to past empirical distortions in that we are better able to get at some truths. However, our minority identity and commitment to be accountable to the people we study may also pose unique problems. These problems should serve to remind us of our political responsibility and compel us to carry out our research with ethical and intellectual integrity. (ibid, pp. 217-18)

I concur with Baca Zinn and hold that part of our ethical, moral, and political responsibility as scholars is to develop paradigms that are not only organic to our culture and values but that can serve as vehicles for ending our oppressive and subordinate condition. It is to this end that I proposed the paradigm of Chicano sociology. Unlike black sociology, which has a long and rich intellectual history and prominent exemplars such as W.E.B. Dubois and E. Franklin Frazier, Chicano sociology and Chicano social science have only recently emerged. It is precisely for this reason that we must recognize that the bulk of our sociological legacy is alien and European and begin to forge our own unique brand of sociological imagination: an imagination drawn not from a foreign ethos, but from our rich cultural heritage, and firmly grounded in the reality of our contemporary experience.

Bringing Culture Back In

An interesting paradox has emerged in Chicano scholarship since the protest literature of the late 1960s and early 1970s. This literature emerged in response to negative and unsympathetic portrayals of Chicano culture in traditional social science. It was critical of social science and proposed that Chicano perspectives were needed to correct the many biases and limitations of mainstream perspectives.

In retrospect, perhaps the basic failing of the protest literature was that it remained largely reactive rather than proactive. It was somehow easier to expose the shortcomings and limitations of social science than it was to offer alternative formulations or new Chicano paradigms. The paradox is that although Chicano scholarship has increasingly grown in acceptance and sophistication, it has failed to provide an adequate reformulation or theoretical conceptualization of Chicano culture. Stereotypes and misconceptions have been widely and vigorously refuted, but they have not been supplanted by new, more positive depictions of our *cultura*. It appears, in fact, that the predominant response of Chicano scholars to negative stereotyping of culture was to avoid the issue of culture altogether.

Most Chicano scholars have discarded internal colonialism because it is not perceived as viable for understanding the contemporary Chicano experience. Some have turned to Marxism, while others, like Baca Zinn (1981), have called for more eclectic approaches that incorporate structural and micro- and macrolevels of analysis. A major criticism of the internal-colony model has been its presumed preoccupation with culture and ethnicity and the neglect of structure and class. What is perhaps most ironic about this criticism is that neither proponents nor detractors of internal colonialism have done much to advance our understanding of Chicano culture.

In the preface to the second edition of *Occupied America* Rodolfo Acuña, one of the pioneers of Chicano scholarship, laments the fact that it does not cover the cultural history of the Chicano people. He also explains why he discarded the internal-colony model.

. . . The first edition of *Occupied America* followed the current of the times, adopting the internal colonial model which was popular during the late 1960s and early 1970s. . . . I have reevaluated the internal colonial model and set it aside as a useful paradigm relevant to the nineteenth century but not to the twentieth. (1981, p. vii)

His rationale for dropping the colonial model is intriguing, for it suggests that the decision was based, at least in part, on the lack of popularity of the model rather than on its intellectual or theoretical merits. The second edition, thus, also appears to follow the current *zeitgeist* in Chicano scholarship. Acuña, however, falls short of openly adopting a Marxist perspective and instead concludes, "After examining a multitude of other paradigms advanced by Chicano scholars in the past ten years, I decided to return to basics and collect historical data" (ibid.).

Perhaps what is most disturbing is that, with a few notable exceptions (see chapter nine), internal colonialism and Marxism have been posed as polar or contradictory perspectives rather than as complementary ones. A related concern is that the rejection of internal colonialism has resulted knowingly or unknowingly in a de-emphasis of the study of Chicano culture. This is unfortunate, for there is no necessary link between the internal-colony model and culture. One can recognize the importance of culture without subscribing to the model, and one can subscribe to the model without recognizing the importance of culture. Maxine Baca Zinn (1981), for example, sees Marxism as only one of several viable social-science theories, but she is a strong advocate of structural explanations, nonetheless (1980a and b, and 1982c). Mario Barrera (1979), on the other hand, subscribes to the internal colonial model, while giving only token attention to culture.

I propose that Chicano scholarship has reached an impasse and that conditions are ripe for a new synthesis that reflects the dynamic interrelationship between structure and culture. That imperialism and capitalism have had a profound effect on Chicanos and radically altered the relationship between Mexico and the United States is unquestionable. We have seen how the war with Mexico and the acquisition of Aztlán were motivated by an expansionist capitalistic system. Chicanos provided much of the cheap and dependent labor in the mines, fields, railroads, and factories that was used to develop American capitalism in the nineteenth and twentieth centuries. Racism became a convenient ideology for justifying the economic exploitation of people of color.

The conflict and tension that has historically characterized relations between Chicanos and the dominant society, however, extends well beyond political economy. In addition to being a conflict between economic systems, it has been a conflict between competing cultures, philosophies, religious systems, and world views.

While political economy is essential to an adequate understanding of the Chicano experience, Chicano paradigms in the social sciences cannot continue to ignore the role of culture in determining and shaping the behavior of Chicanos. Tomás Almaguer has noted that racism has a structural component and a material basis. Race and racism are not simply epiphenomena but manifest a reality of their own.

> . . . This current in Marxian theory has viewed racism simply and primarily as an ideology that the ruling class has used to divide the working class and to deflect attention away from the contradictions between capital and labor and onto social minorities. . . . The result of this has been to minimize the importance of race itself being a central form of oppression and central organizing principle of the class system. (1975, p. 72)

I concur with Almaguer and hold that emergent Chicano paradigms must recognize, moreover, that in a very real sense race transcends class. Chicanos are exploited and subjugated to differential and unequal treatment both between and within social classes.

Mario Barrera has proposed a theory of racial inequality that is a synthesis of internal colonial and Marxist models (see chapter nine). Barrera argues that persons within a particular class have interests in common with all members of that class, regardless of ethnicity.

> . . . A Chicano in the subordinate segment of the working class is still a member of that class, and has interests in common with all members of the working class, for example, in higher wages, better working conditions, the right to bargain collectively, and, ultimately, the establishment of a classless society. These interests are in opposition to those of other classes, particularly the capitalistic class. (1979, p. 214)

Racial segmentation, however, cuts across class lines, so that Chicanos within each class occupy a subordinate segment of that class. This means that Chicanos as a group have certain interests in common (i.e., colonial interests) such as the ending of social discrimination.

> . . . The different Chicano segments also constitute an internal colony in the sense that they share a common culture, at least in part, and this may be reflected in a shared interest in such things as bilingual-bicultural programs in the schools. (1979, p. 216)

Barrera's theory has done much to enhance our understanding of Chicano oppression and represents a significant contribution to Chicano scholarship. Yet what is perhaps most lacking in his theory is a clear vision of

Chicano culture. His theory is, ultimately, a mergence of two structural discrimination theories—internal colonialism and Marxism (ibid., p. 184). Barrera categorizes theories of racial inequality into three basic categories: deficiency theories (i.e., biological, social structural, and cultural), bias theories
(i.e., Anglo prejudice and discrimination), and structural discrimination theories (i.e., caste-class school, internal colonialism, and Marxism). Barrera completely discards deficiency theories and concludes that bias theories are not so
much wrong as incomplete in that they fail to identify the origins of racism,
but he does not present a positive cultural theory of the Chicano experience.
One is therefore led to conclude either that Chicanos have no culture, other
than a common interest in things like bilingual education and Cinco de Mayo
parades, or that culture is epiphenomenon.

Regardless of the spirit of the times there is a need to develop and articulate a positive conception of Chicano culture. Chicanos have a rich
cultural heritage that predates not only the Chicano movement of the 1960s
but the war between Mexico and the United States, and even the landing
of the Pilgrims at Plymouth Rock. A full understanding of the Chicano experience cannot be obtained without incorporating this cultural heritage.
This is to suggest not that political and economic forces are not significant,
but rather that our culture, identity, and sense of self-worth are not simply
reflections of our exploitation at the hands of the Anglo.

A careful reexamination of traditional social science suggests that its
conception of Chicano culture was sometimes not so much wrong as it was
misguided. Many of the cultural traits which were identified by cultural-
deficiency theories have some basis in fact, but they were distorted and viewed
negatively because they ran counter to dominant values. Chicanos were seen
as being present oriented, subjugated to nature, seeking immediate gratification, complacent, nongoal oriented, emotional, fatalistic, dependent, male
dominant, superstitious, and traditional. If these values are transformed into
positive traits, one could say that we are more at one with nature, less concerned with individual success and more oriented to the welfare of the group,
cooperative rather than competitive, more open in the expression of feelings,
and interested in the welfare and feelings of others.

Nathan Murillo (1971, p. 99) proposes, for example, that we have a different orientation toward work, so that we are much more likely to "work
in order to live" than to "live in order to work." We are also much less likely
to judge a person in terms of the presence or absence of material things and
more in terms of their moral character or personal integrity. Our passion for
life has been misperceived as a tendency to live in the present and not plan
for the future. It is interesting to "note that today much of our Anglo society's psychotherapy is aimed at developing or rekindling a here and now time
orientation as a means to improved mental health" (ibid., p. 100). Murillo

also contends that we put much more emphasis on courtesy and manners than Anglos. We emphasize diplomacy and tactfulness, whereas the Anglo "is much more likely to express himself simply, briefly, and frequently bluntly" (ibid., p. 101). As Octavio Paz has observed, the Mexican hides behind a wide assortment of masks in order to obscure his solitude.

Our manner of expression is also more elaborate and indirect, and we take great pains to make interpersonal relations harmonious, at least on the surface. A final cultural trait identified by Murillo is our strong emphasis on familism. For many Chicanos the family is likely to be the most important unit.

The concepts of *machismo* and *hembrismo*, as redefined in chapter eight, now take on added significance, for they incorporate a series of important and interrelated cultural values. They represent not male dominance or female submission and subordination but the pride, dignity, respect, perseverance, and intransigence of our people.

These values enabled Chicanos to cope with economic, political and cultural exploitation, but they often produced conflicts with Anglo society. As José Armas observed,

> The Familia values of cooperation, unity, respect, dignity and honor of individuals which are traditional, are the forces of "La Raza" today.
>
> These attributes have always caused us problems in dealing with the Anglo who has confused our humility for fear, our courtesy for weakness, our respect for inferiority. Yet, we have endured and we are prevailing. (1976, p. 17)

The task before Chicano scholars is to develop paradigms and theoretical perspectives that build on and incorporate these and other cherished *raza* values. Perhaps the call for a Chicano world view or paradigm is premature at this time, given that Chicano scholarship is in a nascent stage. However, even if we are not yet ready to offer or identify a definitive paradigm, demonstrating the need for a Chicano perspective is an essential first step in the process of paradigmatic development.

APPENDIX

Chicano-Police Conflict: A Case Study

Having examined the general processes through which the Chicano people were first displaced and then maintained in a subordinate position, the book concludes with a case study of Casa Blanca, a barrio in Riverside, California, established in the 1880s. Although it would be inaccurate and misleading to term any barrio "typical" or representative of all Chicano communities, the experiences of Casa Blanca residents are a microcosm of those of Chicanos as a whole. This case study, moreover, illustrates the process of isolation or barrioization which has occurred in Chicano communities throughout the Southwest.

The first Mexican *pobladores* of San Salvador (the joint communities of La Placita and Agua Mansa) were subsequently displaced by midwestern and New England Protestants who settled nearby and established what would develop into the present-day city of Riverside (see chapter two). As the Mexican community declined, Mexican settlers became a source of cheap and dependent labor in the emerging agricultural economy. The barrio of Casa Blanca had its origins as housing for citrus workers on the outskirts of the city. As the city grew and expanded, however, Casa Blanca was incorporated within the city limits. Most residents moved out of agricultural work and into low-paying urban occupations outside the barrio. Like other Chicano communities, it is characterized by widespread poverty, an abundance of substandard housing, a high push-out rate in the schools, and the absence of political representation.

Yet perhaps the two most pervasive characteristics of this and other barrios are (1) a pattern of geographic and social isolation and (2) a long history of conflict and tension between the community and the police. These patterns are very much intertwined, as law enforcement has played a critical role in maintaining the isolation of Chicano communities. A study of conflict in a Dallas barrio, for example, reported through testimony before the Greater Dallas Community Relations Commission that residents typically

> . . . felt the police were in West Dallas not to protect the citizenry of West Dallas, but to shield the rest of Dallas from the Mexican-American community. They described the law officers as "troops stationed here to control us rather than to be public servants of the peo-

ple." They expressed fear for their safety and told how many had to stay
in their homes after dark since they believed the law officers had declared "open season on Mexican Americans." (Cited in Achor 1978,
p. 108)

While patterns of police abuse have been common and widespread
throughout the history of the Southwest, Chicano-police conflict has been
a neglected area of study.[1] The prevailing concern of social scientists has been
with lawlessness and criminality among Chicanos themselves. There is a need
for research that questions these beliefs and examines firsthand the attitudes
of barrio residents not only toward law enforcement but toward crime and
civil liberties. This chapter seeks to add to our understanding of Chicano-
police relations by presenting an overview of conflict with police in an urban
barrio, testing several hypotheses concerning fear of the police, attitudes
toward increasing or curtailing police power, support of civil liberties, and
fear of crime. For example, do barrio residents blame the police for major
disturbances in the community or are they basically supportive of police?
Does support for increasing police power increase as fear of crime increases?
Does fear of the police by Chicanos lead to greater support for civil liberties
and increase the desire to curtail police power?

The Setting

The setting for this case study of Chicano-police conflict is a barrio in
Riverside, a Southern California community of approximately 170,000 inhabitants. The barrio was selected for study not only because it has been the
site of recent civil disorders which have gained national attention but because like other barrios in the Southwest it is isolated from Anglo society and
has a long history of conflict with the police. Like most barrios, it is a distinctive community within the city, extending over an area that is approximately
one square mile and includes about 3,000 persons within its boundaries.

From its inception as housing quarters for citrus pickers, Casa Blanca
has been segregated from the city. As early as 1874 the Riverside Board of
Education created a separate school district to exclude Chicano children from
Anglo schools. Initially there were not many Chicano residents in the area,
and during the 1880s and 1890s it was predominantly an Anglo suburb and
the site of several exclusive social clubs, a tennis club, and a polo club. But
segregation prevailed, and within twenty-five years the suburb would be transformed into a Chicano barrio surrounded by large, prestigious homes. Problems with the law were to surface early. In 1916 a citizen's committee chaired
by the mayor requested and obtained the hiring of extra policemen for the
barrio, and the following year an extra officer was hired to patrol on Saturday

nights. In the same year requests were made for as many as eight additional police. Since the 1940s killings, shootings, and beatings of Chicanos by the police have been commonplace.

The barrio shares certain important features with urban slums in that the income and educational level of many residents is low and some of the housing is poor or substandard, but it also differs from the slum in some important respects. First, although there is poverty in the barrio, everyone is not poor. There is considerable variability in the economic and educational attainment of residents.[2] Second, the barrio has emerged partly as a result of prejudice and segregation, but there is an element of voluntarism to barrio residence, and a strong sense of community identification prevails. Barrios are literally *colonias* (colonies), ethnic enclaves within the territorial boundaries of the United States.

This barrio is similarly isolated. Located on the outskirts of the city, it is bounded on the northwest by the freeway, on the southeast by orange groves which separate it from prestigious low-density housing known as the Green Belt area, on the northeast by a modest middle-class suburb, and on the southwest by orange groves and fields that separate it from a commercial district that includes a number of car dealerships. Its isolation has been so extensive that until recent years many of the streets in the barrio were unpaved and residents were not afforded normal city services. Today ambulances are still reluctant to enter the community without a police escort.

The confluence of two diverse though mutually reinforcing forces—residential segregation and a positive identification with barrio residence—have worked to produce a remarkably stable pattern of community residence. Not only are most residents of the community Chicano (about 90 percent), but typically they have lived there all or virtually all of their lives. This, of course, does not necessarily mean that most people born and raised in the barrio would remain there for the rest of their lives, since a community survey obviously excludes those persons who have moved out. What is significant is not that most people who are born in the barrio stay there but that very few new residents move in. New arrivals, moreover, especially if they come from Mexico, are likely to have relatives or friends already living in the community. The stability of the community is further intensified by what appears to be a tendency toward endogamous marriage, so that a strong sense of familism pervades community life. The statement frequently made in jest that "everyone in the barrio is related to everyone else" is not without some factual basis. One person, for example, noted that he had over 260 relatives living in the community.

The stability, cohesiveness, and apparent serenity of the community stand in sharp contrast to the conflict and tension that pervades community-police relations. The police have traditionally been viewed not only as outsiders but as representatives of the dominant, oppressive Anglo society. Over the past seven or eight years prior to the study there had been about one Chicano shot per year. Residents complain of extensive police abuse and harassment. Community-police conflict is especially intense among youth, who are frequently the target of such abuse and harassment.

Community-police conflict culminated in two major incidents in August 1975. One incident occurred on August 2, as the police broke up a bachelor party, tear-gassed the home where the party was being held, and beat up and arrested a large number of the guests. Although fifty-two persons were arrested, almost all charges were subsequently dropped for insufficient evidence, and the city has since settled a number of civil suits out of court. On October 7, 1980, a federal jury in Los Angeles found the Riverside police guilty of violating the civil rights of eight persons involved in the disturbance (Bennett 1980). The second incident was unrelated but served to exacerbate antipolice sentiment. The stabbing of an Anglo male, believed to be a police informer, at a park in the community on August 13 provided the impetus for this incident. The police, in pursuit of the assailant(s), surrounded a corn field throughout the evening of August 13 and the morning of August 14. Tear gas was dropped from a helicopter, and there was extensive gunfire throughout the night. Sheriff's units from Riverside County and San Bernardino County were brought in to reinforce city police, as was the SWAT team from San Diego. The result was a police siege. Residents were stopped and questioned by police as they attempted to go to work or carry on normal daily activities. The August 13 incident was termed a riot by the police and the media. If it was a "riot," it was more of the "commodity" than the "communal" variety, although there was no looting or destruction of business property, which is owned by residents of the community. It was more accurately described as a community-police confrontation, with the police intermittently exchanging gunfire with residents.

The Study

Our survey of community attitudes toward the police was completed within two months of these incidents. Its primary objective was to assess attitudes toward the police not only relative to their handling of the August incidents but in general. The interview schedule covered a number of areas, including (1) general attitudes concerning the police, protection of civil liberties, and fear of crime, (2) specific attitudes toward the police and their handling of the August incidents, and (3) social and demographic characteristics.

Given the extensiveness of police abuse and widespread official violence perpetrated against Chicanos, there is a great need for research that focuses on the conditions under which Chicanos are willing to increase or curtail police power and to support or not support civil liberties. Several hypotheses proposed and tested by Richard L. Block (1971) in a National Opinion Research Center (NORC) study were tested with our barrio respondents. While the hypotheses were tested with white and black respondents, they seemed especially applicable to Chicanos. One hypothesis proposes that since fear provides a rationale for granting the state power, fear of crime should lead to greater support for increasing police power. A second similarly argues that if fear is the primary basis for delimiting the power of the state, then fear of the police should intensify support for civil liberties. The rationale for the hypotheses is as follows:

> . . . If fear is a foundation of support for the state and the police are the state's instrument to control internal threat, then those people with the greatest fear of crime should be most willing to increase the power of the police. Similarly if fear of the state is the basis for limitation of the power of the state, and the police, as an instrument of the state, are a basis of fear of the state, then those respondents who most fear the police would be most likely to want their power limited through the protection of civil liberties. (Block 1971, pp. 93-94)

In applying these hypotheses to Chicanos we expected that while barrio residents would generally not support increasing police power, those who feared crime most would be most willing to support such increases. Also, since police abuse and brutality entail the violation of civil liberties, we expected widespread support for such safeguards with considerable fear of the police, and such support of civil liberties should be especially high among respondents who are most fearful of the police. We hypothesized, finally, that those barrio respondents who were most fearful of the police would want not only to protect civil liberties but to curtail or limit police power.

A random sample of households yielded 170 completed interviews. Though the sample is based on a random selection of households, it is somewhat purposive in the sense that a special effort was made to include youthful respondents, since it is among them that conflict with the police is believed to be most intense. Interviewers were instructed to interview an adult member of the household and a teenaged member whenever possible. This procedure was facilitated by the fact that interviewers normally worked in two-person teams. Inclusion of youth was also deemed important because Chicanos as a group are on the average much younger than the overall population.[3] The sample consists of 38 percent male adults, 35 percent female adults, 16 percent male teenagers, and 9 percent female teenagers. Approximately one out of every four respondents, then, are dependent children.

Interviews were conducted by bilingual-bicultural interviewers, trained and sensitive to the nuances of Chicano culture and the prevailing values of the barrio. Comments and suggestions of various political, civic and community leaders were sought and incorporated into the interview schedule. Interviewers and the principal investigator met with these leaders and were briefed on practices, procedures, and dress and demeanor that leaders believed would elicit maximum cooperation from the community in carrying out the project. Without the help and endorsement of these community members our task would have been difficult, if not impossible.

Basically the same questions used in the NORC survey were included as measures of the four major test variables in the study. Fear of crime was measured by the question

> How likely is it that a person walking around here at night might be held up or attacked—very likely, somewhat likely, somewhat unlikely, or very unlikely?

The index of fear of the police was the person's perception of "police respectfulness toward people like himself." Those respondents who rate police respectfulness as "not so good" are assumed to fear the police more than those who rate it as "pretty good" or "very good." In order to assess support for increases in police power respondents were asked:

> Do you favor giving the police more power to question people, do you think they have enough power already, or would you like to see some of their power to question people curtailed?

The last variable, protection of civil liberties, was measured by two questions regarding support for police review boards and for the right of a suspect to an attorney during police interrogations. Respondents who felt that a suspect has a right to a lawyer and who were in favor of establishing a police review board were said to be in "full support" of civil liberties.

Findings

Attitudes toward Police and Their Handling of the Incidents

A number of open- and close-ended questions were used to ascertain respondent perception of the August incidents and the police handling of them. In response to a close-ended item that asked "What do you see as the major reasons for the August 2 incident?" few respondents blamed the youth at the bachelor party, and most isolated police overreaction as the major factor leading to the disturbance. Specifically, about 17 percent did not respond, but of those that did, some 7 percent felt that the youth were out of control and the police were doing their job, 6 percent felt it was a misunderstanding betweeen the police and the people at the party, 4 percent felt the police overreacted somewhat, 57 percent that the police overreacted a great deal and used force and violence which was not needed, 3 percent gave some other miscellaneous response, and 23 percent did not know the reasons for the incident.

This question was followed up with a close-ended item that asked if they felt the August 2 incident could have been avoided. Most respondents felt that it could have been avoided (59 percent), 14 percent that it could not, and 26 percent either did not know for sure or did not answer. Those who felt it could have been avoided were asked to open-endedly indicate how it could have been avoided. The most common response was that it could have been avoided had the police used better judgment or not overreacted. Approximately 39 percent did not give a reason, but those who did were grouped into five broad categories. Only 4 percent felt that the youth should have listened to the police or shown more restraint (e.g., not thrown bottles at police), 43 percent that the police should have used better judgment, 26 percent that the police overreacted, 13 percent gave miscellaneous responses, and 14 percent did not know how it could have been avoided. The majority of respondents (69 percent) thus clearly blamed the August 2 incident on the police.

Our barrio residents were similarly critical of the police handling of the August 13 incident. In response to an open-ended question on what they saw as the major reasons for this disturbance, 19 percent did not answer. Only 2 percent of those who responded saw young people as causing the problem, and 4 percent thought the police were simply doing their job and enforcing the law. Thirty-five percent, on the other hand, were critical of the police; 7 percent felt the police used poor judgment in handling the situation (e.g., should not have called in the SWAT team), and a significant 28 percent felt that it was caused by police harassment or overreaction (e.g., young Anglo cops bothering the youth). Another 7 percent saw earlier incidents (especially August 2) as contributing to it, 12 percent gave another response, and 41 percent said they did not know what caused the incident. Most persons who responded also felt that the August 13 incident could have been avoided (55 percent), 34 percent that it could not have been, and 11 percent were not sure. Most of those who felt it could have been avoided isolated poor handling of the situation by the police and overpatrolling and harassment as major reasons for it. Only 7 percent said the incident could have been avoided if the youth had not overreacted or antagonized the police, while 40 percent felt the police handled the situation poorly or used too much force. Two percent cited a lack of respect for the police, and another 23 percent saw police overpatrolling and harassment of people as factors that led to the incident. Eight percent gave miscellaneous responses, and 19 percent did not know how it could have been avoided.

In a broader light, a series of open-ended questions asked respondents to indicate what they saw on the whole as the most important reasons for conflict between the community and city police. Ten percent did not respond. Of those who responded, 18 percent blamed the youth of the community for the conflict, another 16 percent saw a lack of communication or misunderstanding between police and residents (especially youth) as an explanation, and 5 percent felt that the youth lacked respect for the police. Another 3 percent saw the police as not respecting youth or Chicanos, 3 percent thought police do not do their job or enforce the law, 6 percent gave miscellaneous responses, and 16 percent did not know. By far the most common reason given for community-police conflict (35 percent), was police prejudice, harassment, and overpatrolling.

This question was followed by another open-ended question asking what they saw as the best way to solve the problem of barrio-police conflict. Although 47 percent did not offer any solution(s), of those who did, most isolated a need to either improve communication with the police or reform them, and, interestingly, few blamed the community for the problem. Five percent indicated that the police were doing a good job or needed to be granted more power, 5 percent that the community or Chicano youth should be reformed, 13 percent called for improving communications without blaming one side or the other for the problem, 13 percent felt that the police needed to learn more about the community or Chicanos in general, 31 percent that there was a need to "clean up" the force and stop their harassment of the community, 9 percent gave miscellaneous answers, and 23 percent indicated they did not know how to solve the problem.

The final open-ended question asked how the city police department could improve its services "to you, your neighbors, and community" and provided an interesting diversity of results. The responses ranged from those that felt the police were "doing a good job" or "needed to enforce the law more" to those that felt the "situation was hopeless" or that the police should "leave us alone"; intermediate between these extremes were persons who simply wanted to improve police services. Though approximately 14 percent did not give any suggestions for improving services, of those who did, 15 percent gave responses that could be interpreted as supportive of the police—6 percent were positive toward the police or said they did "the best they could," and 9 percent called for stronger enforcement of the law or more patrolling. An additional 4 percent called for better police services without offering strong criticism ("be here when needed," "don't be afraid to answer calls at night"), 17 percent called for improved communications ("try to understand us," "more understanding," "try to help people," "be sincere"), and 6 percent called either for having the police learn more about Chicanos, learn Spanish, or for more Chicano police. A substantial number (23 percent) implored the police to treat them with more respect and not abuse their authority ("treat us with respect," "treat us like humans," "treat us equally," "don't stop people all the time"). Three percent expressed the view that the situation was hopeless or that little could be done, 6 percent gave miscellaneous responses, and a full 27 percent said they did not know what could be done to improve police services.

While it is clear from the preceding that most respondents were critical of the police handling of the August incidents and saw their mishandling of these incidents as part of a broader pattern of pervasive police harassment and abuse, their negativity was neither all-encompassing nor predictable. In order to obtain a more direct measure of perceptions of community-police conflict, respondents were asked to "rate relations between police and residents of the barrio" on a five-point scale ranging from excellent to poor. Only 1 percent rated relations between the police and community as excellent, 7 percent saw them as good, 29 percent as average, 12 percent as below average, and as many as 48 percent as poor (3 percent were undecided).

Though relations between the police and the community are rated very low, barrio residents are not unilaterally critical of the police. When asked to give the police department an overall rating, it was rated higher than were relations between the police and the community. Seven percent rated the police department as excellent, 22 percent as good, 33 percent as average, 15 percent as below average, and 20 percent as poor (3 percent were undecided). Yet more persons rated the department as below average or poor than rated it as good or excellent. Differences between the rating of the police department per se and rating of relations between them and the community suggest considerable sophistication on the part of barrio residents and a keen awareness of differential treatment toward them by police. Chicanos do not tend to see the police as ill-trained or inept as much as they see them as treating them differently and unequally relative to others. A common complaint expressed by barrio residents is not that they want special or unusual treatment, only equal treatment with others.

Fear of Crime and Support for the Police in the Barrio

In the preceding section we discovered that though respondents were critical of the police in both their handling of specific disturbances and their general treatment of Chicanos, they were not blindly critical of the police. Their dissatisfaction was relatively specific, in other words, and not generalized to all situations. Not only did Chicano perceptions of the police vary

across situations but there was considerable diversity among them in their
perceptions and evaluations of the police. A number of barrio residents were,
in fact, supportive of the police and in some instances felt that they should
be granted more power to deal with crime and quell disturbances. We now
turn to an examination of certain conditions that may be associated with a
willingness to increase police power and curtail civil liberties. The questions
are worded more broadly, so rather than isolating specific attitudes toward a
given police department or actual incidents, they tap more general and abstract attitudes.

The first hypothesis addresses the question of whether fear of crime
among barrio residents is translated into a greater willingness to support increases in police power. The results are presented in Table 1, but before
discussing them, it should be noted that fear of crime in the barrio appears
to be minimal. Only 23 percent feel that attack in their neighborhood is
"very likely," whereas 28 percent see it as "very unlikely." As expected, few
of our respondents want to increase police power, and many wish to either
curtail or limit police power at its current level. Thirty-two percent wish to
curtail police power, and only about 14 percent wish to increase it from its
current level.

From Table 1 it is clear that the hypothesis is very strongly supported
in our sample. Those barrio residents who say street attack is very likely are
more likely to favor increases in police power, and this difference is statistically significant. Eighteen percent of the respondents who believe attack is
very likely support increasing police power, whereas only 4 percent of those
who feel it is very unlikely do so. Chicanos who see attack as very unlikely,
on the other hand, are much more inclined to want to curtail police power
(54 percent) than those who see attack as very likely (26 percent).

Table 1 shows the effect of several important background variables on
the relationship between fear of crime and support for the police. Age appears
to affect the relationship between fear of crime and support for the police.
That the relationship is strongest among barrio residents under 25 is perhaps
not surprising, since it is Chicano youth who more typically have direct experience with both crime and the police.

Two important patterns are evident when the second control variable,
length of residence in the community, is introduced. First and most obvious
is the great stability of residence among our respondents; only about 13 percent have lived in the community for less than 5 years, whereas 29 percent
have lived there 5 to 15 years, and 58 perent for 16 years or more. Second,
the relationship between fear of crime and support for the police is not as
strong or significant among short-term residents. In fact, among short-term
residents the relationship is inverse, although it is not statistically significant.
Apparently among short-term residents those who fear crime most are least

TABLE 1

Support for the Police and Fear of Attack

	FEAR OF ATTACK			
SUPPORT POLICE	Very likely	Somewhat likely	Somewhat unlikely	Very unlikely
More	18%	18%	19%	4%
Enough	55	69	45	41
Curtail	26	12	35	54
Total	100%	100%	100%	100%
N	38	49	31	46

Gamma = .35   Chi square = 22.42, P < .001

Support for the Police by Fear of Attack Controlling for*:

	Gamma	Chi square	P<
1. *Age*			
24 or less	.60	5.91	.05
25-40	.22	.52	.77
41 or more	.31	2.28	.31
2. *Length of Residence*			
Less than 5 years	-.38	.90	.64
5-15 years	.55	10.42	.005
16 years or more	.58	11.01	.005
3. *Like Living in Community*			
Yes	.58	15.04	.001
No	-.12	.19	.91
4. *Sex*			
Male	.71	18.01	.001
Female	.06	2.08	.35
5. *Family Income*			
Under $7,000	.58	4.68	.10
$7,000-9,999	.21	4.16	.12
$10,000 or more	.11	.32	.85
6. *Education*			
8 years or less	.68	8.65	.01
Some high school	.19	.82	.66
12 years or more	.44	3.94	.14

*Because of the small Ns Fear of Attack was dichotomized into "Likely" and "Unlikely."

supportive of the police. Length of residence in the barrio seems to enhance identification with the community and to intensify the relation between fear of crime and support of the police.

A related control variable is whether the person is satisfied living in the community or is dissatisfied and would like to move. The hypothesis is much more strongly supported among persons who like living in the barrio. This may appear incongruous at first glance if one expects those persons who are dissatisfied with the community to be more fearful of crime and more supportive of the police. Yet it may very well be that community identification increases involvement with community issues such as crime and control of the police, so that the relationship between these variables is most intense among those who identify with and are committed to the barrio.

The effect of gender on fear of crime and support for the police is clear and predictable. Since males in the barrio typically have more direct contact and exposure to crime and to the police, it is not surprising to find that the relationship between these variables is much stronger among men than women. Stated in a different way, the extent to which women in the barrio fear crime is less likely to affect their attitudes toward either increasing or curtailing police power.

The effects of income and education are less clear, but the relationship between fear of crime and support for increasing police power is stronger among respondents with low incomes and little formal education than among those with moderate or high incomes and more education. Chicanos with low incomes and little schooling, like men and youth in the barrio, are more likely to be victims of crime and of police abuse.

Fear of the Police and Support for Civil Liberties in the Barrio

The second major hypothesis to be examined concerns the effects of fear of the police on support for civil liberties among barrio residents. We expected those Chicanos who were most fearful of police also to be more supportive of civil guarantees, since such guarantees are designed to limit police abuses. Table 2 shows that the relationship is in the predicted direction but not statistically significant. Approximately 70 percent of those Chicanos who most fear the police support both measures to protect civil liberties compared to only 50 percent of those who least fear the police. The lack of statistical significance is undoubtedly due at least in part to the overall level of commitment to civil liberties among the Chicanos in our sample.[4] There was, in fact, little variation in the dependent variable, given that *none* were opposed to both measures and about 82 percent supported both measures.[5] In view of the level of support for civil liberties among barrio respondents it was not surprising also to find substantial fear of police among them. Approximately 39 per-

TABLE 2

Support for Civil Liberties and Fear of the Police

	POLICE RESPECT		
SUPPORT CIVIL LIBERTIES	Very Good	Pretty Good	Not So Good
Less support	50%	38%	30%
Full support	50%	62%	71%
Total	100%	100%	100%
N	34	60	61

Gamma = .27   Chi square = 3.95, P < .14

Support for Civil Liberties and Fear of the Police Controlling for*:

	Gamma	Chi square	P<
1. *Age*			
24 or less	.21	.11	.73
25-40	.50	1.16	.28
41 or more	.03	.09	.76
2. *Length of Residence*			
Less than 5 years	-.41	—	.41**
5-15 years	.38	.79	.37
16 years or more	.35	1.98	.16
3. *Like Living in Community*			
Yes	.27	1.31	.25
No	.14	0.00	1.00
4. *Sex*			
Male	.14	.13	.72
Female	.09	0.00	1.00
5. *Family Income*			
Under $7,000	.08	.02	.90
$7,000-9,999	1.00	—	.04**
$10,000 or more	0.00	.15	.70
6. *Education*			
8 years or less	.09	—	.62**
Some high school	.41	—	.26**
12 years or more	.20	.10	.75

* Because of the small Ns the "Very Good" and "Pretty Good" response to Police Respect were combined into a single "Good" category.
**Based on Fisher's Exact Probability test.

cent rated police respect toward persons like themselves as "not so good," and only 22 percent rated it as "very good."

The relationship between fear of the police and support for civil liberties appears stronger among Chicanos who are 25 to 40 years of age than among younger or older ones, and when age is dichotomized, it is considerably stronger among those 30 or older than among those under 30. Perhaps the reason for this is that the relationship between fear of the police and support for civil liberties is more indirect and abstract than the relationship between fear of crime and support for increasing police power, thereby manifesting itself more clearly among older or more mature barrio residents.

The hypothesis is more strongly supported among long-term residents of the community. In fact, among short-term residents the relationship is in the opposite direction: those Chicanos who fear the police most are least supportive of civil liberties. Although not statistically significant, there is also slightly more support for the hypothesis among those who like living in the barrio than those who do not, men than women, Chicanos of moderate rather than low or high income, and those with moderate rather than low or high educational attainment.

Fear of the Police and Support for the Police in the Barrio

The preceding hypotheses have been based on the assumption that much of the willingness of barrio residents to increase police power and limit civil guarantees is grounded in fear: fear both of crime and the police. Fear of crime is likely to lead some residents of the barrio to support increasing the power of the police. Fear of the police, on the other hand, intensifies the support of civil liberties to limit police abuses. Just as fear of the police should lead to greater support for civil liberties, so should it increase the desire to limit the power of police in the barrio, an hypothesis which will now be examined.

From Table 3 it is clear that the relationship between fear of the police and support for the police is strong and significant among our barrio respondents. As predicted, those Chicanos who fear the police most are least likely to support increases in police power. Sixty-three percent of the respondents who fear the police (i.e., who see police respect toward people like themselves as "not so good") desire to curtail or limit police power, whereas only 9 percent of those who do not fear the police desire to curtail it. This difference is, of course, highly significant.

From Table 3 it is also clear that the relationship between fear of the police and support for limiting police power remains significant even when background variables are controlled. The relationship, in other words, cuts

TABLE 3

Support for the Police and Fear of the Police

| | POLICE RESPECT | | |
SUPPORT POLICE	Very Good	Pretty Good	Not So Good
More	32%	20%	2%
Enough	59%	67%	35%
Curtail	9	13	63
Total	100%	100%	100%
N	34	61	60

Gamma = .72   Chi square = 51.84, P < .001

Support for the Police and Fear of the Police*:

	Gamma	Chi square	P<
1. *Age*			
24 or less	.74	10.06	.01
25-40	.94	14.25	.001
41 or more	.63	5.19	.07
2. *Length of Residence*			
Less than 5 years	1.00	9.29	.01
5-15 years	.98	29.39	.001
16 years or more	.73	18.10	.001
3. *Like Living in Community*			
Yes	.84	35.83	.001
No	.89	9.88	.01
4. *Sex*			
Male	.95	38.35	.001
Female	.65	9.60	.01
5. *Family Income*			
Under $7,000	.91	13.38	.001
$7,000-9,999	.95	12.61	.001
$10,000 or more	.71	11.15	.005
6. *Education*			
8 years or less	.96	13.71	.001
Some high school	.56	3.21	.20
12 years or more	.92	11.69	.005

*Because of the small Ns the "Very Good" and "Pretty Good" responses to Police Respect were combined into a single "Good" category.

across age groups in the barrio, although it appears weaker among older respondents. It is similarly supported among newly arrived and long-term residents, those who like living in the community as well as those who wish to move out of the barrio, men and women, persons of low, moderate, and high income, and across educational groups, although not significant among Chicanos with "some high school" education.

Summary and Discussion

This appendix presents a case study of a Southern California barrio that, like many others in the Southwest, has a tradition of conflict with the police. In addition to describing the community and its relations with the police, several hypotheses were tested concerning fear of crime and of the police as well as support for increasing or curtailing police power and protecting civil liberties.

Our survey revealed considerable diversity in attitudes toward the police (both general attitudes and specific ones that pertain to their handling of major disturbances), crime, and civil liberties. With regard to police handling of two major incidents in the barrio, some respondents were supportive of the police and blamed the disturbances on youth or the community, but most were critical of the police and blamed the disorders not only on their mishandling of these particular incidents but on a general pattern of police abuse and harassment. There is a pervasive feeling in the barrio that police do not treat Chicanos with dignity or respect and that they are subjected to differential and unequal treatment. Barrio residents, moreover, distinguish between the way police treat them and the way they treat other citizens and rate the police department higher overall than they rate relations between the police and the barrio.

On a more general level, a majority of barrio residents feel that the police have enough power and wish to either curtail it or keep it at its current level. Contrary to popular belief, fear of crime is not excessive in the barrio. Yet there is considerable fear of the police and a great deal of support for civil liberties among barrio residents.

The hypothesis that fear of crime leads to increases in support for police power, a hypothesis which received only moderate support in the NORC study, was strongly supported by our Chicano respondents. This suggests that the view of Chicanos as uniformly antipolice and supportive of crime should be modified to take into account the diversity of attitudes found among them. There appears to be a significant segment of the barrio who are fearful of crime and seek to increase police power. While it would be wrong to characterize them as a "silent majority" since most barrio residents feel that the police already have enough power, and many more wish to curtail than to increase police power, there is a need to acknowledge the existence of this segment of the Chicano community.

From the aforementioned one might expect that the relationship between fear of crime and support for police power would be stronger among those segments of the community that are ostensibly more fearful of crime and supportive of the police (e.g., the elderly, short-term residents, persons who are dissatisfied with the community, the better educated and more affluent, and women). The findings suggest an inverse pattern, however. The relationship is generally stronger among those groups in the barrio who are more directly involved with both crime and the police. The relationship is also strong among long-term residents and persons satisfied with living in the community because, they too, are more involved with issues such as crime and the police as a result of their greater commitment to, and identification with, the barrio.

The second hypothesis—that Chicanos who most fear the police are most likely to favor the protection of civil liberties—received only limited support in our survey, substantial support among whites and virtually none among blacks in the NORC survey. One reason for the relatively weak support for the hypothesis among Chicanos was their almost universal approval of civil liberties. More than four of five Chicanos supported *both* forms of civil liberties, compared to six of ten blacks and only three of ten whites in the NORC survey who supported both. The almost universal support of civil liberties among Chicanos suggests a need for discarding prevailing measures of civil liberties in favor of more sophisticated ones capable of discerning intragroup differences in such support. If these findings can be generalized to other Chicanos, regarding civil liberties most would believe that a suspect has a right to an attorney when being questioned by police and would be favorably disposed toward civilian review boards. Another possibility is that there is no necessary link between fear of the police and support for civil liberties among Chicanos, and as a result, those who are most fearful of the police are not significantly more likely to be supportive of civil liberties. Finally, it should be noted that the measure of fear of the police is indirect, and more significant results might have been obtained had a more direct and intricate measure been employed.

The final relationship examined was fear of the police and support for increased police power. There was very strong support for the hypothesis that fear of the police among barrio residents increases the desire to curtail police power. As significant as the magnitude of the relationship was the fact that it generally held across age groups, long-, medium-, and short-term residents of the barrio, Chicanos who liked living in the community and those that did not, men and women, persons of low, moderate, and high income, and those of varying educational levels. The strength of this relationship is perhaps not surprising when one considers the history of conflict between Chicanos and the police. As victims of police harassment and abuse, Chicanos have sought to limit and control police power, and much of the desire to curtail their power is grounded in fear of the police and their excesses.

Differences between our findings and those of the NORC study appear consistent with historical differences among the three racial-ethnic groups in attitudes toward crime, treatment by the police, and their relationship to the legal-judicial system. The NORC study reveals that Anglos obviously receive better treatment from the police and are more supportive of them than are blacks or Chicanos. They also have less reason to be fearful of personal attack, since they are less apt to be victims of violent crimes. Predictably, then, fear of crime is least among white and greatest among black respondents. It is interesting that though Chicanos fear crime less than blacks, they appear to fear the police more. This fear is not without justification. The history of Chicano-police relations has been one of conflict and tension, as we have noted. The police have traditionally served as tools for maintaining not only the oppressed position of Chicanos in the Southwest but their spatial and cultural isolation as well. This abuse and mistreatment has contributed not only to greater fear and distrust of the police but to increased support for civil liberties. The police generally are viewed as a vehicle for perpetuating the interests of Anglo-American society rather than as a supportive or protective agency.

The findings of the study have important theoretical and practical implications. Yet, because the study is limited to a single barrio in Southern California, the results are tentative or suggestive rather than conclusive. Although the Riverside barrio appears similar to many other barrios in the Southwest, one cannot be certain the same patterns would be found in other regions, in rural settings, or among nonbarrio Chicanos. Research is needed to substantiate them in other settings. Such research will hopefully not only provide additional insights into the dynamics of Chicano community-police relations but help to ease the conflict and tension which prevail in barrios throughout the Southwest.

Notes

1. Introduction: Toward a Chicano Social Science

1. The term "Chicano" is used here to designate a person of Mexican descent living in the United States on a relatively permanent basis, regardless of place of birth or citizenship status. It has in the past had pejorative connotations in both Mexico and the United States, but it is being increasingly accepted as symbolic of positive identification with a unique ethnic heritage, especially by younger and more politically conscious persons. "Mexican-American," on the other hand, connotes middle-class respectability and a higher level of identification and integration into American society. Thus, while Chicano, Mexican-American, and Mexican as terms for those living on the United States side of the border have different connotations, they are denotatively the same. This confusion of labels is precisely why the unique term Chicano is preferred by many persons of Mexican descent.

2. Edward E. Sampson has similarly called for a scientific revolution in social psychology, arguing that the prevailing paradigm arose in the cultural context of "Puritan Protestantism, individualism, male dominance, selective equality, private property, and capitalism" (1978, p. 1332).

3. Perhaps no term has been more variously defined in social science than culture. As used here it refers to the complex system of shared beliefs, values, and norms among members of a human group or society. It is, in other words, a system of ideas that is shared by group members and organizes their actions. Chicanos participate and are acculturated in varying degrees to the dominant culture, but they also share a distinctive culture that is independent of both United States and Mexican culture.

4. For examples of basically pejorative works see Heller (1966), Rudoff (1971), Madsen (1973), and Carroll (1980).

5. This is not to suggest that all successful or upwardly mobile Chicanos are *vendidos* ("sell-outs") but rather that the dominant society pressures them to adopt its values and world view and resists accepting them as Chicanos. Not only in academia but in politics, law, medicine, business, law enforcement, and other areas as well one is expected to be a professional first and a Chicano second. The society thereby creates the illusion of permeability, while at the same time effectively neutralizing the expression of subordinate group interests. To see this as a problem of individual sell-outs, "*tio tacos*," or "coconuts," however, is to focus on the effects of the problem, not its root causes. The problem is not that too many individual Chicanos assimilate or reject their ethnicity but that cultural hegemony and the minimization of ethnic group consciousness are promoted within the United States.

6. Some, like Joan Moore, have written from both the assimilationist and colonial perspective (see Murguía, 1975 p. 1). Moore, considered by some as the leading

contemporary sociologist writing about Chicanos (as opposed to a Chicano sociologist), advocated a colonial perspective in her earlier work (Moore 1970), but the massive *The Mexican-American People* (Grebler, Moore, and Guzman 1970) and *Mexican Americans* (Moore 1976) are heavily assimilationist in orientation and treat Mexican-Americans as another immigrant group in America. Her most recent major work, *Homeboys*, is not only sympathetic but ostensibly written from the perspective of *pintos* (Chicano convicts) themselves (1978, p. 6). Yet a careful reading of the book would suggest that the underlying theoretical perspective is basically cultural pluralism. According to Moore "Sociologically, we argue that the pluralistic and inductive approach will result in more realistic policies" (ibid., p. 176).

The model adopted is one of "blocked access to legitimate opportunities" first proposed by Robert Merton (1963, pp. 131-60) in his typology of deviant behavior and further developed by Cloward and Ohlin (1960) and others. Moore notes, "We use the word innovation in both its ordinary meaning and as a sociological term from Robert Merton. To sociologists, innovation occurs when normal means to normal ends are inaccessible, and specialized means to those ends are developed. . . . The gangs are innovative stylistically and symbolically. . . . Innovation, both symbolic and stylistic, also affects the patterns of drug use" (ibid., pp. 38-39). Thus, Moore's work, while more sophisticated and sympathetic, still seeks to make Chicano cultural and behavioral patterns fit into existing paradigms rather than to develop new perspectives or interpretations that emanate from within Chicano culture.

7. An "Analysis of Differential Assimilation Rates among Middle-Class Mexican Americans," for example, boldly asserts, "It is the general consensus of students of social mobility that members of most ethnic groups in the United States who are upwardly mobile become acculturated to, and eventually assimilated into, the dominant *American* culture and subsequently lose their ethnic identity" (Teske and Nelson 1976, p. 218).

8. For a discussion of the relationship between Protestantism and the emergence of modern science see Robert Merton's (1963, pp. 574-606) incisive essay "Puritanism, Pietism and Science." His thesis is that the value-attitude complex inherent in the Puritan ethic served as an impetus to the development of modern science. According to Merton (1963, pp. 574-75) "The deep-rooted religious interests of the day demanded in their forceful implications the systematic, rational, and empirical study of Nature for the glorification of God in His works and for the control of the corrupt world."

2. Chicano Labor and the Economy

1. For additional information on this case see Brent 1976 and Robinson 1976.

2. Ironically, in Nueces County over 75 percent of the men reported killed in Vietnam were Chicano (De Anda 1967, p. 221).

3. A study of Mexican immigration from 1910 to 1964 also found that "In comparison with other immigrants, Mexican newcomers are under-represented in high grade occupations such as professional and technical or managerial, and even among clerical workers, craftsmen, and operatives. They are heavily concentrated in the group classified as 'laborers except farm and mine' " (Grebler 1966, p. 45).

3. The United States-Mexico Border: A Chicano Perspective on Immigration and Undocumented Workers

1. The position taken here is consistent with that of groups such as the Committee on Chicano Rights (CCR), based in National City, California (see Committee on Chicano Rights, 1980).

2. A court ruling by Judge William Wayne Justice of the Tyler Division of the United States District Court on September 14, 1978, struck down section 21.031 of the Texas Education Code, which prevented the enrollment of undocumented school children in the public schools unless they paid a $1,000 yearly tuition per student (see Flores 1981, p. 1; MALDEF 1978c). The decision was upheld by the Fifth Circuit Court in New Orleans and eventually by the Supreme Court of the United States.

4. *El Bandido*: The Evolution of Images of Chicano Criminality

1. Although xenophobia prevailed in the early 1940s, concern with the problem of Mexican crime has been a persistent feature of American society since the American take-over of Mexico's northernmost territories. In the 1930s, for example, there was great interest in Mexican crime and delinquency (see the U.S. Wickersham Commission, 1931, and California Governor C.C. Young's Fact-Finding Committee, 1930). The Young committee concluded:

> . . . In the absence of a recent census, it is not possible to draw any close comparison of the incidence of crime among the Mexican population as compared with the general population. It would appear to be very high, but the comparison is affected by the fact that more men than women have entered the country, and the age distribution gives a larger proportion of Mexicans in the age groups most commonly found in prison. (1930, pp. 198-99)

The Wickersham commission results were also inconclusive. Dr. Paul S. Taylor (1931, p. 242) observed: "The statistical record of law violations presented is on the whole, and in varying degrees, somewhat unfavorable to Mexicans." Dr. Max S. Handman argued, moreover, that delinquency was higher among foreign-born Mexicans than among Mexican-Americans. The evidence "seems to indicate that the factor influencing delinquency is either the disorganization of personality incident to a nomadic shift of environment or possibly a selection of those elements in the Mexican population more unstable to begin with than the native-born Mexican" (Handman 1931, p. 264). Much of the problem, according to Handman, was not the result of "the Mexican as Mexican" (i.e., genetics) but rather with the "Mexican environment." The more prevalent use of knives by Mexicans resulted from the fact that the Anglo-Saxon had somehow "outgrown" its use and evolved to a higher level of civilization.

> . . . There is, then, nothing inherent in Anglo-Saxondom which would make it averse to the use of a knife. But the Anglo-Saxon has outgrown it while apparently the Latin has not. That, however, is not a correct way of stating the problem. The Anglo-Saxon has not outgrown the knife; he has outgrown fight-

ing, and when he is angry he fights with his fists, not because he does not want to fight with a knife but because he has been betrayed into fighting by a momentary fit of anger. But among the Mexicans fighting is still a socially approved form of gaining superiority, because they are not in an industrial but an agricultural stage of civilization, and an agricultural stage without much admixture of machine and urban standard after the fashion of our own agricultural population. The result is that aggravated assault is common among Mexicans. (Ibid., p. 256)

5. Education: Problems, Issues, and Alternatives

1. Only native American educational attainment appears lower (Carter and Segura 1979, p. 41).

2. Even more discouraging is the proportion of Chicano teachers. Hispanics constitute only 1.7 percent of all recent bachelor's recipients and also 1.7 percent of all bachelor's recipients who are newly qualified to teach (National Center for Education Statistics 1983, p. 204). This means that only about 1 percent of all recent bachelor's recipients and 1 percent of those newly qualified to teach are Chicano.

3. This ideology has effectively been satirized by Michael Young (1958), who describes a mythical futuristic society in The Rise of the Meritocracy where I.Q. + effort = MERIT.

4. The view of Mexican culture as innately inferior is not new. From the onset many Americans were concerned with the adverse effect that Mexican culture would have on educational standards. In The Near Side of the Mexican Question Jay S. Stowell notes that as early as 1857 W.W.H. Davis, writing in El Gringo, lamented the low level of education in New Mexico.

> . . . The standard of education in New Mexico is at a very low ebb, and there is a larger number of persons who cannot read and write than in any other Territory in the Union. The number attending school is given as 460, which is about one scholar to every 125 inhabitants. . . . This exhibits a fearful amount of ignorance among the people, and it is enough to make us question the propriety of intrusting them with the power to make their own laws. It was always the policy of Spain and Mexico to keep her people in ignorance, and so far as New Mexico was concerned, they seem to have carried out the system with singular faithfulness, and in no country in the world that lays the least claim to civilization has general education and a cultivation of the arts been so generally neglected. . . .There is not a native physician in the country, nor am I aware that there has ever been one. (Stowell 1921, pp. 85-86)

Education in California was also considered inferior by Anglo-American standards. In a report on pioneer schools of Los Angeles H.P. Barrows noted that when he first came to Los Angeles in 1854, there were only two brick school buildings. According to Barrows "Under the Mexican regime, school facilities were very meager. Rancheros who could afford the expense, as a rule, employed private teachers whenever competent persons could be found" (Barrows 1911, p. 61). Education was not a luxury intended for the masses. Major Stephen C. Foster is credited with establishing the public school system in Los Angeles and being its first active superintendent (ibid.).

This attitude continued into the twentieth century, but it was now linked to the influx of a large number of uneducated Mexican immigrants. Vernon Monroe McCombs commented:

> The problem which the large influx of Mexicans into the United States has raised for the public schools in our four border states is a very complex one. The Mexican immigrant brings his family with him to this country, and thousands of boys and girls of school age, who have never been in school a day in their lives and who do not understand the English language, have been crowded into our border communities. (McCombs 1925, p. 98)

5. Horton does not talk about education or Chicanos per se, but his analysis appears to have much relevance for the liberal model of Chicano education and has been adapted for that purpose here.

6. One of the best critiques of the assimilationist model and of research efforts which blame Chicano culture and values for the failure of Chicano children is Deluvina Hernández's *Mexican American Challenge to a Sacred Cow* (1970).

7. Current attacks on bilingual education programs by the general public and the arguments for abolishing them because they are costly to taxpayers and are "not working" are ironic, given that such programs appear from the onset to have been programmed for failure. This pattern is a common one for minorities, however. Programs are designed which are doomed to fail, they are then criticized for not working, and they are finally abolished. There has been a movement for "bilingual" programs to be defined as English-as-a-second-language, (ESL), programs whose ultimate goal is not the maintenance of both languages but teaching English and getting the student to "transfer" from the native language to English as soon as possible. This approach is popular because it is consistent with the assimilationist ideology (Macías et al. 1975, p. 31).

8. For applications of Freire to the Chicano experience see Mares (1974) and Macías et al. (1975, pp. 36-37).

6. The Church and the Chicano

1–2. This quoted material was translated by the author, as was material given in Spanish and English throughout.

3. Another description of the omens by Diego Muñoz Camargo, a Spaniard who married into the nobility of Tlaxcala and wrote from their perspective, closely parallels the account presented by Sahagún's informants (Leon-Portilla 1962, p. 4).

4. Jacques Lafaye, author of one of the most definitive and incisive accounts of the subject, is extremely skeptical with regard to the account of the apparition of Our Lady of Estremadura, noting: "The account I have just transcribed of the pro-

digious event—the oldest account known—was composed at least a century after the origin of the sanctuary of Guadalupe. When it was written by a Jeronymite religious of the convent of Guadalupe, the temple, the convent, the village, the miracles, the pilgrims were no longer a prophetic vision but a daily reality, or at least an image of that reality capable of inspiring popular fervor. . . . For the rest, I believe the Codex of 1440 should be regarded as a piece of pious propaganda" (1976, p. 220).

5. There are clear parallels between the pejorative view of the Anglo toward the Mexican and the attitude of the Spaniard toward the *indio*. In both instances the native population is seen as a heathen and immoral race which is badly in need of religious instruction and guidance. The pejorative view of the Mexican continued into the twentieth century. Commenting on the reception of Mexican immigrants in the United States in the aftermath of the Mexican Revolution, Ortegon observed: "Race prejudice and hatred were rampant in those days. The Mexicans were being looked down on as an inferior ungovernable race, as a barbarian people. 'Greasers' was a very common word on the lips of many Americans" (1932, p. 12).

6. For a somewhat different interpretation of the origin of the Brotherhood see Swadesh (1974). Swadesh argues that the development of the Brotherhood was aided by the scarcity of priests in New Mexico during the late eighteenth century. According to Fray Angelico Chavez the Penitente Brotherhood was introduced by colonists or priests who had come from Mexico at this time (Swadesh 1974, p. 74). The *Penitentes* would tend to the sick and dying when priests were not available and provide physical and spiritual support for bereaved families.

The first to comment on the Brotherhood was Bishop José Antonio Laureano de Zubiria, who in 1833 berated the practice of corporal punishment and ordered the priests not to permit gatherings of *Penitentes* (ibid., p. 75).

7. This is not to suggest that the church has been totally unresponsive. The emergence of groups such as COPS (Communities Organized for Public Service) in San Antonio and UNO (United Neighborhood Organizations) in Los Angeles are indicative of a growing sensitivity on the part of the church. These organizations have proved extremely successful not only in organizing local parishes for political action but in dealing with issues that impinge on Chicano communities (see Trillin 1977 and Valadez 1978). The key to their success has been the support, financial and other, of the church and the effective mobilization of the Chicano middle class. Significantly, however, these organizations have dealt with the more concrete and focused issues such as auto insurance rates and water rates rather than with the more complex and basic social problems facing Chicanos. They have had tremendous success in dealing with short-term issues but have generally avoided more controversial and volatile social problems. The approach taken by them has been reformist, not radical. As a result, their focus has been more on the effects than on the underlying causes of problems.

8. According to Rosino Gibellini (1979, p. ix) "Only the broad outlines of this new approach were indicated by the Medellín Conference. It was articulated much more fully in the now classic work by Gustavo Gutiérrez entitled A *Theology of Liberation*, which first appeared in Peru in 1971." For discussions of the theology of liberation see Gutiérrez (1970, 1973); Gibellini (1979); Mc Fadden (1975); Furfey (1978); Guinea and Moya (1978); Ruiz Maldonado (1975); Kirk (1979); and Dussel (1976).

7. *La Familia Chicana*

1. The landmark Mexican-American Study Project, however, concluded that "compadrazgo, although undoubtedly still viable, appears to be a minor feature of kinship and community social organization in the major urban centers" (Grebler, Moore, and Guzman 1970, p. 355).

2. Poverty, rather than declining, appears to be on the increase. The Census Bureau reported that the poverty level climbed to its highest percentage in 17 years during 1982. A full 15 percent of the population fell below the poverty level, an increase of 8.1 percent over the previous year. For whites the poverty level rose from 11.1 percent in 1981 to 12 percent in 1982; for blacks to 35.6 percent from 34.2 percent. The rate for Hispanics increased from 26.5 percent to 29.9 percent (Schellhardt 1983, p. 1). This means that 3 out of 10 Hispanics were classified as poor.

8. *Machismo*

1. For a negative and stultifying Latina conception of *machismo*, see Ander-Egg, Zamboni, Yáñez, Gissi, and Dussel (1972). They define *machismo* as an oppressive ideology which categorizes individuals as superior or inferior according to their gender (p. 141).

9. Critique and Synthesis

1. See Mirandé (1978) for a more extensive discussion of the paradigm. The perspective on social science presented at the end of chapter one is a substantially revised and expanded statement.

2. This is not to suggest that census data should never be used, but to be aware of restrictions and limitations inherent in their use. Statistics provided by state and federal governmental agencies can be very useful and are often the only information available.

10. Epilogue: Toward a Chicano Paradigm

1. Vaca (1970b, p. 45) notes that in social-science literature all Mexican-American values have their opposite counterparts in Anglo culture except for the value of *machismo*. He has, therefore, taken the liberty of formulating his own counterpart.

2. Murguía (1975, 1982) has published more focused sociological works on Mexican-Americans.

3. Skeptics might wonder whether it is possible to have not only a Chicano but a German, French, or any ethnic methodology or theory. We, in fact, already have German, Russian, European, American, and Mexican sociologies, and within the United States we have regional sociologies and even a "Chicago" school of sociology. Perhaps more significant is that the contributions of all ethnic groups have not been

equally underrepresented within mainstream sociology. The influence of German scholars like Weber and Marx has of course been substantial.

Appendix. Chicano-Police Conflict: A Case Study

1. There have been a number of studies of conflict between blacks and police (see Smith and Hawkins 1973; Furstenberg and Wellford 1973; Phillips and Coates 1971; Chackerian and Barrett 1973; Hahn 1971; Bayley and Mendelsohn 1969: Ennis 1967; Raine 1970; Murphy and Watson 1970; and Boggs and Galliher 1975).

2. The median income in 1970 of all families residing in the census tract where the barrio is located was $6,520, and more than 21 percent of the families were below the poverty level. Approximately 30 percent of the families had incomes below $5,000, 47 percent more than $5,000 but less than $10,000, 18 percent between $10,000 and $24,999, and 4 percent $25,000 or more. The incomes of our respondents were fairly comparable to the census figures, although a smaller proportion of upper-income families ($25,000 or more) were represented in our sample. About 27 percent of our respondents had incomes under $5,000, 41 percent between $5,000 and $9,999, 32 percent $10,000 to $24,999, and 1 percent $25,000 or more. The discrepancy in the proportion of high-income families may have resulted from the fact that the census tract in which the barrio is located contains a number of affluent Anglo residences that are on the fringe of the barrio in the prestigious Green Belt area. The educational attainment of barrio residents is also low. The median years of school completed for persons 25 years old and over residing in the census tract was 8.4 (compared to 11.0 for the city as a whole), and the proportion who had graduated from high school was 18.4 (compared to 42.5 for the city as a whole). The level of educational attainment was higher in our sample because persons under 25 years are included, and younger Chicanos have higher educational attainment. The proportion of high-school graduates was 43.9 in our sample.

3. The median age for persons of Mexican origin living in the United States is about 21 compared to a median age of 31 years for the population as a whole (U.S. Bureau of the Census 1981, p. 5).

4. It should be noted that the measure of support for civil liberties among Chicanos in Table 2 is a conservative estimate of such support, since persons whose response to these questions was "not sure" were treated as though they were not in support of civil liberties. In other words, responses were grouped into those who supported civil liberties and those who definitely did not or were not sure. When "not sure" responses are excluded, the hypothesis is more strongly supported but is still not statistically significant.

5. The figure that 82 percent of the respondents support both measures of civil liberties is obtained when "not sure" responses are excluded. When "not sure" responses are included in the computation, the percentage supporting both measures is sixty-three.

Bibliography

Achor, Shirley. 1978. *Mexican Americans in a Dallas Barrio*. Tucson: University of Arizona Press.

Acuña, Rodolfo. 1972. *Occupied America: The Chicano's Struggle Toward Liberation*. San Francisco: Canfield.

_____. 1981. *Occupied America: A History of Chicanos*. 2d ed. New York: Harper & Row.

Adler, Patricia R. 1974. "The 1943 Zoot-Suit Riots: Brief Episode in a Long Conflict." Pp. 142-58 in *An Awakened Minority: The Mexican-Americans*, ed. Manuel P. Servín. 2d ed. Beverly Hills: Glencoe Press.

Almaguer, Tomás. 1971. "Toward the Study of Chicano Colonialism." *Aztlán: Chicano Journal of the Social Sciences and the Arts* 2 (Spring): 7-21.

_____. 1974. "Historical Notes on Chicano Oppression: The Dialectics of Racial and Class Domination in North America." *Aztlán: Chicano Journal of the Social Sciences and the Arts* 5 (Spring-Fall): 27-56.

_____. 1975. "Class, Race, and Chicano Oppression." *Socialist Revolution* 5 (July-September): 71-99.

_____. 1978. "Chicano Politics in the Present Period: Comment on Garcia." *Socialist Review* 8 (July-October): 137-41.

Alurista, Alberto. 1972. "Campo Cultural de La Raza." Pp. 389-91 in *Aztlán: An Anthology of Mexican American Literature*, ed. Luis Valdez and Stan Steiner. New York: Knopf.

Alvirez, David, and Bean, Frank D. 1976. "The Mexican American Family." Pp. 271-92 in *Ethnic Families in America*, ed. Charles H. Mindel and Robert W. Habenstein. New York: Elsevier.

Ander-Egg, Ezequiel; Zamboni, Norma; Yáñez, Annabella Teresa; Gissi, Jorge; and Dussel, Enrique. 1972. *Opresión y marginalidad de la mujer en el orden social machista*. Buenos Aires: Humanitas.

Anderson, Henry P. 1961. *The Bracero Program in California*. Berkeley: UCB School of Public Health.

Archibald, Robert. 1978. *The Economic Aspects of the California Missions*. Washington, D.C.: Academy of American Franciscan History.

The Arizona Republic. 1977. "'3 Indicted in Torture of Aliens.'" *The Arizona Republic*, Phoenix (August 29): B-1.

Armas, José. 1976. *La Familia de la Raza*. 3d ed. Albuquerque: Pajarito Publications.

Associated Press. 1978. "Third Graders Said Members of Gangs." *The Press*, Riverside, Calif. (March 17): C-4.

Baca Zinn, Maxine. 1975a. "Political Familism: Toward Sex Role Equality in Chicano

Families." *Aztlán: Chicano Journal of the Social Sciences and the Arts* 6 (Spring): 13-26.

_____. 1975b. "Chicanas: Power and Control in the Domestic Sphere." *De colores* 2 (3): 19-31.

_____. 1979a. "Chicano Family Research: Conceptual Distortions and Alternative Directions." *The Journal of Ethnic Studies* 7 (Fall): 59-71.

_____. 1979b. "Field Research in Minority Communities: Ethical, Methodological and Political Observations by an Insider." *Social Problems* 27 (December): 209-19.

_____. 1980a. "Employment and Education of Mexican American Women: The Interplay of Modernity and Ethnicity in Eight Families." *Harvard Educational Review* 50 (February): 47-62.

_____. 1980b. "Gender and Ethnic Identity among Chicanos." *Frontiers: A Journal of Women Studies* 5 (Summer): 18-24.

_____. 1981. "Sociological Theory in Emergent Chicano Perspectives." *Pacific Sociological Review* 24 (April): 255-72.

_____. 1982a. "Chicano Men and Masculinity." *The Journal of Ethnic Studies* 10 (Summer): 29-44.

_____. 1982b. "Mexican-American Women in the Social Sciences." *Signs: Journal of Women in Culture and Society* 8 (Winter): 259-72.

_____. 1982c. "Urban Kinship and Midwest Chicano Families: Evidence in Support of Revision." *De colores* 6 (1 & 2): 85-98.

Barrera, Mario. 1979. *Race and Class in the Southwest: A Theory of Racial Inequality.* Notre Dame: University of Notre Dame Press.

Barrera, Mario; Muñoz, Carlos; and Ornelas, Charles. 1972. "The Barrio as an Internal Colony." In *Urban Affairs Annual Reviews*, ed. Harlan H. Hahn, 6: 465-98. Beverly Hills: Sage.

Barrows, H.D. 1911. "Pioneer Schools of Los Angeles." *Annual Publications, Historical Society of Southern California, 1909-1910.* Vol. 8, pp. 61-66. Los Angeles: J.B. Walters, Printer.

Bayley, David H. and Mendelsohn, Harold. 1969. *Minorities and the Police.* New York: Free Press.

Bean, Frank D., and Bradshaw, Benjamin S. 1970. "Intermarriage Between Persons of Spanish and Non-Spanish Surname: Changes from the Mid-Nineteenth to the Mid-Twentieth Century." *Social Science Quarterly* 51 (September): 389-95.

Becker, Howard S. 1967. "Whose Side Are We On?" *Social Problems* 14 (Winter): 239-47.

Bellah, Robert N. 1964. "Religious Evolution." *American Sociological Review* 29 (June): 358-74.

Bennett, Lorraine. 1980. "Latinos, Police Both Claim Victories in Riverside Suit." *Los Angeles Times* (November 16): cc, II-1, II-6.

Berger, John A. 1941. *The Franciscan Missions of California.* New York: G. P. Putnam's Sons.

Berger, Peter L. 1967. *The Sacred Canopy: Elements of a Sociological Theory of Religion.* Garden City, N.Y.: Anchor.

Bermúdez, María Elvira. 1955. *La vida familiar del mexicano.* Mexico City: Robredo.

Blacker, Irwin R., and Rosen, Harry M. 1962. *Conquest: Dispatches of Cortez from the New World*. New York: Grosset & Dunlap.

Blauner, Robert. 1969. "Internal Colonialism and Ghetto Revolt." *Social Problems* 16 (Spring): 393-408.

_____. 1972. *Racial Oppression in America*. New York: Harper & Row.

Blawis, Patricia Bell. 1977. "Torturers of Mexicans Acquitted." *People's World* (October 29): 4.

Block, Richard L. 1971. "Fear of Crime and Fear of the Police." *Social Problems* 19 (Summer): 91-101.

Boggs, Sara L., and Galliher, John F. 1975. "Evaluating the Police: A Comparison of Black Street and Household Respondents." *Social Problems* 22 (February): 393-406.

Brent, Joseph Lancaster. 1976. "THE LUGO CASE: A Personal Experience. New Orleans, 1926." Searcy & Pfaff. Pp. 1-69, in *Mexicans in California After the U.S. Conquest*, ed. Carlos E. Cortés. New York: Arno Press Reprint Edition.

Briggs, Jr., Vernon M. 1975. *Mexican Migration and the U.S. Labor Market*. Austin: University of Texas Press.

Briggs, Jr., Vernon M.; Fogel, Walter; and Schmidt, Fred. H. 1977. *The Chicano Worker*. Austin: University of Texas Press.

Brownmiller, Susan. 1975. *Against Our Will: Men, Women and Rape*. New York: Simon and Schuster.

Brubacher, John S. 1969. *Modern Philosophies of Education*. 4th ed. New York: McGraw-Hill.

Burke, James Wakefield. 1971. *Missions of Old Texas*. New York: A. J. Barnes & Co.

Burrows, Phyllis Bronstein. 1980. "Mexican Parental Roles: Differences Between Mothers' and Fathers' Behavior to Children." Paper presented at the Annual Meeting of the Society for Cross-Cultural Research, Philadelphia (February).

Bustamante, Jorge A. 1977. "The Immigrant Worker: A Social Problem or a Human Resource." Pp. 165-83 in *Immigration and Public Policy: Human Rights for Undocumented Workers and Their Families*, ed. Antonio José Ríos-Bustamante. Los Angeles: UCLA Chicano Studies Research Center.

_____. 1981. "The Historical Context of Undocumented Mexican Immigration to the United States." Pp. 35-48 in *Mexican Immigrant Workers in the U.S.*, ed. Antonio Ríos-Bustamante. Anthology No. 2. Los Angeles: UCLA Chicano Studies Research Center.

Camarillo, Albert. 1979. *Chicanos in a Changing Society: From Mexican Pueblos to American Barrios in Santa Barbara and Southern California, 1848-1930*. Cambridge: Harvard University Press.

Carranza, Elihu. 1978. *Chicanismo: Philosophical Judgements*. Dubuque, Iowa: Kendall/Hunt Publishing Company.

Carrillo-Beron, Carmen. 1974. *Traditional Family Ideology in Relation to Locus of Control: A Comparison of Chicano and Anglo Women*. Reprinted 1974 by R and E Research Associates, San Francisco.

Carroll, Joseph C. 1980. "A Cultural Consistency Theory of Family Violence in Mexican-American and Jewish-Ethnic Groups." Chapter 5 (pp. 68-85) in *The Social Causes of Husband-Wife Violence*, ed. Murray A. Straus and Gerald T.

Hotaling. Minneapolis: University of Minnesota Press.

Carter, Thomas P., and Segura, Roberto D. 1979. *Mexican Americans in School: A Decade of Change*. 2d ed. New York: College Entrance Examination Board.

Caso, Alfonso. 1958. *The Aztecs: People of the Sun*. Translated by Lowell Dunham. Norman: University of Oklahoma Press.

Castillo, Pedro, and Camarillo, Albert, eds. 1973. *Furia y Muerte: Los Bandidos Chicanos*. Aztlán Publications. Monograph No. 4, Los Angeles: UCLA Chicano Studies Research Center.

Castro, Tony. 1974. *Chicano Power: The Emergence of Mexican America*. New York: Saturday Review Press/E.P. Dutton & Co., Inc.

Católicos por La Raza. 1972. "Catolicos por La Raza." Pp. 391-92 in *Aztlán: An Anthology of Mexican American Literature*, ed. Luis Valdez and Stan Steiner. New York: Knopf.

Centro de Reflexión Teológica. Undated. *¿Cómo es Nuestra Iglesia En América Latina?* (Medellín, 1968). Cuaderno Popular 2, Colección "Hablemos de la Iglesia," 6. Mexico City.: Centro de Reflexión Teológica.

Chackerian, Richard, and Barrett, Richard F. 1973. "Police Professionalism and Citizen Evaluation." *Urban Affairs Quarterly* 6 (March): 345-49.

Chafetz, Janet Saltzman. 1978. *Masculine, Feminine or Human?: An Overview of the Sociology of Gender Roles*. 2d ed. Itasca, Illinois: F.E. Peacock Publishers, Inc.

Chavez, Cesar. 1972. "Peregrinacion, Penitencia, Revolucion." Pp. 385-86 in *Aztlán: An Anthology of Mexican American Literature*, ed. Luis Valdez and Stan Steiner. New York: Knopf.

Cloward, Richard A., and Ohlin, Lloyd E. 1960. *Delinquency and Opportunity: A Theory of Delinquent Gangs*. New York: Free Press.

Comisión pesquisidora de la frontera del Norte 1875. "Reports of the Committee of Investigation: sent in 1873 by the Mexican Government to the Frontier of Texas." Translated from the official edition made in Mexico. New York: Baker & Godwin Printers.

Committee on Chicano Rights. 1980. "Resolutions Passed at the National Chicano Immigration Conference, May 24, 1980." National City, CA: CCR Inc.

Copp, Nelson Gage. 1963. " 'Wetbacks' and *Braceros*: Mexican Migrant Laborers and American Immigration Policy 1930-1960." Ph.D. dissertation, Boston University Graduate School.

Cornelius, Wayne A. 1977. "A Critique of the Carter Administration's Policy Proposals on Illegal Immigration." Pp. 185-96 in *Immigration and Public Policy: Human Rights for Undocumented Workers and their Families*, ed. Antonio José Ríos Bustamante. Los Angeles: UCLA Chicano Studies Research Center.

Cortés, Carlos E. 1976. *Mexicans in California After the U.S. Conquest*. New York: Arno Press Reprint Edition.

Corwin, Arthur F. 1978. *Immigrants—and Immigrants: Perspectives on Mexican Labor Migration to the United States*. Westport, Conn.: Greenwood Press.

Cover Story. 1978. "It's Your Turn in the Sun." *Time* 112 (October 16): 48-61.

Craig, Richard B. 1971. *The Bracero Program: Interest Groups and Foreign Policy*. Austin: University of Texas Press.

Crèvecoeur, J. Hector St. John. 1904. *Letters from an American Farmer*. Reprinted from the original edition. New York: Fox, Duffield & Co.

Cromwell, Vicky L., and Cromwell, Ronald E. 1978. "Perceived Dominance in Decision-Making and Conflict Resolution Among Anglo, Black and Chicano Couples." *Journal of Marriage and the Family* 40 (November): 749-59.

Cromwell, Ronald E., and Ruiz, René A. 1979. "The Myth of Macho Dominance in Decision Making Within Mexican and Chicano Families." *Hispanic Journal of Behavioral Sciences* 1 (December): 355-73.

Davidson, R. Theodore. 1974. *Chicano Prisoners: The Key to San Quentin*. New York: Holt, Rinehart and Winston.

De Anda, James. 1967. "Civil Rights—Need for Executive Branch to Take Positive Steps to Rectify Discrimination in Jury Selection, Voting Eligibility and School Enrollment." Pp. 217-21 in *The Mexican American: A New Focus on Opportunity*. Testimony Presented at the Cabinet Committee Hearings on Mexican American Affairs. El Paso, Texas. October 26-28, 1967.

de Aragon, Ray John. 1978. *Padre Martinez and Bishop Lamy*. Las Vegas, N.M.: Pan-American Publishing Company.

De Hoyos, Angela. 1977. "Words Unspoken." *Hojas poeticas* 1 (mayo): 3.

Delgado, Abelardo. 1974-1975. "Machismo." *La Luz*, vol. 3, no. 9: 6 (December) and vol. 3, nos. 10-11: 7 (January & February).

del Grito, Dolores. 1972. "Jesus Christ as a Revolutionist." Pp. 393-94 in *Aztlán: An Anthology of Mexican American Literature*, ed. Luis Valdez and Stan Steiner. New York: Knopf.

Díaz Del Castillo, Bernal. 1963. *The Conquest of New Spain*. Translated by J.M. Cohen. Baltimore: Penguin.

Díaz-Guerrero, Rogelio. 1975. *Psychology of the Mexican: Culture and Personality*. Austin: University of Texas Press.

Duran, Livie I., and Bernard, H. Russell. 1982. "Introduction: La Raza and Chicano History." Pp. 1-12 in *Introduction to Chicano Studies*, 2d ed., ed. Livie I. Duran and H. Russell Bernard. New York: Macmillan.

Dussel, Enrique D. 1976. *History and the Theology of Liberation: A Latin American Perspective*. Translated by John Drury. Maryknoll, N.Y. Orbis Books.

Dysart, Jane. 1976. "Mexican Women in San Antonio, 1830-1860: The Assimilation Process." *The Western Historical Quarterly* 7 (October): 365-75.

Eisner, Peter. 1982. "Mexican Recession Expected to Hike Illegal Migration to U.S." *Press-Enterprise*, Riverside, Calif. (July 13): A-1.

Endore, Guy. 1944. *The Sleepy Lagoon Mystery*. Los Angeles: The Sleepy Lagoon Defense Committee.

Ennis, Philip H. 1967. *Criminal Victimization in the United States: A Report of a National Survey*. Washington, D.C.: U.S. Government Printing Office.

Ericson, Anna-Stina. 1979. "The Impact of Commuters on the Mexican-American Border Area." Pp. 238-56 in *Mexican Workers in the United States: Historical and Political Perspectives*, ed. George C. Kiser and Martha Woody Kiser. Albuquerque: University of New Mexico Press.

Fanon, Frantz. 1963. *The Wretched of the Earth*. New York: Grove Press.

———. 1967. *Black Skin, White Masks*. New York: Grove Press.

Fehrenbach, T.R. 1968. *Lone Star: A History of Texas and the Texans*. New York: Macmillan.

Fernandez, Raul A. 1977. *The United States-Mexico Border: A Politico-Economic Profile*. Notre Dame: University of Notre Dame Press.

Firestone, Shulamith. 1972. *The Dialectic of Sex*. New York: Bantam.

Flores, Estevan T. 1981. "Mexican Immigrant Children and Public Education: International Implications from the Texas Case." Paper delivered at the Mexico-United States Relations: A Focus on the Mexican American Community Symposium, UCLA, Los Angeles, Calif., April.

Fogel, Walter. 1967. *Mexican Americans in Southwest Labor Markets*. Mexican-American Study Project, Division of Research, Graduate School of Business Administration, Advance Report 10. University of California, Los Angeles.

———. 1978. *Mexican Alien Workers in the United States*. Monograph No. 20. Los Angeles: University of California, Institute of Industrial Relations.

Forrest, Earle R. 1965. *Missions and Pueblos of the Old Southwest*. Chicago: Rio Grande.

Freeman, Jo. 1975a. *The Politics of Women's Liberation: A Case Study of an Emerging Social Movement and Its Relation to the Policy Process*. New York: McKay.

———. 1975b. *Women: A Feminist Perspective*. Palo Alto, Calif.: Mayfield Publishing Co.

Freire, Paulo. 1970. *Pedagogy of the Oppressed*. Translated by Myra Bergman Ramos. New York: Herder and Herder.

———. 1973. *Education for Critical Consciousness*. Translated by Myra Bergman Ramos. New York: The Seabury Press.

Fuentes, Carlos. 1970. *Todos los gatos son pardos*. Mexico City: Siglo Veintiuno.

Furfey, John Hanly. 1978. *Love and the Urban Ghetto*. Maryknoll, N.Y.: Orbis Books.

Furstenberg, Jr., Frank F., and Wellford, Charles F. 1973. "Calling the Police: The Evaluation of Police Service." *Law and Society Review* 7 (Spring): 393-406.

Gaines, Dan. 1979. "Three Held After Renewed Sniping in Casa Blanca." *The Press*, Riverside, Calif. (March 20): B-1, B-2.

Galarza, Ernesto. 1964. *Merchants of Labor: The Mexican Bracero Story*. Santa Barbara: McNally & Loftin.

———. 1970. *Spiders in the House and Workers in the Field*. Notre Dame: University of Notre Dame Press.

———. 1977. *Farm Workers and Agri-business in California, 1947-1960*. Notre Dame: University of Notre Dame Press.

Galicia, H. Romero. 1973. *Chicano Alternative Education*. Hayward, Calif.: Southwest Network of the Study Commission on Undergraduate Education and the Education of Teachers.

Gamio, Manuel. 1971a. *Mexican Immigration to the United States*. New York: Dover Publications. (First published by the University of Chicago Press, 1930.)

———. 1971b. *The Life Story of the Mexican Immigrant*. New York: Dover Publications. (First Published by the University of Chicago Press, 1931, as *The Mexican Immigrant: His Life Story*.)

García, Juan Ramon. 1980. *Operation Wetback: The Mass Deportation of Mexican Undocumented Workers in 1954*. Westport, Conn.: Greenwood Press.

García, Mario T. 1976. "MERCHANTS AND DONS: San Diego's Attempt at Modernization, 1850-1860." (Reprinted from the *Journal of San Diego History*, vol. 21, no. 1., Winter 1975). Pp. 52-80 in *Mexicans in California After the U.S. Conquest*, ed. Carlos E. Cortés. New York: Arno Press Reprint Edition.

_____. 1981 *Desert Immigrants: The Mexicans of El Paso, 1880-1920*. New Haven: Yale University Press.

Garcia, Richard A. 1978. "The Chicano Movement and the Mexican American Community, 1972-78: An Interpretative Essay." *Socialist Review* 8 (July-October): 117-36.

Gardner, Bill. 1977. "Mexican Mafia." *Press-Enterprise*, Riverside, Calif. (October 8): A-1, A-4.

Geiger, Maynard, O.F.M. 1965. *Mission Santa Barbara 1782-1965*. Santa Barbara: Franciscan Fathers of California.

Gibellini, Rosino. 1979. *Frontiers of Theology in Latin America*. Translated by John Drury. MaryKnoll, N.Y.: Orbis Books.

Gibson, Charles. 1966. *Spain in America*. New York: Harper & Row.

Gilbert, G. M. 1959. "Sex Differences in Mental Health in a Mexican Village." *International Journal of Social Psychiatry* 3 (Winter): 208-13.

Gilbert, M. Jean. 1978. "External Family Integration Among Second-Generation Mexican Americans." Pp. 25-48 in *Family and Mental Health in the Mexican American Community*, ed. J. Manuel Casas and Susan E. Keefe. Monograph No. Seven. Los Angeles: UCLA Spanish Speaking Mental Health Research Center.

Glazer, Nathan, and Moynihan, Daniel Patrick. 1963. *Beyond the Melting Pot*. Cambridge, Mass.: The M.I.T. Press.

Goldfinch, Charles W. 1949. "Juan N. Cortina, 1824-1892: A Re-Appraisal." M.A. thesis, University of Chicago.

Gómez, David F. 1973. *Somos Chicanos: Strangers in Our Own Land*. Boston: Beacon Press.

Gómez-Quiñones, Juan. 1970. "Plan de San Diego Reviewed." *Aztlán: Chicano Journal of the Social Sciences and the Arts* 1 (Spring): 124-32.

_____. 1981. "Mexican Immigration to the United States and the Internationalization of Labor, 1848-1980: An Overview." Pp. 13-34 in *Mexican Immigrant Workers in the U.S.*, ed. Antonio Ríos-Bustamante. Los Angeles: UCLA Chicano Studies Research Center.

_____. 1982. "Critique of the National Question, Self-Determination and Nationalism." *Latin American Perspectives* 33 (Spring): 62-83.

Gómez-Quiñones, Juan, and Arroyo, Luis Leobardo. 1976. "On the State of Chicano History: Observations on Its Development, Interpretations, and Theory, 1970-74." *Western Historical Quarterly* 7 (April): 155-85.

Gonzales, Ron. 1979. "CBS Asks News Council Review of '60 Minutes' " *The Press*, Riverside, Calif. (March 20): B-1, B-2.

González, Gilbert G. 1974. "A Critique of the Internal Colony Model." *Latin American Perspectives* 1 (no. 1): 154-61.

Goodman, Mary Ellen, and Beman, Alma, 1971. "Child's-Eye-Views of Life in an Urban Barrio." Pp. 109-22 in *Chicanos: Social and Psychological Perspectives*, ed.

Nathaniel N. Wagner and Marsha J. Haug. Saint Louis: Mosby.

Gordon, Milton M. 1964. *Assimilation in American Life*. New York: Oxford University Press.

Gouldner, Alvin W. 1962. "Anti-Minotaur: The Myth of a Value-Free Sociology." *Social Problems* 9 (Winter): 199-213.

Governor C.C. Young's Mexican Fact-Finding Committee. 1930. *Mexicans in California*. State of California. San Francisco: State Building (October).

Granado, Virginia. 1974. "Para mi jefe." *De colores* 2 (Spring): 37.

Grebler, Leo. 1966. *Mexican Immigration to the United States*. Mexican-American Study Project, Division of Research, Graduate School of Business Administration, Advance Report 2. University of California, Los Angeles.

Grebler, Leo; Moore, Joan W.; and Guzman, Ralph C. 1970. *The Mexican-American People*. New York: Free Press.

Griffin, John S. 1976. "LOS ANGELES IN 1849: A Letter from John S. Griffin, M.D. to Col. J.D. Stevenson, March 11, 1849. Los Angeles, 1949." Pp. 1-19 in *Mexicans in California After the U.S. Conquest*, ed. Carlos E. Cortés. New York: Arno Press Reprint Edition.

Griswold del Castillo, Richard. 1979. *The Los Angeles Barrio, 1850-1890: A Social History*. Berkeley: University of California Press.

Guinea, Wifredo, S.J., and Moya, Rafael, S.J. 1978. *Un grito a los obispos de Puebla: Sáquenme de Aquí*, 78. Mexico City: Ideas y Servicios Editoriales.

Guinn, J.M. 1911. "The Sonoran Migration." *Annual Publications, Historical Society of Southern California, 1909-1910*. Vol. 8, pp. 31-36. Los Angeles: J.B. Walters, Printer.

Gutiérrez, Gustavo. 1970. *Líneas pastorales de la Iglesia en América Latina, análisis teológico* Lima: Editorial Universitaria.

———. 1973. *A Theology of Liberation*. Maryknoll, N.Y.: Orbis Books.

Gutiérrez-Christensen, Rita. 1976. "EULOGY FOR A MAN FROM JALOSTITLAN." *GRITO del SOL* 1 (Book Four): 59-68.

Hahn, Harlan. 1971. "Ghetto Assesments of Police Protection and Authority." *Law and Society Review* 6 (November): 183-94.

Hammarley, John. 1977. "Inside the Mexican Mafia." *New West* 2 (December): 67-71.

Hawkes, Glenn R., and Taylor, Minna. 1975. "Power Structure in Mexican and Mexican-American Farm Labor Families." *Journal of Marriage and the Family* 37 (November): 807-11.

Hayden, Robert G. 1966. "Spanish-Americans of the Southwest: Life Style Patterns and Their Implications." *Welfare in Review* 4 (April): 14-25.

Heller, Celia S. 1966. *Mexican American Youth: Forgotten Youth at the Crossroads*. New York: Random House.

———. 1971. *New Converts to the American Dream? Mobility Aspirations of Young Mexican Americans*. New Haven, Conn.: College and University Press.

Hernández, Deluvina. 1970. *Mexican American Challenge to a Sacred Cow*. Monograph No. 1. Mexican American Cultural Center. University of California, Los Angeles.

Ho, Ping-ti. 1965. "An Historian's View of the Chinese Family System." Pp. 15-30 in *The Family's Search for Survival*, ed. Seymour M. Farber, Piero Mustacchi, and Roger H. L. Wilson. New York: McGraw-Hill.

Hobsbawm, Eric J. 1959. *Primitive Rebels: Studies in Archaic Forms of Social Movements in the 19th and 20th Centuries*. New York: Praeger.

_____. 1969. *Bandits*. London: Weidenfeld and Nicolson.

Hoffman, Abraham, 1974. *Unwanted Mexican Americans in the Great Drepession*. Tucson: University of Arizona Press.

Horton, John. 1973. "Order and Conflict Theories of Social Problems." Pp. 21-38 in *Radical Perspectives on Social Problems*, ed. Frank Lindenfeld. 2d ed. New York: Macmillan.

Hoult, Thomas Ford. 1968. ". . . Who Shall Prepare Himself to the Battle?" *American Sociologist* 3 (February): 3-7.

Huang, Lucy Jen. 1976. "The Chinese American Family." Pp. 124-47 in *Ethnic Families in America*, ed. Charles H. Mindel and Robert W. Habenstein. New York: Elsevier.

Hufford, Charles H. 1929. *The Social and Economic Effects of the Mexican Migration into Texas*. M.A. thesis, University of Colorado, Boulder. Reprinted 1971 by R and E Research Associates, San Francisco.

Humphrey, Norman Daymond. 1944. "The Changing Structure of the Detroit Mexican Family: An Index of Acculturation." *American Sociological Review* 9 (December): 622-26.

Hurtado, Juan. 1976. "An Attitudinal Study of Social Distance Between the Mexican American and the Church." Ph.D. dissertation, United States International University. San Diego: Mexican American Cultural Center.

_____. 1979. "The Social Interaction Between the Chicano and the Church: An Historical Perspective." *GRITO del SOL* 4 (Book One): 25-45.

Isáis-A., Raoul E. 1979. "The Chicano and the American Catholic Church." *GRITO del SOL* 4 (Book One): 9-24.

Janowitz, Morris. 1969. "Patterns of Collective Racial Violence." Pp. 412-44 in *The History of Violence in America: Historical and Comparative Perspectives*, ed. Hugh Davis Graham and Ted Robert Gurr. New York: Praeger.

Johnson, Kenneth F., and Ogle, Nina M. 1978. *Illegal Mexican Aliens in the United States*. Washington, D.C.: University Press of America.

Johnston, Tracy J. 1979. "La Vida Loca." *New West* 4 (January 29): 38-46.

Jones, Lamar Babington. 1965. "Mexican-American Labor Problems in Texas." Ph.D. dissertation, University of Texas, Austin. Reprinted 1971 by R and E Research Associates, San Francisco.

Jones, Robert C. 1948. "Ethnic Family Patterns: The Mexican Family in the United States." *American Journal of Sociology* 53 (May): 450-52.

Kaplan, Abraham. 1964. *The Conduct of Inquiry*. San Francisco: Chandler Publishing Co.

Kessell, John L. 1976. *Friars, Soldiers, and Reformers: Hispanic Arizona and the Sonora Mission Frontier 1767-1856*. Tucson: University of Arizona Press.

_____. 1980. *The Missions of New Mexico Since 1776*. Albuquerque: University of New Mexico Press.

King, G. 1936. "The Psychology of a Mexican Community in San Antonio Texas."

M.A. thesis, University of Texas, Austin.

Kirk, J. Andrew. 1979. *Liberation Theology*. Atlanta: John Knox Press.

Kirsch, Jonathan. 1978. "The Decade of the Chicano." *New West* 3 (September 11): 35-47.

Kirstein, Peter Neil. 1973. "Anglo Over Bracero: A History of the Mexican Worker in the United States from Roosevelt to Nixon." Ph.D. dissertation, Saint Louis University.

Kiser, George, and Silverman, David. 1979. "Mexican Repatriation During the Great Depression." Pp. 45-66 in *Mexican Workers in the United States*, ed. George C. Kiser and Martha Woody Kiser. Albuquerque: University of New Mexico Press.

Kiser, George C., and Kiser, Martha Woody, ed. 1979. *Mexican Workers in the United States*. Albuquerque: University of New Mexico Press.

Kluckhohn, Clyde. 1965. "Foreword." Pp. xi-xii in *Reader in Comparative Religion: An Anthropological Approach*, ed. William A. Lessa and Evon Z. Vogt. 2d ed. New York: Harper & Row.

Kuhn, Thomas S. 1962. *The Structure of Scientific Revolutions*. Chicago: University of Chicago Press.

Ladner, Joyce A. 1971. *Tomorrow's Tomorrow: The Black Woman*. New York: Doubleday.

_____. 1978. *The Death of White Sociology*. New York: Random House.

Lafaye, Jacques. 1976. *Quetzalcóatl and Guadalupe: The Formation of Mexican National Consciousness 1531-1813*. Translated by Benjamin Keen. Chicago: University of Chicago Press.

Latta, Frank F. 1980. *Joaquín Murrieta and His Horse Gangs*. Santa Cruz, Calif.: Bear State Books.

Law, Glen. 1977. "U.S. Intervention Is Sought in Alien-Torture Acquittals." *The Arizona Republic*, Phoenix (October 11): B-1.

Lazzareschi, Carla. 1979. "Hispanics Protest '60 Minutes' TV Show on Casa Blanca Crime." *The Press*, Riverside, Calif. (January 19): B-1.

Lee, Shu-Ching. 1953. "China's Traditional Family: Its Characteristics and Disintegration." *American Sociological Review* 18 (June): 272-80.

Leon-Portilla, Miguel. 1962. *The Broken Spears: The Aztec Account of the Conquest of Mexico*. Boston: Beacon.

Leslie, Gerald R. 1973. *The Family in Social Context*. 2d ed. New York: Oxford University Press.

Levy, Jr., Marion J. 1968. *The Family Revolution in Modern China*. New York: Atheneum.

Lipshultz, Robert J. 1962. "American Attitudes Toward Mexican Immigration, 1924-1952." M.A. thesis, University of Chicago. Reprinted 1971 by R and E Research Associates, San Francisco.

López, Ronald W.; Madrid-Barela, Arturo; and Flores Macías, Reynaldo. 1976. *Chicanos in Higher Education: Status and Issues*. Chicano Studies Center Publications, Monograph No. 7. University of California, Los Angeles.

Luzod, Jimmy A., and Arce, Carlos H. 1979. "An Exploration of the Father Role in the Chicano Family." Paper presented at the National Symposium on the Mexican American Child. Santa Barbara, California.

McCaleb, Walter Flavius 1954. *The Spanish Missions of Texas*. San Antonio: Naylor Company.

McCombs, Vernon Monroe. 1925. *From Over the Border: A Study of the Mexicans in the United States*. New York: Council of Women for Home Missions and Missionary Education Movement.

McFadden, Thomas M. 1975. *Liberation, Revolution, and Freedom*. New York: The Seabury Press.

McWilliams, Carey. 1949. "California and the Wetback." *Common Ground* 9 (Summer): 15-20.

———. 1968. *North from Mexico*. New York: Greenwood Press.

Macías, Reynaldo Flores, Webb de Macías, Carolyn; De La Torre, William; and Vásquez, Mario. 1975. *Educación Alternativa*. Hayward, Calif.: Southwest Network of the Study Commission on Undergraduate Education and the Education of Teachers.

Madsen, William. 1973. *The Mexican-Americans of South Texas*. 2d ed. New York: Holt, Rinehart and Winston.

Mares, E.A. 1974. "Fiesta of Life: Impressions of Paulo Freire." Pp. 167-77 in *Parameters of Institutional Change: Chicano Experiences in Education*, ed. Southwest Network. Hayward, Calif.: Southwest Network of the Study Commission on Undergraduate Education and the Education of Teachers.

Martinez, Joe L. 1977. *Chicano Psychology*. New York: Academic Press.

Martínez, Oscar J. 1980. *The Chicanos of El Paso: An Assessment of Progress*. El Paso: Texas Western Press.

Martínez, Thomas M. 1969. "Advertising and Racism: The Case of the Mexican-American." *El Grito: A Journal of Contemporary Mexican American Thought* 2 (Summer): 3-13.

Meier, Matt S., and Rivera, Feliciano. 1972. *The Chicanos: A History of Mexican Americans*. New York: Hill and Wang.

Meinig, Donald William. 1969. *Imperial Texas: An Interpretive Essay in Cultural Geography*. Austin: University of Texas Press.

Mejia, Daniel P. 1976. "Cross-Ethnic Father Role: Perceptions of Middle Class Anglo American Parents." Ph.D. dissertation, University of California, Irvine.

Memmi, Albert. 1965. *The Colonizer and the Colonized*. Translated by Howard Greenfeld. New York: Orion Press.

Mendoza, Vicente T. 1962. "El machismo en México a través de las canciones, corridos, y cantares." Pp. 75-86 in *Cuadernos del instituto nacional de Antropología III*. Buenos Aires: Ministerio de Educación y Justicia.

Merton, Robert K. 1963. *Social Theory and Social Structure*. Rev. ed. Glencoe, Ill.: Free Press.

———. 1972. "Insiders and Outsiders: A Chapter in the Sociology of Knowledge." *American Journal of Sociology* 78 (July): 9-48.

Mexican American Legal Defense and Education Fund (MALDEF). 1978a. "MALDEF Documents Official Abuse of Authority Against Mexican-Americans in Letter to Attorney General Griffin Bell." San Francisco.

———. 1978b. "Dallas Brutality Conference Displays Chicano Unity." *MALDEF* 8 (Summer): 1-8.

_____. 1978c. "MALDEF Win Protects Alien Rights." *MALDEF* 8 (Fall): 1-6.

Miller, Walter B. 1958. "Lower Class Culture as a Generating Milieu of Gang Delinquency." *Journal of Social Issues* 14 (no. 3): 5-19.

Mindel, Charles H., and Habenstein, Robert W. 1976. *Ethnic Families in America.* New York: Elsevier.

Mirandé, Alfredo. 1975. *The Age of Crisis: Deviance, Disorganization, and Societal Problems.* New York: Harper & Row.

_____. 1977. "The Chicano Family: A Reanalysis of Conflicting Views." *Journal of Marriage and the Family* 39 (November): 747-56.

_____. 1978. "Chicano Sociology: A New Paradigm for Social Science." *Pacific Sociological Review* 21 (July): 293-312.

_____. 1979. "A Reinterpretation of Male Dominance in the Chicano Family." *The Family Coordinator* 28 (October): 473-79.

_____. 1982a. "Machismo: Rucas, Chingasos, y Chingaderas." *De colores* 6 (1 & 2): 17-31.

_____. 1982b. "Sociology of Chicanos or Chicano Sociology?: A Critical Assessment of Emergent Paradigms." *Pacific Sociological Review* 25 (October): 495-508.

Mirandé, Alfredo, and Enríquez, Evangelina. 1979. *La Chicana: The Mexican-American Woman.* Chicago: University of Chicago Press.

Montiel, Miguel. 1970. "The Social Science Myth of the Mexican American Family." *El Grito: A Journal of Contemporary Mexican American Thought* 3 (Summer): 56-63.

_____. 1973. "The Chicano Family: A Review of Research." *Social Work* 18 (March): 22-31.

Moore, Joan W. 1970. "Colonialism: The Case of the Mexican Americans." *Social Problems* 17 (Spring): 463-72.

_____. 1973. "Social Constraints on Sociological Knowledge: Academics and Research Concerning Minorities." *Social Problems* 21 (Summer): 65-77.

_____. 1976. *Mexican Americans.* 2d ed. Englewood Cliffs, N.J.: Prentice-Hall.

Moore, Joan W. (with Garcia, Robert; Garcia, Carlos; Cerda, Luis; and Valencia, Frank). 1978. *Homeboys: Gangs, Drugs, and Prison in the Barrios of Los Angeles.* Philadelphia: Temple University Press.

Morales, Armando. 1972. *Ando Sangrando (I Am Bleeding): A Study of Mexican American-Police Conflict.* La Puente, Calif.: Perspectiva.

Morales, Patricia. 1982. *Indocumentados mexicanos.* Mexico City: Editorial Grijalbo.

Moreno, Manuel M. 1971. *La organización política y social de los aztecas.* Mexico City: Instituto Nacional de Antropología e Historia.

Muñoz, Jr., Carlos. 1970. "Toward a Chicano Perspective of Political Analysis." *Aztlán: Chicano Journal of the Social Sciences and the Arts* 1 (Fall): 15-26.

_____. 1983. "The Quest for Paradigm: The Development of Chicano Studies and Intellectuals." Pp. 19-36 in *History, Culture and Society: Chicano Studies in the 1980s,* eds. Mario T. García, Francisco Lomelí, Mario Barrera, Edward Escobar, and John García. National Association for Chicano Studies, Proceedings. Ypsilanti, MI: Bilingual Press.

Murguía, Edward. 1975. *Assimilation, Colonialism and the Mexican American People.*

Mexican American Monograph Series No. 1, Center for Mexican American Studies. University of Texas at Austin.

———. 1982. *Chicano Intermarriage: A Theoretical and Empirical Study.* San Antonio: Trinity University Press.

Murguía, Edward, and Frisbie, W. Parker. 1977. "Trends in Mexican-American Intermarriage: Present Findings in Perspective." *Social Science Quarterly* 53 (December): 374-89.

Murillo, Nathan. 1971. "The Mexican American Family." Pp. 97-108 in *Chicanos: Social and Psychological Perspectives,* ed. Nathaniel N. Wagner and Marsha J. Haug. Saint Louis: Mosby.

Murphy, Raymond J., and Watson, James W. 1970. "The Structure of Discontent: Relationship Between Social Structure Grievance and Riot Support." Pp. 140-257 in *The Los Angeles Riots,* ed. Nathan Cohen. New York: Praeger.

Murphy, Suzanne. 1978. "A Year with the Gangs of East Los Angeles." *Ms.* 7 (July) 56-64.

Murray, Paul V. 1965. *The Catholic Church in Mexico: Historical Essays for the General Reader, Vol. I (1519-1910).* Mexico City: Editorial E. P. M.

Myrdal, Gunnar. 1944. *An American Dilemma.* New York: Harper.

Nadeau, Remi. 1974. *The Real Joaquin Murieta: Robin Hood Hero or Gold Rush Gangster?* Corona del Mar, Calif.: Trans-Anglo.

Nance, Joseph Milton. 1963. *After San Jacinto: The Texas-Mexican Frontier, 1836-1841.* Austin: University of Texas Press.

———. 1964. *Attack and Counter Attack: The Texas-Mexican Frontier, 1842.* Austin: University of Texas Press.

National Center for Education Statistics. 1983. *The Condition of Education.* Statistical Report, 1983 Edition. U.S. Department of Education. Washington: U.S. Government Printing Office.

National Chicano Research Network. 1982. "Selected Indicators from the 1980 Census." *La Red/The Net* 55 (June): 1.

National Hispanic Conference. 1980. "A Report from the National Hispanic Conference on Law Enforcement and Criminal Justice." (July 28-30) Washington, D.C.

Neal, Joe W. 1941. "The Policy of the United States Toward Immigration from Mexico." M.A. thesis, University of Texas, Austin.

Negri, Sam. 1977. "FBI Probes Alien-Torture Case for Civil Rights Act Violations." *The Arizona Republic,* Phoenix (October 19): B-1, B-2.

Nomad, Max. 1961. *Apostles of the Revolution.* New York: Collier Books.

North, David S. 1970. *The Border Crossers: People Who Live in Mexico and Work in the United States.* Washington, D.C.: Trans Century.

North, David S., and Houstoun, Marion F. 1976. *The Characteristics and Role of Illegal Aliens in the U.S. Labor Market: An Exploratory Study.* Washington, D.C.: Linton & Company.

Orozco, E.C. 1980. *Republican Protestantism in Aztlán.* Glendale, Calif.: The Petereins Press.

Ortegon, Samuel M. 1932. "The Religious Status of the Mexican Population of Los

Angeles." Master of theology thesis, University of Southern California, Los Angeles.

Paredes, Américo. 1958. *"With His Pistol in His Hand"*: *A Border Ballad and Its Hero*. Austin: University of Texas Press.

_____. 1967. "Estados Unidos, México y El Machismo." *Journal of Inter-American Studies* 9 (January): 65-84.

_____. 1977. "On Ethnographic Work Among Minority Groups: A Folklorist's Perspective." *New Scholar* 6 (Fall and Spring): 1-33.

Parkes, Henry Bamford. 1969. *A History of Mexico*. 3d ed. Boston: Houghton-Mifflin.

Paz, Octavio. 1961. *The Labyrinth of Solitude*. Translated by Lysander Kemp. New York: Grove.

Peñalosa, Fernando. 1968. "Mexican Family Roles." *Journal of Marriage and the Family* 30 (November): 680-89.

Phillips, Jerri Linn, and Coates, Robert B. 1971. "Two Scales for Measuring Attitudes Toward Police." *Wisconsin Sociologist* (Spring): 3-19.

Pitt, Leonard. 1966. *The Decline of the Californios: A Social History of the Spanish-Speaking, 1846-1890*. Berkeley: University of California Press.

Raine, Walter. 1970. "The Perception of Police Brutality in South Central Los Angeles." Pp. 380-412 in *The Los Angeles Riots*, ed. Nathan Cohen. New York: Praeger.

Ramírez, Manuel III, and Castañeda, Alfredo. 1974. *Cultural Democracy, Bicognitive Development, and Education*, New York: Academic Press.

Ramos, Reyes. 1973. "A Case in Point: An Ethnomethodological Study of a Poor Mexican American Family." *Social Science Quarterly* 53 (March): 905-19.

Ramos, Samuel. 1962. *Profile of Man and Culture in Mexico*. Translated by Peter G. Earle. Austin: University of Texas Press.

Reisler, Mark. 1974. "Passing Through Our Egypt: Mexican Labor in the United States, 1900-1940." Ph.D. dissertation, Cornell University.

Rendon, Armando B. 1972. *Chicano Manifesto*. New York: Macmillan.

Reynolds, Annie. 1933. *The Education of Spanish-Speaking Children in Five Southwestern States*. Washington, D.C.: United States Government Printing Office.

Ricard, Robert. 1966. *The Spiritual Conquest of Mexico*. Translated by Lesley Byrd Simpson. Berkeley: University of California Press.

Ridge, John Rollin [Yellow Bird]. 1955. *Life and Adventures of Joaquín Murieta, the Celebrated California Bandit*. Norman: University of Oklahoma Press.

Rist, Roy C. 1978. *The Invisible Children: School Integration in American Society*. Cambridge: Harvard University Press.

Ritzer, George. 1975. "Sociology: A Multiple Paradigm Science." *American Sociologist* 10 (August): 156-67.

Robinson, W. W. 1976. *PEOPLE VERSUS LUGO: Story of a Famous Los Angeles Murder Case and Its Amazing Aftermath*. Los Angeles, 1962. Dawson's Book Shop. Pp. 1-46 in *Mexicans in California After the U.S. Conquest*, ed. Carlos E. Cortés. New York: Arno Press Reprint Edition.

Rocco, Raymond A. 1977. "A Critical Perspective on the Study of Chicano Politics." *Western Political Quarterly* 30 (December): 558-73.

Rodriguez, Richard. 1974-75. "Going Home Again: The New American Scholarship Boy." *American Scholar* 44 (Winter): 15-28.

Romano, Octavio Ignacio-V. 1968a. "Editorial." *El Grito: A Journal of Contemporary Mexican-American Thought* 2 (Fall): 2-4.

_____. 1968b. "The Anthropology and Sociology of the Mexican-Americans: The Distortion of Mexican-American History." *El Grito: A Journal of Contemporary Mexican-American Thought* 2 (Fall): 13-26.

_____. 1970. "Social Science, Objectivity, and the Chicanos." *El Grito: A Journal of Contemporary Mexican-American Thought* 4 (Fall): 4-16.

Rosenbaum, Robert J. 1973. "Las Gorras Blancas of San Miguel County, 1889-1890." Pp. 128-33 in *Chicano: The Evolution of a People*, ed. Renato Rosaldo, Robert A. Calvert, and Gustav L. Seligmann. Minneapolis: Winston Press.

Rubel, Arthur J. 1966. *Across the Tracks: Mexican Americans in a Texas City.* Austin: University of Texas Press.

Rudoff, Alvin. 1971. "The Incarcerated Mexican-American Delinquent." *Journal of Criminal Law, Criminology and Police Science* 62 (June): 224-38.

Ruiz Maldonado, Enrique, ed. 1975. *"Liberación y cautiverio: debates en torno al método de la teología en América Latina.* Conference Publication *Encuentro Latino Americano de Teología.* Mexico City: Comite Organizador.

Russell, Philip. 1977. *Mexico in Transition.* Austin: Colorado River Press.

Sahagún, Fray Bernardino de. 1946. *Historia general de las cosas de Nueva España.* Vols. 1-3. Mexico City: Nueva España.

Samora, Julian. 1975. "Mexican Immigration." Pp. 60-80 in *Mexican-Americans Tomorrow*, ed. Gus Tyler. Albuquerque: University of New Mexico Press.

Samora, Julian; Bernal, Joe; and Peña, Albert. 1979. *Gunpowder Justice: A Reassessment of the Texas Rangers.* Notre Dame: University of Notre Dame Press.

Samora, Julian, and Lamanna, Richard A. 1967. *Mexican-Americans in a Midwest Metropolis: A Study of East Chicago.* Mexican-American Study Project, Division of Research, Graduate School of Business Administration, Advance Report 8. University of California, Los Angeles.

Sampson, Edward E. 1978. "Scientific Paradigms and Social Values: Wanted—A Scientific Revolution." *Journal in Personality and Social Psychology* 36 (November): 1332-43.

Sánchez, George I. 1940. *Forgotten People.* Albuquerque: University of New Mexico Press.

_____. 1974. "Concerning Segregation of Spanish-Speaking Children in the Public Schools. Austin, 1951." Pp. 1-75 in *Education and the Mexican American.* Advisory ed. Carlos E. Cortés. New York: Arno Press Reprint Edition (Reprint of 1951 edition).

Schellhardt, Timothy D. 1983. " '82 Poverty Rate Said Highest in 17 Years." *The Press-Enterprise*, Riverside, Calif. (August 3): A-1.

Schlesinger, Andrew B. 1971. "Las Gorras Blancas, 1889-1891." *Journal of Mexican American History* 1 (Spring): 87-143.

Schrieke, B. 1936. *Alien Americans: A Study of Race Relations.* New York: Viking Press.

Scruggs, Otey M. 1979. "Texas and the Bracero Program, 1942-1947." Pp. 85-97 in

Mexican Workers in the United States, ed. George C. Kiser and Martha Woody Kiser. Albuquerque: University of New Mexico Press.

Secrest, William B. 1967. *Joaquin: Bloody Bandit of the Mother Lode*. Fresno, Calif.: Saga-West.

Sena-Rivera, Jaime. 1977. "La Familia Chicana as Mental Health Resource—A Trigenerational Study of Four Mexican-Descent Extended Families in the Michigan-Indiana-Illinois Region." Advance Report, National Institute of Mental Health (Spring).

_____. 1979. "Extended Kinship in the United States: Competing Models and the Case of La Familia Chicana." *Journal of Marriage and the Family* 41 (February): 121-29.

Shaull, T. Richard. 1975. "Grace: Power for Transformation." Pp. 76-87 in *Liberation, Revolution, and Freedom: Theological Perspectives*, ed. Thomas M. McFadden. New York: Seabury Press.

Shockley, John Staples. 1974. *Chicano Revolt in a Texas Town*. Notre Dame: University of Notre Dame Press.

Silva Herzog, Jesús. 1960. *Breve historia de la revolución mexicana: los antecedentes y la etapa maderista*. Vol. 1. Mexico City: Fondo de Cultura Económica.

Sleepy Lagoon Defense Committee. 1942. *The Sleepy Lagoon Case*. Los Angeles: Citizens' Committee for the Defense of Mexican-American Youth.

Smith, Dorothy E. 1977. "A Sociology for Women." Paper delivered at a conference organized by the Women's Research Institute of Wisconsin. October.

Smith, Paul E., and Hawkins, Richard O. 1973. "Victimization, Types of Citizen-Police Contacts, and Attitudes Toward the Police." *Law and Society Review* 8 (Fall): 135-52.

Sommers, Joseph. 1981. "The Problem of the Undocumented Worker: A View from the United States." Pp. 151-60 in *Mexican Immigrant Workers in the U.S.*, ed. Antonio Ríos-Bustamante. Los Angeles: UCLA Chicano Studies Research Center.

Sonnichsen, Charles L. 1961. *The El Paso Salt War 1877*. El Paso: Carl Hertzog and the Texas Western Press.

Sorenson, John L. 1964. "Some Field Notes on the Power Structure of the American Anthropological Association." *American Behavioral Scientist* 7 (February): 8-9.

Sosa Riddell, Adaljiza. 1974. "Chicanas and El Movimiento." *Aztlán: Chicano Journal of the Social Sciences and the Arts* 5 (Spring-Fall): 155-65.

Soto, Antonio R. 1979. "The Church in California and the Chicano: A Sociological Analysis." *Grito del sol* 4 (Book One): 47-74.

Southwest Network. 1974. *Parameters of Institutional Change: Chicano Experiences in Education*. Hayward Calif.: Southwest Network of the Study Commission on Undergraduate Education and the Education of Teachers.

Stanner, W. E. H. 1965. "The Dreaming." Pp. 158-67 in *Reader in Comparative Religion: An Anthropological Approach*, ed. William A. Lessa and Evon Z. Vogt. 2d ed. New York: Harper & Row.

Staples, Robert. 1973. "What Is Black Sociology? Toward a Sociology of Black Liberation." Pp. 161-72 in *The Death of White Sociology*, ed. Joyce A. Ladner. New York: Random House.

———. 1976a. "The Black American Family." Pp. 221-47 in *Ethnic Families in America*, ed. Charles H. Mindel and Robert W. Habenstein. New York: Elsevier.

———. 1976b. *Introduction to Black Sociology*. New York: McGraw-Hill.

Staples, Robert, and Mirandé, Alfredo. 1980. "Racial and Cultural Variations among American Families: A Decennial Review of the Literature on Minority Families." *Journal of Marriage and the Family* 42 (November): 887-903.

Steiner, Stan. 1970. "The Shrunken Head of Pancho Villa." Pp. 208-29 in *La Raza*. New York: Harper and Row.

Stoddard, Ellwyn R. 1973. *Mexican Americans*. New York: Random House.

Stowell, Jay S. 1921. "The Mexican at Work in the United States." *The Near Side of the Mexican Question*. New York: George H. Doran Company.

Stumphauzer, Jerome S.; Aiken, Thomas W.; and Veloz, Esteban V. 1977. "East Side Story: Behavioral Analysis of a High Juvenile Crime Community." *Behavioral Disorders* 2 (February): 76-84.

Swadesh, Frances Leon. 1974. *Los Primeros Pobladores: Hispanic Americans of the Ute Frontier*. Notre Dame: University of Notre Dame Press.

Szymanski, Albert. 1972. "Trends in the American Class Structure." *Socialist Revolution* 10 (July-August): 101-22.

Talmon, Yonina. 1961. "Aging in Israel, a Planned Society." *American Journal of Sociology* 67 (November): 284-95.

Taylor, Paul Schuster. 1930. *Mexican Labor in the United States*. Vol. 1. Berkeley: University of California Press.

———. 1934. *An American-Mexican Frontier, Nueces County, Texas*. Chapel Hill: University of North Carolina Press.

Teske, Jr., Raymond H.C., and Nelson, Bardin H. 1976. "An Analysis of Differential Assimilation Rates among Middle-class Mexican Americans." *Sociological Quarterly* 17 (Spring): 218-35.

Tirado, Miguel David. 1970. "Mexican American Community Political Organization." *Aztlán: Chicano Journal of the Social Sciences and the Arts* 1 (Spring): 53-78.

Trillin, Calvin. 1977. "U.S. Journal: San Antonio, Some Elements of Power." *New Yorker* 53 (May): 92-94, 96, 98-100.

———. 1979. "U.S. Journal: Riverside, Calif., Todo Se Paga." *New Yorker* 54 (February 5): 101-5.

Trujillo, Larry D. 1974. "La evolución del 'Bandido' al 'Pachuco': A Critical Examination and Evaluation of Criminological Literature on Chicanos." *Issues in Criminology* 9 (Fall): 43-67.

Tuck, Ruth D. 1946. *Not With the Fist: Mexican-Americans in a Southwest City*. New York: Harcourt, Brace and Company.

United States Bureau of the Census. 1976. *Persons of Spanish Origin in the United States: March 1976*. Current Population Reports, Series P-20, no. 310 (July). Washington, D.C.: U.S. Government Printing Office.

———. 1978a. *Persons of Spanish Origin in the United States: March 1978*. Current Population Reports, Series P-20, no. 328 (August). Washington, D.C.: U.S. Government Printing Office.

————. 1978b. *Persons of Spanish Origin in the United States: March 1977*. Series P-20, no. 329 (September). Washington, D.C.: U.S. Government Printing Office.

————. 1979. *Persons of Spanish Origin in the United States: March 1979*. Current Population Reports, Series P-20, no. 347 (October). Washington, D.C.: U.S. Government Printing Office.

————. 1980. *Persons of Spanish Origin in the United States: March 1979*. Current Population Reports, Series P-20, no. 354 (October). Washington, D.C.: U.S. Government Printing Office.

————. 1981. *Persons of Spanish Origin in the United States: March 1980*. Current Population Reports, Series P-20, no. 361 (May). Washington, D.C.: U.S. Government Printing Office.

————. 1982. *Household and Family Characteristics: March 1981*. Current Population Reports, Series P-20, no. 371 (May). Washington, D.C.: U.S. Government Printing Office.

————. 1983a. *Population Profile of the United States: 19 82*. Current Population Reports, Series P-23, No. 130 (December). Washington, D.C.: U.S. Government Printing Office.

————. 1983b. *Marital Status and Living Arrangements: March 1982*. Current Population Reports, Series P-20, no. 380 (May). Washington, D.C.: U.S. Printing Office.

————. 1984a. *Fertility of American Women: June 1982*. Current Population Reports, Series P-20, No. 387 (April). Washington, D.C.: U.S. Government Printing Office.

————. 1984b. *Conditions of Hispanics in America Today*. Population Division. Washington, D.C.: U.S. Government Printing Office.

U.S. Commission on Civil Rights. 1970. *Mexican Americans and the Administration of Justice in the Southwest*. Washington, D.C.: U.S. Government Printing Office.

————. 1971. *The Unfinished Education: Outcomes for Minorities in the Five Southwestern States*. Report II: Mexican American Educational Series. Washington, D.C.: U.S. Government Printing Office.

————. 1973. *Teachers and Students: Differences in Teacher Interaction With Mexican American and Anglo Students*. Report V: Mexican American Education Study. Washington, D.C.: U.S. Government Printing Office.

————. 1974. *Toward Quality Education for Mexican Americans*. Report VI: Mexican American Education Study. Washington, D.C.: U.S. Government Printing Office.

U.S. Congress Senate Committee on Immigration. 1928. "Restriction of Western Hemisphere Immigration." A bill to subject certain immigrants, born in countries of the Western Hemisphere, to the quota under the immigration laws. Washington, D.C.: U.S. Government Printing Office.

U.S. Senate Immigration Commission (Dillingham Commission). 1911. Reports of the Immigration Commission. *Immigrants in Industries*. Vol. 3, p. 25. Washington, D.C.: U.S. Government Printing Office.

Vaca, Nick C. 1970a. "The Mexican-American in the Social Sciences, 1912-1970." Part 1: 1912-1935. *El Grito: A Journal of Contemporary Mexican-American Thought* 3 (Spring): 3-24.

_____. 1970b. "The Mexican-American in the Social Sciences, 1912-1970." Part 2: 1936-1970. *El Grito: A Journal of Contemporary Mexican-American Thought* 4 (Fall): 17-51.

Valadez, Kathy L. 1978. "UNO: A Study in Community Development." *Somos* 1 (April/May): 16-19.

Valdez, Luis. 1972. Introduction to *Aztlán: An Anthology of Mexican American Literature*, ed. Luis Valdez and Stan Steiner. New York: Knopf.

Valdez, Luis, and Steiner, Stan. 1972. *Aztlán: An Anthology of Mexican American Literature*. New York: Knopf.

Valeriano, Antonio. Undated. Historia de las apariciones. Escrita en náhuatl por Antonio Valeriano. Traducida por Primo Feliciano Velásquez. Mexico City: Obra Nacional de la Buena Prensa.

Vickery, Joyce Carter. 1977. *Defending Eden: New Mexican Pioneers in Southern California, 1830-1890*. Riverside: Dept. of History, University of California, Riverside and Riverside Museum Press.

Villalpando, Manuel. 1977. *A Study of the Impact of Illegal Aliens on the County of San Diego on Specific Socioeconomic Areas*. San Diego: San Diego County Human Resources Agency.

Watson, Wilbur H. 1976. "The Idea of Black Sociology: Its Cultural and Political Significance." *American Sociologist* 11 (May): 115-23.

Webb, Walter Prescott. 1965. *The Texas Rangers*. Austin: University of Texas Press.

_____. 1975. *The Texas Rangers in the Mexican War*. Austin: Jenkins Garrett Press.

Weintraub, Sidney, and Ross, Stanley R. 1980. *The Illegal Alien from Mexico*. Austin: University of Texas Press.

Wickersham Commission Reports (U.S. National Commission on Law Observance and Enforcement). 1931. *Report on Crime and the Foreign Born*. No. 10. Originally Published by United States Government Printing Office. (Publication No. 6: Patterson Smith Reprint Series in Criminology, Law Enforcement, and Social Problems, 1968).

Wilson, William J. 1974. "The New Black Sociology: Reflections on the 'Insiders and Outsiders' Controversy." Pp. 327-38 in *Black Sociologists: Historical and Contemporary Perspectives*, ed. James E. Blackwell and Morris Janowitz. Chicago: University of Chicago Press.

Wolf, Eric. 1972. "The Virgin of Guadalupe: A Mexican National Symbol." Pp. 149-53 in *Reader in Comparative Religion: An Anthropological Approach*, ed. William A. Lessa and Evon Z. Vogt. 3d ed. New York: Harper & Row.

Ybarra, Leonarda. 1977. "Conjugal Role Relationships in the Chicano Family." Ph.D. dissertation, University of California, Berkeley.

_____. 1982a. "When Wives Work: The Impact on the Chicano Family." *Journal of Marriage and the Family* 44 (February): 169-78.

_____. 1982b. "Marital Decision-Making and the Role of Machismo in the Chicano Family." *De colores* 6 (1 & 2): 32-47.

Young, Michael. 1958. *The Rise of the Meritocracy, 1870-2033: An Essay on Education and Equality*. Baltimore: Penguin Books.

Zea, L. 1952. *Conciencia y posibilidad del mexicano*. Mexico City: Porrúa y Obregón.

Index